WAR

A Concise History of Austria

For a small, prosperous country in the middle of Europe, modern Austria has a very large and complex history, extending far beyond its current borders. Today's Austrians have a problematic relationship with that history, whether with the multi-national history of the Habsburg Monarchy, or with the time between 1938 and 1945 when Austrians were Germans in Hitler's Third Reich. Steven Beller's gripping and comprehensive account traces the remarkable career of Austria through its many transformations, from German borderland, to dynastic enterprise, imperial house, Central European great power, failed Alpine republic, German province, and then successful Alpine republic, building up a picture of the layers of Austrian identity and heritage and their diverse sources. It is a story full of anomalies and ironies, a case study of the other side of European history, without the easy answers of more clearly national narratives, and hence far more relevant to today's world.

STEVEN BELLER is an independent scholar. He has already published a number of books on Austrian history, including *Vienna and the Jews, 1867–1938: a Cultural History* (1989), *Theodor Herzl* (1991) and *Francis Joseph* (1996).

CAMBRIDGE CONCISE HISTORIES

This is a series of illustrated 'concise histories' of selected individual countries, intended both as university and college textbooks and as general historical introductions for general readers, travellers and members of the business community.

For a list of titles in the series, please see the end of the book.

A Concise History
of Austria

STEVEN BELLER

CAMBRIDGE
UNIVERSITY PRESS

CAMBRIDGE UNIVERSITY PRESS
Cambridge, New York, Melbourne, Madrid, Cape Town, Singapore, São Paulo,
Delhi, Dubai, Tokyo, Mexico City

Cambridge University Press
The Edinburgh Building, Cambridge CB2 8RU, UK

Published in the United States of America by Cambridge University Press, New York

www.cambridge.org
Information on this title: www.cambridge.org/9780521478861

First published 2006
6th printing 2011

Printed in the United Kingdom at the University Press, Cambridge

A catalogue record for this publication is available from the British Library

ISBN 978-0-521-47305-7 Hardback
ISBN 978-0-521-47886-1 Paperback

CONTENTS

ILLUSTRATIONS

*Photograph taken by the author.
**Photograph taken by Esther Diane Brimmer.

MAPS

ACKNOWLEDGEMENTS

Many years ago, when Bill Davies asked whether I knew of anyone interested in writing a Concise History of Austria, it was an easy, if immodest decision on my part to suggest myself. Writing such a book seemed a challenging prospect, but one that could be done fairly simply and in not too much time. It took me a long time to realize that conciseness is very time-consuming, and that a Concise History of *Austria* is, in any case, verging on a *non sequitur* – and for such a small state too. It took me even longer to write the book, but now that it has finally been completed, my hope is that it will help to give both an understanding of the broad outlines of Austria's fascinating history, and some sense of how its extensiveness and its complexity make an easy, concise rendering of it more problematic than might at first appear (or at least as it appeared to me back then). It is also true that part of the fascination lies in that very extensiveness and complexity, but I leave readers to make that discovery for themselves in the following pages.

At the outset of research for this project I benefited greatly from being a Member of the Institute for Advanced Study at Princeton, and subsequently a Fellow of the International Research Centre for Cultural Studies (IFK) in Vienna. I would also like to thank the History Department of George Washington University for giving me the opportunity to teach a course on the Habsburg Monarchy. Apart from that, I would like to thank Doris and Andrew Brimmer for their generosity, and my beautiful and patient wife, Esther Diane

Brimmer, whose support is the main reason why I was able to bring this book to completion.

Many friends and colleagues – far too numerous, I fear, to be each named in such a short acknowledgement – helped, stimulated and advised me in the writing of this book, even when they on occasion did so through disagreement. To all of them, in Austria, the United States, Britain and elsewhere, I give my thanks. There are also more specific debts of gratitude: Bruce Martin at the Library of Congress was most helpful in facilitating my research; Derek Beales graciously replied to my ill-informed query about an illustration, which is now in the book; Erhard Stackl at *Der Standard* in Vienna was also most helpful on several questions concerning the book; Klaus Nellen at the Institute for the Human Sciences in Vienna is always helpful and a good listener. I would like to thank Julian Sofaer for his generosity concerning permission to reproduce two of Gerhart Frankl's paintings for this book, and Mag. Franz Huemer, for allowing several pictures from the *Heimatbuch* of Bad Leonfelden to be printed here. I am also most grateful to Hans Haider, Regina Huber, Wolfgang Leschanz, Gerhard Milchram, Renate Pein, Rudolf Semotan and Wilhelm Wadl for their generosity concerning illustrations.

Evan Bukey, Allan Janik, Aviel Roshwald and David Sorkin were kind enough to read parts of the manuscript and offer suggestions as to how the text could be improved, for which I am very thankful. They are not responsible for any mistakes in the end result.

I also would like to thank the personnel at Cambridge University Press, starting with Bill Davies, who gave me this opportunity, and stuck with me as long as possible. Marigold Acland, Chris Harrison and Elizabeth Howard also are to be thanked for their extreme patience with this author. Isabelle Dambricourt, Jo Breeze, Carol Fellingham Webb and the production team have been both patient and helpful in finally bringing this book to publication.

Finally, I would like to acknowledge several people not yet mentioned whose hospitality and example over the years have done much to give this book what character it possesses: George and Christl Clare; Elisabeth de Gelsey; Werner Eichbauer; Christl Fabrizii; Marcel Faust; Kurt Rudolf Fischer; Mascha Hoff; Ingeborg Lau; Hilde Spiel; Nike Wagner and all the members of the extended Haiboeck family, whether in Bad Leonfelden, Marseilles,

Salzburg, Linz or New York. Alan and Bea Corgan, and Jan and Herta Palme also contributed, in ways they might not always have realized. During the course of my writing this book, many in the above list have passed on, as has my father, Milton 'Mickey' Beller. It is because he loved an Austrian so, my mother, Hermi Beller, that I – and this book – exist. It is only fitting, therefore, that this book be dedicated to my parents, and to their grandson Nathaniel, for the story in these pages is also part of his.

Steven Beller
Washington DC

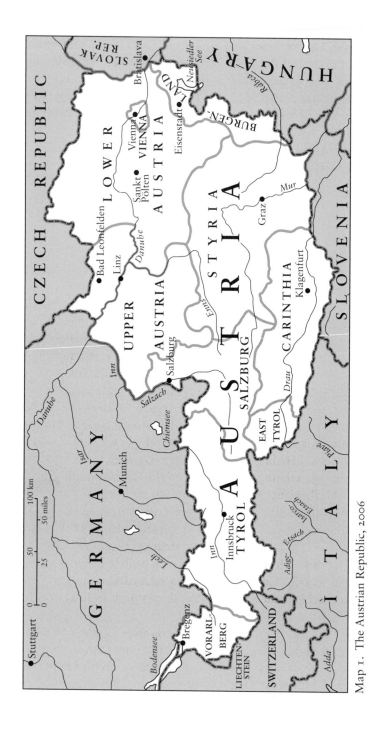

Map 1. The Austrian Republic, 2006

INTRODUCTION

Austrians, it might be said, are a nation without a history, and Austrian history is a history without a nation. Only since 1945 have Austrians seriously tried to construct a national identity separate from that of Germans, and succeeded; yet Austria as an identifiable historical concept long antedates even the idea of the nation-state. For a small country such as modern-day Austria, with a population of only about 8 million, there is an awful lot of Austrian history.

Yet little of that history is straightforwardly 'national', and much of it refers to places and peoples far beyond Austria's current borders. Until 1918 'Austria' was a multi-national, dynastic empire, otherwise known as the Habsburg Monarchy, in which the Germans of the Alpine hereditary lands (modern-day Austria, more or less) were only one ethnic 'nationality' among other 'Austrians' (such as Czechs, Ruthenians and so forth). While there was an 'Austria' in the form of the First Austrian Republic after 1918, few 'Austrians' regarded this as the best response to the Monarchy's collapse, most preferring *Anschluss* (union with Germany) instead. Between 1938 and 1945 this wish was fulfilled, but with horrific consequences, as National Socialist Germany incorporated Austrians in its war-and-murder machine and made them both complicit in the Holocaust and partners in total defeat.

After 1945 a newly independent Austria arose. A new identity was consciously constructed by Austria's leadership, both to create the solidarity so sorely missing between the wars, and also to distance 'Austrians' from what 'Germans' had perpetrated between 1938 and

Illustration 1. Austrian archetype: Salzburg.

1945. The resurrection of Austria after 1945 is one of the more miraculous stories of Europe's post-war recovery. A combination of political and economic peace at home, neutrality abroad and a general agreement to let the sleeping dogs of the past lie, resulted by the latter part of the twentieth century in one of the most prosperous and pacific countries on Earth.

On the face of it Austria, even today, deserves to be called an 'island of the blessed'. Its per capita GDP is one of the highest in the European Union, and the Austrian economy has successfully transformed itself, using the population's high level of technical education to move from an industrial to a service base. Austrians benefit from an extensive and generous welfare state, coupled with some of the world's lowest crime rates, especially as concerns violent crime.

The country's geographical position at the heart of Europe, once a huge liability, is now potentially a large advantage. Its landlocked position between Germany and Italy made it the prey of both powers in the interwar period, but now, as part of the European Union's internal market, gives the country strategic commercial significance. Being surrounded by successor states to the Habsburg Monarchy, Czechoslovakia, Hungary and Yugoslavia, meant political hostility and economic dislocation in the interwar period. After the post-1945 communist takeovers of its neighbours, with the Iron Curtain on much of its frontier, Austria found itself on the edge of the 'West'.

Since the fall of communism and the enlargement of the European Union in 2004, Austria now has burgeoning economies on its borders, and hence large economic opportunities. Moreover, this enlargement has finally put Austria in what Austrians always thought was its proper place, at the heart, rather than the eastern edge, of 'Europe'. One might have thought that the Austrians would consider themselves very fortunate at their nation's remarkable transformation.

And yet the weight of Austrian history, especially what happened when Austria was not 'Austria' between 1938 and 1945, continues to mark, complicate and trouble national self-understanding. From 1986 the Waldheim Affair raised old ghosts from the time of the Second World War and scandalized foreign opinion. For a time thereafter the actions of the Vranitzky government suggested that Austrians were seriously trying to come to terms with 'their' past. Yet the resistible rise of Jörg Haider and his far-right Freedom Party to power (albeit in coalition with moderate conservatives) suggested otherwise. It is very paradoxical: Austrians, renowned for their 'happy-go-lucky' temperament, and living in one of the most successful states in the world, continue to be extremely sensitive, even self-conscious, insecure and defensive, when asked about their 'national' past.

There are powerful reasons for this discomfort with Austrian history. There is the central paradox with which we started, that there is a very strong discontinuity between what Austria and Austrians are today, and what Austria and 'Austrians' were before. There is the question of the labyrinthine complexity of historical 'Austrian' identity, which stems from the inability of 'Austria' to fit itself into the 'modern' world of nation-states in the past two centuries. This left a problematic legacy to Central Europe, yet at the same time allowed 'Austria' to be at the centre of many of the twentieth century's intellectual, ideological and cultural currents, for good or ill.

Many modern-day Austrians would like to embrace the double legacy of imperial, supra-national Habsburg Austria and cosmopolitan 'Vienna 1900'. Yet this involves many difficulties, not the least being how to do so without falling foul of the guilt-laden mire of the 'caesura' of 1938 to 1945. This whole enterprise of claiming the other 'Austrian' past to bolster modern-day Austrian national identity is morally perilous. It is impossible to pick and choose which parts of the 'Austrian' past to claim, and the parts omitted in pursuit of a workable national past have bitten back in a very incisive way. Whether contemporary Austrians will fully come to terms with their past, including the history of that past's attempted suppression, remains to be seen.

Even the apparently 'usable' parts of the past are not always what they seem. On 19 September 1991 a body was discovered on the Ötztal glacier high up in the Alps, at Hauslabjoch. A rescue crew from Innsbruck was called on the assumption that this was some unlucky mountaineer, but this was not the case. The body was of a man killed thousands of years ago, and was in fact the best-preserved body from the Bronze Age ever found. Austrian public opinion, especially the tabloid press, responded with a certain degree of national pride in the fact that the 'oldest man ever found' was an Austrian. 'Ötzi the Iceman' had, admittedly, died thousands of years before there was any idea of Austria, but claiming 'ancestors' from time immemorial is not unusual, as British national pride in Stonehenge attests. The Austrian claiming of Ötzi was dealt a devastating blow, however, when, on revisiting the site of discovery, it was realized that the Iceman had in fact been discovered in *Italy*, the Austro-Italian frontier running right through the middle of the Hauslabjoch. After much debate, the two countries agreed that the Austrians could keep Ötzi temporarily for research purposes in Innsbruck, but he would then have to be handed over to the Italians for permanent safekeeping. The 'oldest Italian ever found' (and indeed the Iceman seems to have come from the area of the Mediterranean) now resides in Bolzano, in the Italian province of Alto Adige, otherwise known as South Tyrol.

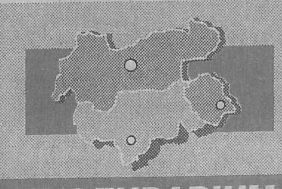

TIROLER
TAGESZEITUNG - 9

KALENDARIUM

Namenstag: Alice, Barnabas, Roselinde, Paula, Adelheid, Johannes Facundo, Jolenta.

Illustration 2. Tyrolean identity: logo from the *Tiroler Tageszeitung*, 11 June 1996

And thereby hangs a tale. As far as most Austrians are concerned, South Tyrol should be part of Austria. The province is largely inhabited by German speakers, and Italy's sovereignty over it has been disputed ever since it was handed over by the Allies in the post-First World War settlement to reward Italy for entering the war in 1915. The matter has largely been laid to rest, but Tyroleans on both sides of the border continue to see South Tyrol as really part of a greater Tyrol. One of the leading newspapers in Innsbruck, the *Tiroler Tageszeitung*, until very recently had as its header a map of Tyrol, with the two parts in Austria (North and East) in full shading, and South Tyrol in a lighter shade. South Tyroleans themselves seem largely content with the autonomy and other concessions gained from the Italian government, but there is no doubt that they continue to see themselves as Tyroleans. Arguably, Ötzi is neither Austrian nor Italian, but a Tyrolean.

The case of Ötzi highlights one startling fact about modern-day Austria: for a country of only 8 million it has surprisingly large regional variety, and strong particularist identities among its nine provinces. This is partly a result of the country's mountainous terrain and its elongated western segment. In the far west, abutting Lake Constance and hence the Rhine, Vorarlberg remains far more integrated into German and Swiss transportation networks than to Austrian. It takes longer to get to Vienna by train from Bregenz than it does to get to Paris. Tyrol is largely composed of the Alps, and has therefore been central in modern Austria's identity as a tourist destination. Yet it is similarly remote from the main, 'fat' part of Austria and has a heritage of rugged provincial independence which stems in part from its relatively late absorption into the Habsburgs' 'Austrian' domains in the fourteenth century. Another province central to modern Austrian cultural identity, and Austria's tourist industry, Salzburg, was only fully incorporated into the Habsburg Monarchy in 1816. When Mozart was born there in 1756, he was not an 'Austrian'.

The provinces, or *Länder*, to the south and east, Styria and Carinthia, have a longer tradition of being Austrian, Styria having been united with the core Austrian lands in the time of the Babenbergs, and Carinthia coming under Habsburg rule in 1336, yet the Alpine ranges which restrict access to the north and the rivers which

flow south have resulted historically in these provinces having different concerns from their northern neighbours. The latter are the
core Austrian lands, Upper and Lower Austria, astride the Danube.
Vienna, the capital, was once also the capital of Lower Austria but
is now a province in its own right. Burgenland, the most easterly
province, abutting Hungary and the puszta, is the province with the
shortest Austrian tradition, having been historically part of Hungary
before becoming Austrian in 1919.

The geographical breadth, stretching from the Rhine to the puszta,
the Alpine barriers which range across the country and the historical diversity of the provinces have fostered regional identities and
loyalties that make any claims to straightforward Austrian identity
very strained. Part of this particularistic tendency is tempered by the
fact that the bulk of the population lives in the flatter part of the
country, in Vienna and the Danube valley. The two Austrias, Upper
and Lower, combined with Vienna, comprise over half the country's population. Nevertheless, the smaller provinces' identities, with
their emphasis on alpine traditions – over half of the country's area
is either forested or barren – have done much to inform modern-day
Austrian identity. The central theme of that identity can indeed be
viewed as the tension between these two 'Danubian' and 'Alpine'
sides of Austria, roughly corresponding to Bruno Kreisky's 'valley
people' and 'mountain people'. Others see a split between the eastern and western halves of the country, or, more simply, Vienna versus
the rest of the country, a tension rich in tradition.

The most critical problem embedded in Austrian history is encap-
sulated in an incident from the Waldheim Affair. Responding to
questions about his wartime record, presidential candidate Kurt
Waldheim stated: 'What I did during the war was nothing more
than what hundreds of thousands of other Austrians did, namely
fulfilled my duty as a soldier.'

This seemingly reasonable defence becomes strange, once you ask
to whom or to what he was fulfilling his 'duty'. Given that Austria
had been 'conquered' by Nazi Germany, Waldheim was fulfilling
his duty not to Austria but to the Third Reich, the supposed foreign
usurper. In most understandings of 'duty' it can only be performed
towards legitimate authority, and in the modern nation-state only
towards one's own nation, ultimately to one's own higher moral

self. If the Third Reich was, as most Austrians have claimed, not a legitimate authority, then it would have been impossible to fulfil one's *duty* to it. Waldheim's statement thus cast doubt on Austria being the 'first invaded country' and highlighted the deep ambivalence over the national identity of 'Austrians' during the Second World War. Imagine a Czech politician saying the same thing about his fighting for the Germans during the war.

Waldheim's statement has been seen as part of Austria's continuing problem with the Nazi past, as an inadvertent, vestigial identification of the Third Reich as a legitimate authority, inasmuch as Austrians considered themselves as Germans and the *Anschluss* as legitimate, if in retrospect a mistake. There could have been an element of this. Yet I think another explanation is more likely.

The sense of 'duty' used by Waldheim was not that of Western Europe, or even northern, Kantian Germany, but rather a Central European form, with a centuries-old tradition in the Habsburg Monarchy. Under this understanding of 'duty' (*Pflicht*), it makes no difference who is giving the orders; orders are there to be obeyed because by definition whoever is giving the orders is an authority, or 'the authorities', and therefore to be obeyed – the basis of their authority left unquestioned. It is the 'duty' of a subject, and not of a citizen.

Waldheim's claim about Austrians during the Second World War points to a far deeper legacy of Austrian history, the troubled search over centuries for a basis of legitimacy and authority for the Habsburg dynasty to rule over its realms without fear of contradiction. After 1945 Austrians used their history selectively to construct a historical identity which could confer legitimacy and hence authority on an Austrian nation-state, but this behaviour was not new. Austrian history's central theme has been the search for a definition of 'Austria', an identity, a meaning, which would confer legitimacy and authority on what otherwise was simply family rule over a dynastic agglomeration of territories.

The Habsburgs started as the opponents of Swiss proto-democracy, became the opponents of the Protestant nation-states, then of the French Revolutionary liberal nation-state, before ultimately succumbing to the nationalisms of its own peoples (and neighbours). All along 'Austria' strove to define itself in ways which would make it appear legitimate to itself and others. Sometimes it succeeded, but never for long, and never fully, always with a slight lack of conviction. Austrian history is a case study in the other side of European history, of those concepts of political coherence left in the wake of the triumphant nation-state. Austria's post-war awkwardness with its past and its sense of identity is part of a very long tradition.

1

The Eastern March, to 1439

Austria began its history in the late tenth century as an eastern march of the duchy of Bavaria. It was during this period that an area in the Danube valley came to be known as 'the eastern land', in Latin 'terra orientalis', or 'ostarrichi' in the local German of the time. The first written evidence of this early medieval equivalent of 'Österreich' dates from 996. In the eleventh century the march was sometimes referred to as 'Osterlant'; the Latin version of 'Austria' first appears in a document in 1147.

As Austrian historians were at pains after 1945 to prove, the march was never actually called the 'Ostmark'. Nevertheless, it was as an eastern march of the German kingdom under Bavarian suzerainty, a military district on the Germans' south-east frontier, that Austria started its career.

As the discovery of Ötzi indicates, human activity in the area began thousands of years before any concept of 'Austria'. The mountainous terrain meant that there were few early settlements. The region was not at the forefront of human civilization, and the Iron Age culture evident at Hallstatt appeared relatively late, around 800 BCE. From then until around 400 BCE the main group in the region was the 'Illyrians', who were largely displaced by Celts, chief among them the tribes of the Norici and Taurisci. The Raetii remained in control of the mountain stronghold of what is now Vorarlberg and Tyrol, but in the eastern part the Celts set up the kingdom of Noricum around 200 BCE. In the second century BCE, Noricum came under increasing pressure from Germanic tribes to the north, and was peacefully incorporated into the Roman Empire in 15 BCE. Raetia, by contrast, suffered coercive Roman occupation, with much of the population deported.

Roman rule lasted for more than five hundred years. The Romans additionally conquered the rich province of Pannonia, to the east of Noricum, and also tried to conquer the Germanic tribes to the north. The catastrophic defeat at the hands of the Cheruscii in the Teutoburg Forest in 9 CE resulted in Roman retreat to the Danube, so that Noricum became an imperial border area, its frontier eventually a part of the Limes, the Romans' military wall across Europe. Existing Celtic settlements became Roman *municipia*, such as Lentia (Linz), Juvavum (Salzburg), Brigantium (Bregenz) and Vindobona (Vienna). Carnuntum, the capital of Pannonia, and at the eastern end of the Limes, appears to have been a major Roman city. The culture of the vine was introduced, an extensive road system was built and Roman civilization flourished.

In the relatively peaceful first century CE Rome exerted hegemony over the Germanic tribes to the north of the Limes, the Naristi, Marcomannii and the Quadii, but thereafter the threat of Germanic invasion became ever greater. Marcus Aurelius came to the region in 172 to repel Marcomannii invaders; his death in Vindobona in 180 was Vienna's first claim to fame. From the third century, the Alemannii were a major threat. The Romans increased their military presence, but the border was increasingly porous. By Constantine's rule much of the Roman army consisted of German mercenaries. In the latter half of the fourth century the Romans allowed some Germanic tribes fleeing the Huns to settle *within* the Limes as part of the Roman defence system.

Yet attacks, by Ostrogoths, East Germans and Huns, continued. In 433 the Romans evacuated Pannonia in the face of the Huns, and after Attila's death in 453 the Goths took over. By then Noricum was at the mercy of the Germanic Rugii, and in 488 Noricum's Christianized and Romanized population was ordered to evacuate. Raetia had already been lost to the Alemannii. From 493 the area of the eastern Alps was part of Theodoric's Ostrogothic empire, and the Roman era was over.

The tribal 'migrations' continued, and the Danube valley was a prime route for them. The Langobardii (Lombards) appeared around 500 in the northern and eastern parts of the region, only to be chased out by the Avars from the east in 567. The Langobardii ended up in northern Italy in 569. The Avars then moved in, accompanied by Slavic tribes. From the north and west another Germanic tribe, the Bajuvarii, vassals of the Franks, had also entered the region. Thus began the contest of Avars and Slavs against Bajuvarii (Bavarians) for control of the region.

By the early seventh century the Avars controlled a territory stretching from the Baltic coast deep into the Balkans. They swept in from the Eurasian steppes on their horses and took all before them. Byzantium employed them against the Huns and the Slavs, who had appeared in the Balkans in the early sixth century. The Avars had subjugated the Slavs and made them their vassals, so that they could resettle the conquered area to the benefit of their Avarian masters. By 600 the Bavarians and the Slavs were contesting large areas of the eastern Alps. In 626 the Avars, allied with the Persians, threatened Constantinople. Their failure, however, led their Slav vassals to rebel. The northern Slavs chose a Frank, Samo, as their king; the Alpine Slavs, the Carantanii, chose a Bavarian, Odilo, as their count. The Avars reconquered Samo's kingdom to the north, but the lands of the Carantanii (Carinthians) remained under Bavarian control. In between, in the relatively fertile Danube valley and surrounding foothills, Bavarians battled it out with Slavs and their Avar masters, with Slav settlement reaching the Pustertal in around 650. From then on, Slav settlement retreated in face of Bavarian pressure, so that the Enns River divided Bavarian and Slav by 780.

The ascendant power in the region was now the Bavarians. Originally vassals of the Ostrogoths and then of the Franks, the Bavarians had been left to their own devices for much of the sixth and seventh centuries, with only intermittent Frankish control. They had pushed east and south in their settlement of the Danube valley and eastern Alps, and had gained overlordship of Carantania.

In the eighth century the Carolingian Frankish kings restored their power over the Bavarians, and Charlemagne led the Franks and Bavarians against the Avars from 791. By 803 the Avars had been driven back to the Fischa and Leitha rivers, opening up a large area for settlement. A system of marches, stretching from the Danube to the Adriatic, was set up in the region, and was clearly necessary: the region continued to be beset by various conflicts, whether owing to Slavonian rebellion, Bulgar attacks, internal rivalries or the interventions of the 'Great Moravian Kingdom', a large Slav power to the north. Worst of all was the onslaught of the Magyars in the late ninth century.

As with the Avars, Magyar power was created on the hoof. They began appearing in the region in 862, fleeing from the steppes before more powerful tribes. At first their numbers were small, and they were used as mercenaries in the conflict between Franks and Moravians, but in 896 the Magyars came en masse to what was to be called the Hungarian Plain, and the 'Hungarian storm' began in earnest. The horse-based Magyar armies were initially vastly superior to the Frankish forces. From their base in the Danube valley, Magyar armies raided the surrounding lands with impunity. In 906 they defeated the Moravians, and in 907 they destroyed the Bavarian army at Pressburg. The Carolingian marches collapsed. The Bavarian frontier fell back to the Enns, but even this was often passed by Magyar raiders. For fifty years or more the Magyars terrorized the region. Then, on 10 August 955, King Otto I and the Germans defeated a combined army of Magyars and Bavarian rebels at the Lechfeld (outside Augsburg).

Lechfeld had dramatic consequences for Central European history. Otto I used his new-found power and prestige to become Holy Roman Emperor in 962, the first in a continuous line of 'emperors' of the German-centred polity which was to extend to 1806.[1] In the Danube valley, Lechfeld was followed by a slow reconquest of the land east of the Enns that found much of the pre-Magyar society still present. Otto I established another march there, which after 976 was headed by Margrave Luitpold, the first Babenberg ruler. Bavarian armies pushed the new march's border ever eastward along the Danube, until in 1002 it reached to the

---

[1] From Otto I on, the ruler of the Holy Roman Empire was the German king, elected by his princely peers (later known as the prince electors); the German king was also known as the 'king of the Romans'; only when the elected German king was then anointed by the pope in Rome was he officially the Holy Roman Emperor. Many 'emperors' were therefore only officially kings.

area around Vienna. Meanwhile, in 976 Carantania had become the separate dukedom of Carinthia and marches were established in what would become Carniola and Styria. Although the mention of 'ostarrichi' in 996 is not a definitive start of Austrian history, it did occur at a historic turning point for the region. The 'dark ages' of invasion by one tribe after another had come to an end, and the territorial kernel had been established of what was to become 'Austria'.

The region already had a complex heritage. The various waves of peoples who had inhabited the area each left their mark, and none of the groups had entirely disappeared. The Bavarians provided the bulk of the area's population, with the other Germanic tribe of the Alemannii providing most of the population in the west, towards Lake Constance. Yet, as the various tribes had swept in, the present population often had either stayed under some form of subjugation, or gone higher up into the mountains or deeper into the forest. There had been deportations, evacuations and slaughters, but these had been incomplete. The Roman era had seen a largely Celtic population 'Romanized', and, after the fourth century, gradually Christianized.

When the Roman regime in the area collapsed before the Germanic invasions, pockets of 'Roman' population remained, for instance around Salzburg. Many Roman place names survived, such as Grödig (Crethica), a suburb of Salzburg. Salzburg itself was still known in the eighth century by its Latin name of Juvavum. Former 'Romans', or, as they were known in German, *Walchen* or *Welsche* (with which 'Welsh' shares an etymological root), survived in various communities, retaining both their language, a dialect of Latin later known as Romansch, and their Christian religion. When Christianity was reintroduced into the area in the seventh and eighth centuries, with missions often led by English and Irish clergy such as Winfrid (Bonifatius) and Columbanus (Kolumban), the missionaries found many 'Roman' Christian communities already present.

The Austrian region was one in which Roman and Christian influence never wholly died out. The Roman regime had collapsed around 500, but by 739 Salzburg had already become a bishopric and in 798 an archbishopric. The dominant cultural and linguistic power in the region was that of the Germanic tribes, especially the Bavarians, as the adoption of a dialect of German in the region and the disappearance of all but a few Romansch communities attests, but the Germanic communities also adopted Roman practices, such as cultivation of the vine, existing Roman street patterns in the cities and also Roman field patterns on the land. From the seventh century the Bavarians had also been slowly Christianized, and, with the competition of Byzantine Orthodoxy thwarted in the ninth century, the region had become once again a part of the religious Roman sphere.

The Avar invasion and the settling of much of the eastern Alps by Slavs had added another dimension to an already complicated mix. Here again, while the Germans eventually won out, many Slav communities survived, even if they eventually adopted the German language of their overlords. The Magyar episode shook up the picture a little more. Far from being a land with one pure ethnic origin, the population of the Austrian area, as in so many parts of Europe, represented a rich concatenation of peoples and cultures, even if the Bavarian element predominated.

THE BABENBERGS, 1000–1278

In 1000, King Stephen of Hungary converted to Christianity. By making the Magyar power a Christian one, Stephen blunted the Bavarian drive eastward into the Danubian Plain. Admittedly, it took a resounding military defeat by Stephen and the Magyars in 1030 actually to stop and partly reverse the German advance, and the German–Magyar conflict remained active. Yet the fact of being faced with a Christian adversary set new limits on German actions in the eastern march. From being a region beset by massive swings in power, the Danubian area became relatively stable, enabling power blocs to develop and consolidate.

The Austrian march under the Babenbergs was only one of such power blocs, and not obviously the strongest. To its north and east were non-Germanic kingdoms – Bohemia, Hungary and Poland – with Christian monarchs. Compared with these royal entities, the

Illustration 3. Power from below? 'The Investment of the
Carinthian Duke at the Prince's Stone (Fürstenstein)'. Josef
Ferdinand Fromiller, 1748.

mere margrave of Austria was a bit player, and until 1156 he was
subordinate to the duke of Bavaria.

   The first Babenberg margraves controlled very little of the territory even of modern-day Austria. To the west, Salzburg had long
been part of Bavaria and was developing into a clerical territory,
governed by the archbishop. West of Salzburg, in Tyrol, small lord-
ships remained the norm until the counts of Tyrol (named for their

castle near Merano) won control in the twelfth century. What is now Vorarlberg remained a feudal patchwork. It was even further from the Babenberg powerbase and largely Alemannic.

To the south and south-west, Carinthia and the new march of Styria (Steiermark) were developing as territories in their own right. Carinthia had become a duchy in 976 and could trace its traditions back to the time of its formation as a union of chiefs of the Slav Carantanii. Into the fifteenth century a new duke had to undergo a double ceremony, first in Karnburg being ensconced by a symbolic representative of the Carinthian people on the Fürstenstein, the remains of a Roman pillar, and only then sitting at the Herzogsstuhl on the Zollfeld to enfeoff his nobles. The first rite, pagan and symbolizing power coming from below, was abandoned in 1414. The second rite, Catholic and representing power coming from above, survived into the seventeenth century. Carinthia, for all its continuity, was a waning power; debilitated by feudal infighting, the duchy had lost much of its territory as march after march broke away, Carniola, Friuli, Istria and Verona among them.

Styria also began as a set of three Carinthian marches, established after Lechfeld. The four easternmost counties of Carinthia were added soon after for military support against the continuing Magyar threat. The territory, initially populated largely by Slavs, eventually was ruled by the Traungauer family. From their fortress in Steyr (hence Styria), the family, also known as the Otakars, built up their power through the usual feudal methods of both military and marital campaigns. In 1180, Otakar IV achieved ducal status, casting off the last vestiges of subordination to Bavaria. Styrian independence did not last long, however. The failure of Otakar to produce an heir led to the Treaty of Georgenberg of 1186, and the Babenbergs taking over Styria in 1192.

The Babenbergs' march was thus only one powerbase among many in the region. Inside the march as well, Babenberg power was far from complete. Much of the best land was possessed by clerical authorities, most notably the archdiocese of Salzburg and the diocese of Passau. In the feudal scheme of things, most of the rest of the territory was controlled by the march's nobility, the Babenbergs only having their demesne lands for truly reliable support. Over time the family was able to increase its direct holdings substantially, by inheritance, purchase and forfeit, but other noble families remained powerful. There was thus a constant struggle to pacify the march's nobility, either by agreement or by force. To help in this pacification, the Babenbergs introduced *ministeriales*, such as the Kuenringer family, indentured servants who were nevertheless given large administrative and military responsibilities. Over time the *ministeriales* became a new service nobility, intent on shedding its servile status, and hence potentially another source of resistance to ducal power. At the same time, the Babenbergs shared a mutual dependence with their nobilities in defending the march against its often more powerful neighbours.

In medieval power politics a family such as the Babenbergs needed great entrepreneurial and diplomatic skills to negotiate the fine line between keeping domestic vassals in line and maintaining and improving its external position. It also needed good fortune and the ability to reproduce itself, hence outlasting its dynastic rivals. For almost three centuries the Babenbergs played this game quite well. By the thirteenth century they had become ducal rulers of a vast swathe of the south-eastern Holy Roman Empire, of both Austria and Styria, and were maritally allied to the imperial, Hohenstaufen family.

This success was achieved by the skill of several Babenbergs, as well as by great risk-taking. The success or failure of dynasties was often a lottery, with best-laid plans foiled by a death in battle or from disease. With so many levels of power and so many players involved, any prince was reliant on the success or failure of his allies, and the often unpredictable consequences.

Imperial politics were dominated by the battles between the emperor and the papacy, which began with the Investiture Crisis in 1075, and then transmuted into the Guelph–Ghibelline Wars. The Babenbergs proved astute in backing one side or another, or both, depending on circumstances. Two Babenbergs were particularly adept at navigating the shoals of the imperial–papal conflict while strengthening their domestic base. After his father, Leopold II, had temporarily been dispossessed of the march by opposing Emperor Henry IV, Leopold III ended up in the good books of both Church and Empire by supporting the rebellion of Henry IV's son, Henry V. For his services, Leopold won the hand of the emperor's sister in 1106, greatly enhancing Babenberg prestige. Thereafter he kept his distance from imperial politics, concentrating on pacifying the Austrian nobility. He also was very generous towards the Church, founding both Klosterneuburg and Heiligenkreuz. He was canonized in 1485, and eventually became the Austrian patron saint.

His namesake Leopold VI followed a similar pattern at the turn of the thirteenth century. He was a staunch supporter of his relatives, the Hohenstaufen, in the Guelph–Ghibelline conflict; yet he was also a great patron to the Church, founding various monasteries and going on various crusades, both in the Middle East and in Western Europe (against the Albigensians and the Muslims in Spain). He married his daughter to Henry VII, Emperor Frederick II's son, and also mediated a settlement to the imperial–papal conflict in 1230. Within Austria, Leopold VI kept the nobility in check, and, seeing the future basis of wealth and power, bought several towns from their overlords, including Wels, Linz and Freistadt, as well as greatly enhancing the prospects of Vienna. By increasing his resource base at home, he enhanced control of his duchy, and made his value as an ally in imperial politics that much greater.

Other Babenbergs were less astute, but somehow managed to end up ahead, even when they lost. Henry II 'Jasomirgott', the first Austrian duke, achieved that title in 1156, and independence from Bavaria, in the *Privilegium minus* from Frederick Barbarossa, but only as a consolation prize for having to surrender the duchy of Bavaria itself, which his predecessor, Leopold IV, had gained in 1139.

Henry II's successor, Leopold V, was both astute and a brazen risk-taker. He managed to gain territory at the expense of Bavaria, and negotiated the Georgenberg Treaty with the Styrians. His arrest and imprisonment of Richard I of England in 1192 at Dürnstein then led to his excommunication for imprisoning a crusader; yet he was prepared to risk the spiritual consequences, for the ransom money which the English paid built the road from Vienna to Styria and new walls for many cities, as well as providing a new coinage. That this infamous episode took place as a result of a quarrel between Leopold and Richard at the siege of Acre during the Third Crusade also illustrates the risks feudal princes took, were bound to take, in pursuing their duties.

Illustration 4. Henry II Jasomirgott, on crusade. Detail from
the Babenbergerstammbaum, Klosterneuburg.

Illustration 5. Power from above: Göttweig Monastery.

Babenberg success was not merely based on skilful risk-taking and astute dynastic politics, however. The Babenbergs' march happened to be in one of the more fertile and hence prosperous parts of Central Europe. Once the Magyar threat receded, the land could be cleared and settled in earnest. There were huge opportunities, for the area was very lightly populated. In this 'Wild East', land grants to a noble or a religious order would be made by the emperor, or the margrave. Religious orders, such as the Benedictines and the Cistercians, were prominent recipients: many of Austria's most famous monasteries, such as the Benedictine Melk, Klosterneuburg and Göttweig, and the Cistercian Heiligenkreuz and Zwettl, were founded either in the late eleventh or early twelfth century, and were major agents of settlement.

The grantee then recruited his workforce from a peasantry that was largely enserfed. The attraction for a serf of becoming a settler was a relatively light level of feudal burdens, and the possibility of more land to work. This explains why many Bavarians were prepared to move east into the new areas, so much so that they soon predominated in areas which had originally been by majority Slav.

As the choicer territory was taken, the remoter and less fertile areas became targets of settlement, but this process took time. Into the thirteenth century the area north of Linz and into southern Bohemia was a massive forest, with only a few trade routes traversing it, and the border between Bohemia and Austria undefined – the archetypal forest of fairytales. It was only in the middle of the thirteenth century that local noblemen, among them the Wilherings, lords of Waxenberg, established settlements. The communities of the northern Mühlviertel were very late foundations. Leonfelden was first established as a parish in 1292.

As most of the land came under cultivation, with the growing of high-value crops such as grape vines expanding and new farming technologies, such as the iron-wheeled plough, introduced, the regional economy became more sophisticated, and towns became important commercial and administrative centres. The Danube became a significant trade route, and Vienna the most important entrepôt on it. Connected to the German heartland by the river westwards, the town was the gateway to Hungary, and beyond Hungary to the Byzantine Empire, giving Vienna, and Austria, an oriental orientation. Two of the most prominent Babenbergs, Henry II and Leopold VI, married Byzantine princesses.

Vienna's strategic commercial advantages were reinforced by Babenberg policy. Moving their residence along the Danube as their power expanded, the Babenbergs established themselves at Klosterneuburg in 1108, and Vienna in 1150. Leopold V spent part of his ill-gotten gains on improving Vienna, including building a lavish new wall, but it was Leopold VI who really established it as the urban centre of the duchy. He gave Vienna a crucial commercial advantage in 1221, when he conferred the right of the staple on the city's merchants. This gave them a monopoly on trade between Germany and Hungary on the Danube. The acquisition of Styria in 1192 also augmented Vienna's trading position by increasing contacts with Venice, as well as bringing the large revenues generated from the Erzberg, one of Europe's largest iron mines, into the Austrian ducal coffers.

The resulting prosperity was reflected in the cityscape, most notably in the lavish rebuilding of St Stephen's Church in the centre of the city from 1230. Vienna also played host to many of the great figures in early German literature. Minnesingers such as Dietmar von Aist, Walther von der Vogelweide, Neidhart von Reuental and the Tannhauser played at the court, whether under Leopold VI or his son, Frederick II. Perhaps most significantly, it was in Austria in the early thirteenth century that the *Nibelungenlied* was written. The story of the Nibelungs, in the original, takes place largely in the valley of the Danube, and not the Rhine.

The good fortune of Babenberg Austria did not last. Leopold VI died in 1230 and was succeeded by his son, Frederick II, who lacked his father's diplomatic and political skills. His antagonistic character – he was to be known as Frederick the Quarrelsome – left him ill prepared to manage the new forces in the land, whether religious institutions, towns or the new nobility of the *ministeriales*, let alone negotiate relations with his neighbours or Emperor Frederick II. *Duke* Frederick II's first years were a political rollercoaster, which saw noble rebellion and the emperor outlawing the duke, only for the emperor to be distracted by events in Italy, so that the duke could regain full control over his rebellious lands. The Mongol invasion of Eastern Europe (but not Austria) and the renewal of the imperial–papal conflict saw Duke Frederick II in control of his territories, and actively courted by emperor and pope alike.

The duke eventually settled down to managing his territory. In 1238 he divided the duchy into two administrative parts, Austria above the Enns (Upper Austria) and Austria below the Enns (Lower Austria), giving the Traungau (and Steyr) to Upper Austria at the expense of Styria. Another notable administrative action was the granting of a Patent of Protection for Jews in his land in 1244, largely to regulate the financial services offered by this group. Then fate took another turn: in June 1246, Duke Frederick II was killed fighting the Hungarians on the Leitha. Crucially, he had no male heir. The basis of ducal power, the *Privilegium minus*, provided for succession through the female line, but that was also unclear. By not ensuring a male heir, the Babenbergs had committed the cardinal sin of feudal European politics. It took decades of crisis and warfare before another dynasty was able to take their place in the region's politics: at that complex game, the Habsburgs were to prove masters.

Illustration 6. a) Leopold VI and b) Frederick II the Quarrelsome (with Vienna in background). Details from the Babenbergerstammbaum, Klosterneuburg.

Illustration 6. (*cont.*)

Illustration 7. Austrian Gothic: Saint Stephen's Cathedral, Vienna.

ENTER THE HABSBURGS, 1278–1439

On 26 August 1278 the army of Rudolf of Habsburg, the German king, defeated the forces of Otakar, king of Bohemia, near Dürnkrut on the Marchfeld, north-east of Vienna. Marchfeld was a major turning point in Austrian history, for it made the Habsburgs rulers of Austria. From then until 1918, Austrian history is inseparable from the career of this paragon of dynastic politics. The Habsburg family was to foster pretensions of a divine right to imperial rule, and eventually to world dominion. In the Habsburg cosmos Austria was often only a small element, swept along in the wake of the dynasty's grandeur, its giddying successes as well as its humbling failures. The entry of the Habsburgs was to change the meaning of what was Austrian.

Marchfeld came about as a result of the dying out of the male line of the Babenbergs in 1246, and the crisis and disorder unleashed by the ensuing succession contest. Seeking to restore order, a group of Austrian nobles invited Otakar, king of Bohemia, to take over as ruler in 1251. Otakar then married one of the female heirs, Margarete, subdued the nobles who had invited him, and established effective rule over Austria, Styria, Carinthia, Carniola, Friuli and even Aquileia. (In the process he divorced Margarete to gain a marriage alliance with Hungary.) With his Bohemian lands to the north, Otakar seemed on the verge of establishing an empire from the Baltic to the Adriatic sea. This was only possible, though, because of the collapse of the Empire into chaos on the death of Emperor Frederick II in 1250. It was to remedy this that the German princes elected Rudolf of Habsburg German king in 1273 – against Otakar's own candidacy.

Rudolf had followed a policy of restoring the imperial rights lost since 1250, especially as regards the main offender, Otakar. In the face of the overwhelming force amassed by Rudolf, Otakar submitted in 1276, handing back his Austrian territories to Rudolf. When it became clear that Rudolf intended to endow his own Habsburg family with these Austrian lands, much of his support, also within Austria, fell away. Otakar rebuilt much of his coalition, and Rudolf looked vulnerable. So Otakar took his chance on the Marchfeld. As a result of his victory, Rudolf was able to claim Austria, Styria and Carniola for his family, enfeoffing the territories to his two sons, Albrecht and Rudolf, in 1282, with Albrecht becoming sole heir by mutual agreement in 1283. Carinthia was enfeoffed in 1286 to Meinhard II, scion of the Gorizian counts and *de facto* lord of Tyrol, as reward for his support against Otakar.

The acquisition of the Austrian lands was a major step up for the Habsburg family. With their control of the Sundgau in Upper Alsace and the Aargau in what is now northern Switzerland (where the Habsburg, originally 'Habichtsburg', (hawk's fortress) was situated), the family had become prominent lords in southern German Swabia. Rudolf had expanded Habsburg control over more of the northern approaches to the St Gotthard Pass, one of the most important geopolitical points in medieval Europe, and was already a player of some weight in imperial politics. It was, however, his relative weakness that made him a good (malleable) candidate for king in the eyes of the prince electors. His gaining the Babenberg territories therefore represented a vast increase of prestige – and power. It was now the Habsburgs who were threatening to subdue the other German princes by realizing the potential of imperial-royal power.

Albrecht almost managed this. Initially passed over by the electors on his father's death in 1291, he forced his election as king in 1292. He then set about using his Austrian and Swabian powerbase to achieve real imperial-royal power in the Empire, on the successful French model of the time. Albrecht's plans were only foiled by his murder in 1308 at the hands of his dispossessed nephew, graphically known subsequently as Johann Parricida.

Reacting adversely to the prospect of Habsburg domination offered by Albrecht's reign, the prince electors chose another dynasty to provide his successor, Henry VII of Luxemburg. The politics of Luxemburg imperial ambition, however, had positive results for Albrecht's sons, Frederick and Leopold. Henry's plans for imperial coronation in Rome and acquiring the crown of Bohemia for his son, John, led him to ally with the Habsburg brothers, enabling them to put down rebellion and establish themselves in their Austrian lands.

When Henry died in 1313, the Habsburgs tried to regain the imperial mantle, but the election was contested, with Ludwig IV of Bavaria having the better claim over Frederick of Habsburg. The conflict between the Bavarian Wittelsbachs and the Habsburgs took years to resolve and was only (partially) settled in 1325, by the Treaty of Munich, which saw Ludwig and Frederick ruling jointly as kings. This was a Habsburg failure, for Frederick was king in name only, the real power being wielded by Ludwig. When Frederick died in 1330, the new Habsburg rulers, his two younger brothers Albrecht II and Otto, were quite prepared to trade Habsburg imperial ambitions for more local gains.

The distractions of the imperial contest had severely undermined Habsburg interests in their original powerbase north of the St Gotthard Pass. Habsburg pretensions had led to a coalescing of opposition in the Everlasting League of 1291, the nucleus of the future Swiss Confederation. The Swiss viewed Habsburg attempts to realize their feudal rights in the area with alarm and anger, for even at this point Swiss society did not follow the feudal norm. Swiss forces raided the abbey of Einsiedeln in 1313, and impudently beat back Leopold's army at Morgarten in 1315. It was a turning point

Illustration 8. Power from above: Hochosterwitz, Carinthia

in Habsburg – and Swiss – history. The Confederation, renewed in 1315, gradually became the counterpart, and then successor, to Habsburg power. By the beginning of the fifteenth century, the Habsburgs would be virtually excluded from their original home-land, and in 1415 ejected from the Habsburg itself.

It was during Frederick's reign that the Habsburgs, by origin Alemannic Swabians, began to style themselves as the 'dominium Austriae', rulers of Austria. Frederick's successors concentrated on their Austrian-centred powerbase at the expense of their Swabian or imperial interests. Albrecht II and Otto struck a secret deal with Ludwig IV whereby their acquiescence to his rule was met with his connivance in their acquiring Carinthia and Carniola in 1336. Albrecht II, sole ruler from 1339, avoided imperial squabbles and concentrated on consolidating his grip on Austria and his new ter-ritories to the south, even while the Habsburgs' Swabian position weakened further, with both Lucerne and Zurich joining the Swiss. Albrecht II's reign also saw the Black Death in 1348 and 1349, and a succession of other natural disasters, but the strong fiscal and political position that he had skilfully built up meant he could respond to these effectively, amongst other things stopping attacks in Vienna and elsewhere against Jews, whom a superstitious population blamed for their calamities.

His successor, his eldest son, Rudolf IV (1358–65), continued his father's policies, repairing the Habsburg position in Swabia and reforming administration and taxation in his Austrian lands. He lavished ducal largesse on his residence, Vienna, founding the city's university in 1365 and having the nave of St Stephen's rebuilt, thereby earning himself the soubriquet 'the Founder'. This founding zeal arose, however, partly from relative Habsburg weakness, as a response to the foundation of Prague University in 1348 and the renovation of St Vitus's Cathedral by the Luxemburg king of Bohemia, and since 1348 undisputed German king, Charles IV.

The Luxemburgs, also a family from the western German lands who had acquired even richer territories in the eastern parts of the Empire, now overshadowed the Habsburgs. Rudolf IV had married Charles IV's daughter in 1353, but he initially was resentful of his more powerful father-in-law. Most notoriously, he countered Charles IV's Golden Bull of 1356, which codified imperial law but also diminished the role of Bavaria and Austria (the lands of the Luxemburgs' rivals, the Wittelsbachs and the Habsburgs), by committing one of the great acts of fraud of medieval Europe: the *Privilegium maius*. 'Rediscovered' in 1359, this collection of five forged documents purported to be a grant of privileges from Emperor Frederick Barbarossa to the Babenberg dukes, which greatly enhanced Austrian status in the Empire. Amongst other things it granted the Austrian duke the title of archduke. Charles IV rejected most of these Habsburg claims, but he accepted some, and fiction became fact a century later when in 1442 the Habsburg emperor, Frederick III, accepted the *Privilegium maius* as valid.

Rudolf IV became much more co-operative when it became clear that Charles IV's support might garner Tyrol for the Habsburgs. This occurred in 1363 when the last in the Meinhard line of Gorizian counts, Margarete 'Maultasch' (already dispossessed by the Habsburgs of Carinthia and Carniola), gave Tyrol to the Habsburgs. With Charles IV's backing, Rudolf IV held on to it, against the Wittelsbach claimants and the Tyrolean nobility. With Tyrol under Habsburg control and the Habsburg position north of the St Gotthard relatively strong, the old Habsburg ambition of controlling all the major roads between Italy and Germany seemed achieved, a fact which Rudolf IV triumphantly proclaimed to the Venetian doge.

Co-operation with the Luxemburgs led to a dynastic inheritance treaty in 1364. At the same time Rudolf planned to strengthen his position astride the Alps by a marriage alliance with the Viscontis, dukes of Milan. Dynastic alliances with Milan, Bohemia and also Hungary promised an even stronger base for Habsburg ambitions, albeit as a junior partner to the Luxemburgs. Then, on the way to Milan for the marriage of his brother, Leopold, to Viridis Visconti, Rudolf, aged only twenty-seven, died.

Initially his brothers, Albrecht III and Leopold III, ruling jointly, continued his successful policies. They kept Tyrol, and acquired territory in Istria and Gorizia, as well as Freiburg im Breisgau, and land in Vorarlberg to link up their Austrian with their Swabian territories. Joint rule, however, proved unsatisfactory to Leopold, and in 1379 the Habsburg lands were divided, with Albrecht III gaining the heartland of Upper and Lower Austria, and Leopold III the rest. Divided rule of the Habsburg lands was to last more than a century.

By this time the Habsburg political entity was being referred to as 'domus Austriae', the House of Austria, and this was apt. The territories might still be under one roof, but different apartments were ruled by various family members. The Habsburg lands split in 1379, and split again in 1396, with more adjustments in the 1400s, as the brothers in the Leopoldine line, the sons of Leopold III – Wilhelm, Leopold IV, Ernst ('the Ironman') and Frederick IV – quarrelled over who should get what. The 'House of Austria' thus came to be split into three parts: Lower Austria (present-day Lower and Upper Austria); Inner Austria (Styria, Carinthia, Carniola and the Adriatic territories); and Upper Austria (Tyrol and the Habsburg possessions in Swabia and Alsace).

The actual situation was much more complicated than this simple triumvirate would suggest: in the late fourteenth and early fifteenth century the Habsburgs acted like characters in a soap opera. The Habsburg house kept being divided up differently, and parts swapped between brothers. Overshadowing and complicating these quarrels was the fraternal conflict in the House of Luxemburg between Charles IV's two sons, Wenceslas IV, king of Bohemia, and

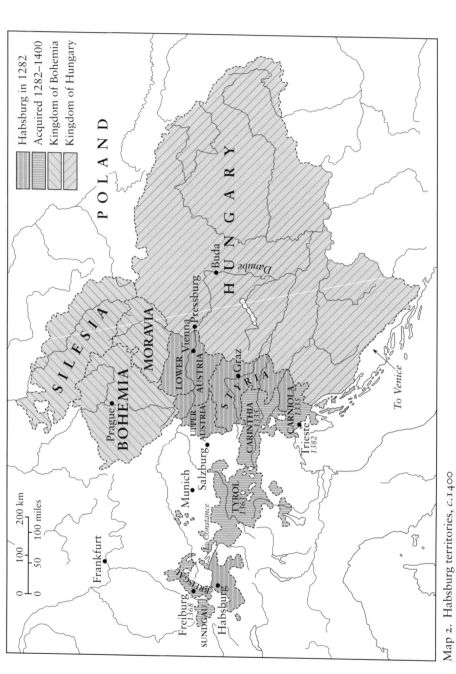

Map 2. Habsburg territories, c.1400

Legend:
- Habsburg in 1282
- Acquired 1282–1400
- Kingdom of Bohemia
- Kingdom of Hungary

POLAND

SILESIA

BOHEMIA
Prague

MORAVIA

LOWER AUSTRIA
Vienna
Pressburg

UPPER AUSTRIA

STYRIA
Graz

HUNGARY
Buda

Danube

CARINTHIA
1335

CARNIOLA
1335

Trieste
1382

To Venice

Munich

Salzburg

L. Constance

TYROL
1363

BREISGAU
1368

SUNDGAU

Habsburg

Freiburg

Frankfurt

0   100   200 km
0   50   100 miles

Sigismund, king of Hungary. The Habsburgs were in effect bit players in the major drama that saw Sigismund eventually replace his brother as German king in 1411, and as Bohemian king in 1419.

These divisions were not good for Habsburg power and status. Leopold III's aggressive policy of territorial expansion brought him Trieste in 1382, but his campaign in Swabia led to his death in 1386 at Sempach, and the effective end of Habsburg hegemony in Switzerland at Näfels in 1388. When Leopold III's sons divided up his lands, 'Upper Austria', Tyrol and the lands to its west, was left to Frederick IV. Frederick's reckless action in arranging the escape of Pope John XXIII from the Council of Constance in 1415 so infuriated Sigismund that he had him put under imperial ban and imprisoned at Constance. In Frederick's absence the Swiss Confederation conquered the remaining Habsburg territories in Switzerland, including the Habsburg itself in 1415. Frederick IV escaped from Constance in 1416, and managed to restore his position in Tyrol, but not in Switzerland.

His brothers, meanwhile, continued to argue over their Leopoldine inheritance, and then from 1404 over guardianship of the minor, Albrecht V, heir to the Albertine line in 'Lower Austria'. This led to civil war throughout the core Austrian lands. Foreign mercenaries, Hungarian and Moravian bands, local nobles, Vienna and other towns, all joined the fray, with devastating results. Eventually, in 1411 the (Lower) Austrian estates[2] resolved the situation by kidnapping a willing Albrecht V and installing him as duke.

Albrecht V's effective rule brought a return to order, although his close alliance with Sigismund, including his marriage to Sigismund's daughter, Elisabeth, involved Austria in the Hussite Wars, leading to turmoil in the duchy's northern reaches. The Viertel (quarter) organization of present-day Upper and Lower Austria was a response to the Czech Hussite threat. The horrendous persecution of the Jews of Vienna in 1421 was also largely owing to their being perceived as allies of the Hussites, although the duke's support of the persecution,

---

[2] The constituent 'estates' of the duchy of Lower Austria were the local Church prelates, the lords, the knights and the towns, in other words the local power-brokers, represented in the duchy's proto-parliamentary 'Landtag' or diet. Other Habsburg provinces had similar representative bodies, and similar estates structures were the political norm in late medieval and early modern Europe.

Illustration 9. The Erzberg (Iron Mountain), Styria: one of Europe's largest iron mines, a major source of revenue for Austrian rulers in the Middle Ages.

resulting in the death by burning of 212 of the wealthier Jews (and confiscation of their property), had more to do with his material self-interest.

Albrecht V was only a junior partner of the Luxemburgs, but playing the willing subordinate might have worked out well. On Sigismund's death in 1437, Albrecht V inherited the crowns of both Bohemia and Hungary, as well as being elected German king. Had he not died of dysentery in October 1439, while on campaign against the new threat of the Ottoman Turks, Habsburg hegemony in Central Europe might have begun a century earlier than it did. That he left only a posthumous heir, Ladislaw, proved a disaster for the Albertine line; it proved an immense boon for the heir's guardian, Frederick V of Styria. Himself once a ward of Frederick IV of Tyrol, Frederick V became guardian of both Ladislaw and Frederick IV's son, Siegmund. For the moment he held all the cards in the Habsburgs' dynastic game; he was to make good use of them.

It is hardly coincidence that Albrecht V died on campaign against the Turks. The ins and outs of the Habsburg and Luxemburg quarrels took place against the backdrop of two events that were harbingers of the future. The emergence of Jan Hus, the Council of Constance and the Hussite Wars that followed presaged the religious turmoil of subsequent centuries. Meanwhile, the Ottoman Turks had arrived in south-eastern Europe. Both events were recognized at the time to be of the greatest significance: the Turkish threat was the occasion for the first meeting of the Austrian Landtag. Yet just *how* significant only became clear later; the Habsburg response to these potent forces was to shape the region's history for the next three centuries.

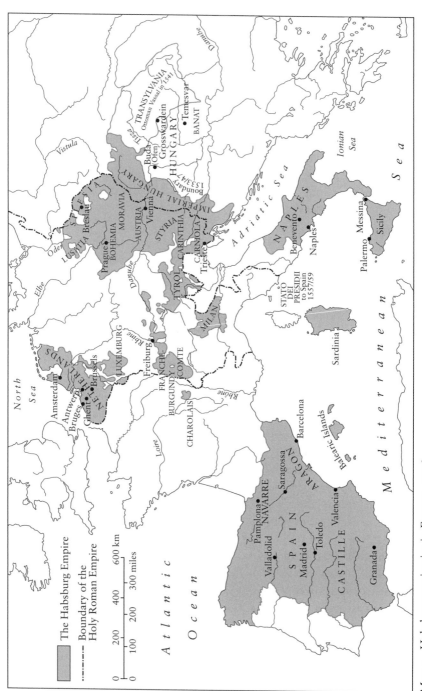

Map 3. Habsburg territories in Europe, 1556

The Habsburg Empire

Boundary of the Holy Roman Empire

North Sea

Atlantic Ocean

Vistula

Oder

Elbe

Danube

BOHEMIA
Prague
SILESIA
LUSATIA
Breslau
MORAVIA
AUSTRIA
Vienna
STYRIA
CARINTHIA
CARNIOLA
Trieste
TYROL
Freiburg
MILAN
Danube
Rhine
LUXEMBURG
NETHERLANDS
Amsterdam
Antwerp
Bruges
Ghent
Brussels
FRANCHE COMTE
BURGUNDY
CHAROLAIS
Loire
Rhône

TRANSYLVANIA
Ottoman Vassal in 1541
Buda (Ofen)
Grosswardein
Temesvar
BANAT
HUNGARY
IMPERIAL HUNGARY
Tisza
Boundary 1533/47

Adriatic Sea

Ionian Sea

NAPLES
Benevento
Naples
Palermo
Messina
Sicily

STATO DEI PRESIDII
to Spain 1557/59

Sardinia

Mediterranean Sea

NAVARRE
Pamplona
Saragossa
ARAGON
Barcelona
Balearic Islands
Valladolid
SPAIN
Madrid
Toledo
CASTILLE
Valencia
Granada

600 km
400
300 miles
200
200
100
0
0

2

AEIOU, 1439–1740

In 1451 Frederick V of Styria, elected King Frederick III of Germany in 1440, began his march on Rome, where, on 18 March 1452, he became the first Habsburg, and the last German king, to be crowned emperor by the pope in Rome, as tradition prescribed. With Frederick III began the Habsburg monopoly on imperial office until 1806 (excepting 1740–5), and the dynastic policies that were to bring his successors to the brink of universal monarchy. Yet Frederick III undertook his impressive procession to the imperial title in near bankruptcy and with little territory of his own. He could not pay for the march's expenses (the pope paid), and while he was proceeding to Rome the Austrian estates were in virtual rebellion, demanding the return of their rightful ruler, Ladislaw, Frederick's cousin and ward, whom Frederick had taken to Rome with him.

The rise of the Habsburgs to world power thus began with a claim to imperial and hence divine sanction quite at variance with modern notions of political reality. Over three centuries, from Frederick's becoming family head in 1440 to the accession of Maria Theresa in 1740, the Habsburgs sought to realize their divine right to rule, and not only to rule their own patrimony, but to preside as God's chosen dynasty over the entire civilized (Christian) world. Their sense of a special divine duty and hence right, the *pietas austriaca*, stretched back to Rudolf I, but it was given its most famous formulation by Frederick III in the acronym AEIOU, in notes made before he was even crowned emperor. In German this stood for: 'Alles erdreich ist Österreich unterthan'; in Latin: 'Austriae est imperare

37

omni universo.' In English: 'It is for Austria to rule the whole world.' Remarkably, for much of the sixteenth and seventeenth centuries, this claim to universal monarchy was almost realized. 'Austria' – the House of Austria, the Habsburg dynasty – at times threatened to achieve in reality the hegemony in Europe to which it felt entitled; as Holy Roman Emperors, the Habsburgs in any case could claim a formal superiority over Western Christendom.

This exalted position in Europe's political firmament was asserted against the political realities of early modern Europe, and against most of the current of early modern European thought. There was also the irony that the three instruments of 'divinely ordained' Habsburg hegemony in Central Europe, the crowns of the Holy Roman Empire, Bohemia and Hungary, were theoretically all elective.

One of the Habsburgs' great achievements as a dynasty was to turn all three of these elective offices into hereditary positions, *de facto* in the case of the Holy Roman Empire, *de jure* in the case of Bohemia and Hungary. Their success was a spectacular endorsement of the habit of bold assertion and dogged persistence, of the opportunistic invention and then defence of prerogative, which characterized the dynasty in its heyday. The Habsburgs always had a complicated relationship to fact and fiction: one of Frederick III's first acts after becoming emperor was confirmation of the forged *Privilegium maius* as the law of the Empire.

By necessity, the Habsburg rationale for their divine right to global rule changed markedly from 1440 to 1740, and their pretensions, eventually, became more modest. Competing justifications of power emerged, independent of the late medieval complex of the universalist imperial tradition with which the Habsburgs identified. These new sources of power and legitimacy – economic, religious and ultimately national – were eventually to threaten the very existence of the Habsburg Monarchy.

UNIVERSAL MONARCHY, 1439–1556

Frederick III had a very exalted view of his office and of the Habsburgs' mission, but he was a very weak monarch. For the first twenty years of his reign he was overshadowed by his brother, Albrecht VI, the Hungarian general, John Hunyadi, and the Czech leader, George Podiebrad. Frederick III's main source of power in this period was his wardship of Ladislaw, king of Bohemia and Hungary and duke of Austria. Frederick's dogged refusal to release Ladislaw, even after he had reached the traditional Austrian age of majority, twelve, combined with negligent rule of his ward's territories, eventually led to the Austrian estates forming the League of Mailberg in 1451 to force Frederick to hand over Ladislaw and restore legitimate government. By the time Frederick III returned from Rome in 1452, the League had grown to include Hunyadi and Podiebrad as well. Thus it was that the Holy Roman Emperor, besieged by his ward's subjects, was forced to release Ladislaw in September 1452.

Over the next years Frederick was a study in impotence and inaction. Byzantium fell in 1453, and the Turks advanced towards Hungary, but the emperor did little to help defend Christendom's borders. It was John Hunyadi who successfully withstood the Turkish siege of Belgrade; hence on Ladislaw's death in 1457 the Hungarian estates elected Hunyadi's son, Matthias Corvinus, as king. In Bohemia George Podiebrad was preferred as king to any continuation of Habsburg rule. Frederick was even challenged by his brother, Albrecht, whose invasion of Lower Austria in 1461 was widely welcomed as salvation from the previous state of brigandage. It was only Albrecht's death in 1463 that returned control of Upper and Lower Austria to Frederick.

In the 1460s Frederick ruled his territories fairly competently. He gained bishoprics for Vienna (a long-term Austrian ambition), Wiener Neustadt and Laibach; he also astutely bought the port of Fiume. Yet relations with the Austrian nobility remained poor, and Frederick did little to respond to renewed Turkish attacks on Hungary and the south-eastern Habsburg borderlands, except found the Order of Saint George in 1468. Prestige was no substitute for actual resources, and these Frederick III did not provide. The region's peasants ended up organizing their own defence units, but these were smashed by the Turks at Gloggau in 1478.

By then Frederick III was preoccupied with another threat: Matthias Corvinus, angered by Frederick's frustration of his plans against the Turks, declared war on Frederick, and, with help from the archbishop of Salzburg, swept through Austria. Vienna fell in

1485, Wiener Neustadt in 1487. Frederick was forced to flee to Linz, apparently a beaten man.

Yet Frederick III had also presided over a huge gain for the Habsburgs: the dynastic marriage alliance with Burgundy. The lands of the duke of Burgundy were strewn between France and Germany, from what is now southern France all the way to the Dutch coast, and included, in the 'netherlands' (as opposed to the 'upperlands' of Burgundy proper), some of the most prosperous areas of Europe. Although it had no legal standing as a realm on its own, and was bisected by Lorraine, Burgundy had become one of the leading powers in Europe in the fifteenth century, and one of the richest, with ambitions to match. Duke Philip 'the Good' had established the Order of the Golden Fleece in 1430, and his son, Charles 'the Bold', duke from 1465, had plans for an independent kingdom of Burgundy, similar to the medieval 'middle kingdom' of Lotharingia. The Burgundian court at Malines was one of the most lavish in Europe, and Burgundy a power to reckon with, especially in the upper Rhine.

It was to obtain Burgundian support that Siegmund of Tyrol persuaded his cousin Frederick III to negotiate a marriage alliance between Frederick's son, Maximilian, and Charles's only daughter, Maria, and the couple were betrothed at Trier in late September 1473. Negotiations stalled, however, and then Siegmund switched sides, making peace with the Swiss at Constance in 1474 in the 'Everlasting Settlement' (ending Habsburg interest in Switzerland). After setbacks for Burgundy, negotiations resumed and the marriage alliance was agreed in May 1476. When Charles was killed at Nancy in January 1477, Maximilian rushed to Burgundy to ensure the engagement with Maria. On 10 August, Matthias Corvinus invaded Austria; on 19 August, Maximilian married Maria at Ghent, setting the Habsburgs on the path to being the greatest of dynasties.

Maximilian now had to defend his wife's territories against Burgundy's liege-lord, the French king Louis XI. Maria died in 1482, and Maximilian was forced into large concessions to France in the Peace of Arras of 1482, but he proved remarkably resilient. In 1486 he was elected king of the Romans (German king); in 1488 he was almost handed over by the citizens of Bruges to the city of Ghent for execution; by 1490 he was able to buy out his cousin, Siegmund, and acquire Tyrol for himself.

Maximilian clearly liked Tyrol: he made Innsbruck, situated as it was midway between the Burgundian and Austrian territories, his capital. He had an elaborate chapel for his tomb built there (in which he is not buried), which is a three-dimensional piece of dynastic propaganda, with statues to such Habsburg ancestors as Arthur, king of the Britons. He was rarely able to reside for long, however, as he was constantly on the move defending old rights and establishing new ones.

To the west he continued to struggle with the French over the Burgundian inheritance, which he largely regained in 1493. To the east, the death in April 1490 of Matthias Corvinus allowed Maximilian to reconquer occupied Austria, and the Peace of Pressburg of 1491 with Wladislaw II Jagellon, king of Hungary and Bohemia, saw the Habsburgs retain a subsidiary right to succession in Hungary and in full control of their Austrian lands. Frederick III died on 19 August 1493 – as a huge success, leaving his son as head of the houses of both Austria and Burgundy.

Maximilian became *de facto* emperor, and continued his father's propagandistic assertion in word and image of the Habsburgs' divine right to be the imperial dynasty. He also proved to be the great master of expanding Habsburg influence through marriage, fully justifying the often quoted saying:

> Bella gerant alii, tu felix Austria nube,
> Nam quae Mars aliis, dat tibi regna Venus.[1]

Maximilian realized two marriage alliances, with the house of Castile in Spain and the house of Jagellon in Central Europe, which together garnered the Habsburgs Spain, the New World, much of Italy, as well as most of Central Europe. He could do this because the Habsburgs presented themselves as a counterweight to the other two emerging great powers in early modern Europe: France and the Ottoman Empire. Yet marriage as a strategy was only part of the secret to Habsburg success. When both marriage alliances brought the Habsburgs much more than had originally been envisaged, they were able to assert their rights not only in propaganda and ritual, but

---

[1] 'Let the others wage war, you, happy Austria, marry!/What Mars gives to others, will be Venus's gift to you.'

also on the battlefield. Despite what the adage implies, Maximilian and his successors waged wars aplenty.

If the complex power relations on the upper Rhine helped the Habsburgs acquire the Burgundian inheritance, the even more intricate balance in Italy led to the Spanish inheritance. In 1494 France's invasion of Italy shocked the endemically warring parties there into forming the Holy League of 1495. In the accompanying negotiations Maximilian and Ferdinand of Aragon undertook a marriage alliance: Maximilian's son, Philip, married Juana, the daughter of Ferdinand and Isabella, in 1496, and Maximilian's daughter, Margaret, married the *infante*, Juan, in 1497. The death of Juan in October 1497 then made Philip and Juana heirs to the Spanish lands. Philip's death in 1506, and the subsequent grief of his widow, declared madness, meant that it was their son, Charles of Ghent (his birthplace in 1500), who became sole heir to the Spanish domains. This constituted a huge boost in Habsburg power.

Maximilian also attempted to shape the Holy Roman Empire into an effective counter to the French Valois kingdom, unsuccessfully. His attempts to create a more effective, centralized imperial government were opposed by a concerted effort to institutionalize the federal, decentralized nature of the Empire. A constitutional framework was created, with the Imperial Chamber Court (*Reichskammergericht*), an imperial tax (the *Reichspfennig*) and a federal structure of twelve districts (*Kreise*), but although the Empire might assume the forms of a state, like those emerging in France, Spain and England, it lacked substance.

In the Austrian lands proper, Maximilian also attempted fiscal and administrative reform with a view to the hereditary lands becoming a base for strengthening imperial power. Their mineral wealth, the iron mines of Styria and the copper and silver mines of Tyrol, especially the mine at Schwaz, had been crucial in securing him the loans needed to fight his wars and finance his imperial politics. Hence he instituted the beginnings of centralized government in the Regiment, in effect regent councils, for Tyrol in 1490 and for Lower (i.e. modern-day Upper and Lower Austria) and Inner Austria in 1493. Maximilian was one of the first Habsburgs to adopt a bureaucratic approach to governing, but he deferred to the estates when they resisted the expansion of the newfangled executive bodies, and the initiatives for more radical change died on the vine.

Illustration 10. Maximilian I as Sovereign of the Order of the Golden Fleece. Flemish, *c.*1519.

Maximilian's half-heartedness in domestic reform was owing partly to the distraction of his constantly waging war. In 1498 he was fighting the French, in 1499 the Swiss. In 1504 he intervened in the conflict between the Palatinate and Bavaria, picking up territories such as Bavarian Kitzbühel. In 1507 he was at war with

Hungary, as a negotiating tactic. Venetian hostility meant that the Most Serene Republic blocked his way to Rome and coronation as Holy Roman Emperor. In response, on 4 February 1508, Maximilian declared himself 'elected Roman emperor', a huge step in the separation of the German polis from its originally universalist and italocentric traditions.

Maximilian spent years caught up in the vicissitudes of the wars over Italy, criss-crossing the continent to do battle. In August 1513 he led an English army against the French at Guinegate, and a few weeks later in October joined the Spanish in defeating the Venetians at Vicenza. The eventual result of all this hectic campaigning was an exhaustion of his resources, without much to show for it. The peace treaties of 1516 with France and Venice left Maximilian with a few gains, such as Cortina d'Ampezzo, but also losses, such as Verona.

He tried to mobilize the Empire against the French threat, and was one of the first German monarchs to play the German national card, but without much response from the Empire's princes. He was a master at employing the majesty of the emperor; he even had an autobiographical poem, *Theuerdank*, published to embellish his image. Yet his efforts were not matched by his resources, despite the Tyrolean mines and the wealth of the Burgundian lands. He spent too much time warring, and not enough persuading the particularist forces in the Empire and his territories to accept more efficient governmental and fiscal structures. In the early modern world of emerging nation-states he remained more the 'last knight' than a Machiavellian 'prince'.

He was, however, expert at arranging dynastic marriage alliances. Near the end of his reign he achieved another double marriage, of his grandchildren, Maria and Ferdinand, with the children of Wladislaw II Jagellon, Louis and Anna. With the Turkish threat providing the incentive, a pact over mutual rights to succession in 1491 became a dynastic agreement in 1506 and the double marriage alliance of 1515. Maximilian himself served as proxy groom to Anna in the betrothal ceremony. It was only in 1516 that his grandson, Ferdinand, agreed to the marriage, which took place in 1521.

Maximilian had died on 12 January 1519 in Wels, having been booted out of Innsbruck for not paying his bills. He had not yet been able to secure the election of his grandson Charles as German king, but he had left him a panoply of territories, with dynastic opportunities in yet more. His marriage alliances with Spain and in Central Europe were to shape Habsburg destiny for the next four centuries.

Maximilian's heir, Charles V, had become duke of Burgundy and king of Castile in 1506. He had reached his majority in 1515, and the death of Ferdinand of Aragon in 1516 had left him king of all Spain, to which he went in 1517 to secure his throne. After Maximilian's death, and heavy bribery, Charles was unanimously elected German king on 28 June 1519, but it was only in October 1520 that he journeyed from Spain for his coronation at Aachen. Meanwhile a delegation from the Austrian estates had gone to Spain to demand the abolition of the Regiment, only to be sharply rebuffed; nevertheless, the estates of the various hereditary lands each in turn pledged allegiance to their new ruler, who appeared to have the world at his feet.

Apart from Spain, the Burgundian lands and the hereditary Austrian lands, Charles was ruler of extensive territories in Italy and the Mediterranean thanks to the Aragonese inheritance. Overseas, Spain already had colonies in the Caribbean, and Hernán Cortez had landed in Mexico in February 1519. (The conquest of Peru by Pizarro was to follow in 1532.) In the Holy Roman Empire, Charles was not only king and (elected) emperor, but, shortly after his accession, he had also acquired Württemberg. The Habsburg territorial inventory seemed such a powerful combination that the apparently impossible dream of universal monarchy implicit in Frederick III's AEIOU now looked realizable. As Charles V's chancellor, Mercurino Gattinara, put it to him in 1519, he did seem 'on the path to universal monarchy' so as to 'unite all Christendom under one sceptre'.[2] With his motto being 'Plus ultra' (Still further), it seems that this was a path that Charles had confidently chosen to take.

Yet the claim to universal monarchy was never realistic. The France of Francis I also had ambitions and had some decided advantages, such as internal lines of communication and relatively efficient

---

[2] Jean Bérenger, *A History of the Habsburg Empire, 1273–1700* (Harlow, 1994), pp. 144–5.

administration. Even when bullion flowed in from the New World, French revenues were still a match for Habsburg finances. The sheer extent of Habsburg lands made them virtually unmanageable as a coherent platform for universal monarchy. Even as Charles V had been crowned emperor, his Austrian subjects were refusing to recognize the old Regiment in Vienna, and setting up their own. Similar unrest among local ruling castes intent on preserving their autonomy marked many of Charles's other territories, most notably the Netherlands.

Two other factors militated against Charles's goal of universal monarchy. One was very material. If France resisted from within Christendom, the Turks posed an immense threat from without. The other was more ethereal, but with even greater consequence, and that was the appearance of Martin Luther. In the same year that Maximilian had published his chivalric poem, *Theuerdank*, Luther, on 31 October 1517, had posted his ninety-five theses on the door of the Castle Church in Wittenberg. The emergence of Protestantism was a direct and mortal threat to the world view of traditional Catholic Christianity, on which the Holy Roman Empire's authority, and hence that of the Habsburgs, depended. With Lutherans, then Calvinists and other sects on the scene, Charles V might have a great deal of power, but the concept of 'uniting Christendom under one sceptre' was spiritually hollow. There was, moreover, a link between the threat of the Turkish infidel and the challenge of the Lutheran heretic: while fending off the former, Charles found it impractical to suppress the latter.

The great size of Charles V's Empire made it a threat to everyone else, and yet its sheer extent and lack of integration made it unwieldy as an instrument of power. Charles V made things worse with his immense pretensions to world hegemony, in the Habsburg tradition. A more modest and charismatic ruler might have persuaded his fellow princes that the threat was so great from the French, Turks and Protestants (to say nothing of rebellious lower orders) that Habsburg hegemony was necessary for their own protection. Yet Charles V could never make himself loved, and though he might make himself feared for extended periods, he could never do so for long enough to achieve his aims. But then, Machiavellian *raison d'état* was not Charles V's style.

To mitigate the consequences of his inevitable absences from his wide-ranging territories, Charles V adopted an old Habsburg tradition by parcelling them out to be governed by various family members. This was also a form of consolation for those family members, especially his younger brother, Ferdinand. The consolation prize for the cadet line in 1521 was the original Habsburg hereditary lands of 'Lower Austria' (Austria above and below the Enns, and Inner Austria). This was improved in 1522 by adding Tyrol with its silver mines, but it was still very much the lesser portion of the Habsburg domains. The farming off of the original Austrian lands to Ferdinand was also, at this point, only temporary: Charles V, as head of the family, was still their ultimate ruler.

Charles V was fully occupied in ruling his domains, and fighting for them. His early years were taken up with war against the French in Italy, in the course of which Charles's troops, unpaid and looking for compensation, sacked Rome in 1527. This disgraceful event diminished Charles's prestige, but he was still militarily in the ascendant. At the Peace of Cambrai in 1529, Charles accepted the loss of the duchy of Burgundy, but forced the French to give up Milan. At the ceremony on 24 February 1530 in Bologna – Rome still not having recovered from the sacking of 1527 – Pope Clement VII crowned Charles Holy Roman Emperor and duke of Milan. This was the last time any Holy Roman Emperor was crowned by the pope.

That year, 1530, saw Charles V concentrating on the Empire for the first time since he had interrogated Luther at the Diet of Worms of 1521. In the emperor's absence Lutheranism had spread rapidly, *especially* in the Habsburgs' Austrian territories. By the Augsburg Diet of 1530, the Lutherans had become an organized, established factor in the Empire, as exemplified by the presentation of their *confessio Augustana*. This transformed imperial politics, and the emperor's role in them. Charles V succeeded in getting his brother, Ferdinand, elected as king of the Romans (and hence his successor) on 5 January 1531; but the rejection by Charles V of the Lutheran position and the election of his Catholic brother led the Protestant princes and estates in the Empire to form the Schmalkaldic League in February 1531, which soon had French backing. The Turkish advance on Vienna in 1532 revealed the new dynamics of imperial politics: Charles V had to appeal to the Nuremberg Diet to provide an imperial army to defend Vienna, and could thus no longer move against the Lutherans. Instead, Protestant forces in the Empire, with French – and English – backing, invaded Württemberg, forcing Habsburg surrender of it in 1534.

Charles V, foiled, again lost interest in the Empire. In 1535 he launched a strategically foolish but symbolically prestigious invasion of Tunis, near the former site of Carthage, the ancient Roman enemy. Charles continued in the mode of Roman emperor by celebrating his victory with a triumphal march in Rome in 1536. By the 1540s Charles's victories elsewhere had emboldened him to attempt the smashing of the Schmalkaldic League and the restoration of Catholic supremacy. He had the pope call a General Council at Trent, a Church territory abutting Habsburg territory, in 1545, and an imperial army defeated the League at Mühlberg in 1547. Now apparent master of Germany, Charles imposed in the Interim of Augsburg of 1548 a re-establishment of Catholicism throughout the Empire.

Charles had over-reached. In 1552 the Protestant princes allied with the French king, Henry II, at Chambord. Charles's erstwhile ally, Maurice of Saxony, led a mainly Protestant but partly Catholic army to rein in the emperor. While Charles managed to elude the humiliation of capture at Innsbruck, and was able to respond by besieging Metz in the winter of 1552, this turn of events proved a decisive blow. The failure of the siege of Metz in January 1553 led to Charles's decision to resign his political offices, beginning in 1555.

The Religious Peace of Augsburg of 1555 saw the principle of *cuius regio, eius religio* (the religion of the ruler is the religion of his subjects) established in the Empire. It was left to Ferdinand to sign, for the emperor himself would not put his name to this recognition of the end of Catholic supremacy and religious unity that was his ideal. Charles resigned as ruler of the Netherlands in 1555; of Spain in 1556. In September 1556 he surrendered the imperial office to Ferdinand (who was only actually elected emperor in 1558). Charles retired to Spain, where he died in 1558.

With him died any credible Habsburg attempt to establish universal monarchy. Philip II of Spain, Charles's son, still pursued that goal, and he registered some success. The defeat of the French at St Quentin in 1557 led to Habsburg control of Italy. With France sliding into religious civil war, and silver flooding in from South America, Philip II was clearly the most powerful ruler in Europe. If, as Charles had wished, Philip had succeeded him (or at least Ferdinand) as Holy Roman Emperor; if the dynastic marriage of Philip to Mary of England in 1554 had borne fruit, or his overtures to Elizabeth of England in 1559 had succeeded, something approaching universal monarchy might have been realized and Habsburg, world, history been quite different. Yet the religious revolution could not be negated even by the king of Spain's great wealth and power, try as he might.

In the wake of the failure of Charles V's project of universal monarchy, the cadet branch was left with many of the House of Austria's responsibilities but not that much of the dynasty's resources. Stuck with by far the poorer part of the patrimony, Ferdinand I and his successors had to deal with the largely Protestant and restless Austrian lands, the divisions of the Empire and the Turkish threat. How they nevertheless adapted to meet these challenges is the story of the founding of the Habsburg Monarchy.

THE BASTION OF CHRISTENDOM, 1521–1648

The territories which Charles V ceded to Ferdinand – effectively in 1521, formally in 1556 – were not the most prized in the Habsburg portfolio. Compared with Spain, the Netherlands and the Habsburgs' Italian territories, their German and Central European lands were of only moderate worth, and they were directly threatened by two of the Habsburgs' greatest problems: the Turks and the Protestants.

Economically, the Danubian region had declined relative to Western Europe as trade had shifted to the Atlantic, and trade to the east was blocked by the Turkish invasion. There was still a flourishing mining industry, although much of it was controlled by the Habsburgs' south German financiers and it was soon to be undercut by New World bullion inflows. There was also a partial commercialization of agriculture in the region, which meant prosperity for large landowners, but also a 'second serfdom' for many peasants, causing serious unrest. The Austrian lands paled in economic significance even compared with Bohemia, let alone the Habsburg Netherlands.

When Ferdinand arrived in 1521, he even had a revolt of the estates in Lower Austria to face.

Ferdinand nevertheless quickly recovered the situation and proved a remarkably effective ruler. If he did not solve the religious question to his satisfaction, he was able to make good on the Jagellonian windfall of 1526, and he provided the rudimentary structures of an Austrian Monarchy that proved able to withstand the Turks, the religious problem and the particularist forces of the estates. His initial years were occupied by suppressing estates' revolts in Lower Austria and elsewhere, and peasant revolts in the mid-1520s, both quite bloodily. What he could not stop was the rapid spread of Lutheranism to most of the populace in the Austrian lands.

His position was transformed on 26 August 1526, when the Hungarian army was decimated by the Turks at the Battle of Mohács, and the young King Louis II Jagellon was killed. According to the dynastic marriage alliance of 1515, Ferdinand was now heir to the Bohemian and Hungarian crowns. Yet both crowns were in theory elective, and Ferdinand could only achieve his 'rights' if he could 'win' an election, by a majority of electors or *force majeure*. In Bohemia, Ferdinand's election proved straightforward if expensive. In Hungary, however, his election was contested by John Zápolya, and a power struggle ensued with large parts of Hungary beyond Habsburg control.

Then in 1528, having withdrawn after Mohács, the Turks reappeared. In 1529, Suleiman the Magnificent advanced on Vienna and laid siege to it in September. The siege was lifted in October, as the Turks withdrew for the winter, but in 1532 there was another major attack, causing Charles V to summon an imperial army, including Protestants, to defend Christendom. The Turks retreated on that occasion, but were still in charge of much of Hungary. From 1537 to 1547 Ferdinand tried to reconquer his Hungarian territory, the Turks continued to raid Austrian territory, and the Zápolya party pressed its cause from Transylvania. The ceasefire of 1547 saw Ferdinand having to pay the Turks 30,000 ducats per annum to maintain the peace, and Hungary split roughly into three areas: Royal Hungary, a western/north-western band from Croatia to largely Slovakian north-west Hungary; autonomous Transylvania under Zápolya's son, John Sigismund, in the north-east; and the bulk of the kingdom under Turkish control. Hostilities soon resumed, without much effect. The Treaty of Constantinople in 1562 recognized the borders of 1547, and continued the annual 30,000 ducat payment. Between Royal and Turkish Hungary there was now a designated 'military frontier', with fortresses on both sides.

Ferdinand was left with only part of his 'rightful' inheritance of 1526, but he had still achieved much. He had stopped the Turks, and his Bohemian and Hungarian acquisitions dramatically changed the nature of the junior Habsburgs' territories. What before had been an almost entirely German-speaking populace (apart from some Italians and Slovenes) had now become polyglot. The Bohemian acquisition was also a large gain for Habsburg power. Not only did the Bohemian crown automatically confer electoral status, but its lands were also much richer than the hereditary Austrian lands. When the Estates General of the newly united territories met in 1542 to pay for the Turkish wars, the Bohemian lands were invited to pay two-thirds of the bill.

Territorial expansion and the Turkish threat necessitated a recasting of Habsburg government. Building on Maximilian's reform attempts, and using the Burgundian government as his model, Ferdinand adroitly introduced the core elements of centralized government. In 1527 his *Hofstaatsordnung* established a Privy Council (*Geheime Rat*) as the supreme executive organ of his new, amalgamated Monarchy; an Aulic Council (*Hofrat*) as the supreme court of justice; and a Court Chancellery (*Hofkanzlei*) for administration. In 1556 the Aulic War Council (*Hofkriegsrat*) was established to co-ordinate the Hungarian campaign.

The successful imposition of this new, centralizing regime reveals a prince with much political acumen, especially considering Ferdinand had come to Austria not speaking German, but Ferdinand also knew not to over-reach. Only the bare bones of central government were introduced. In 1537 both the Bohemian lands and Hungary were exempted from the purview of the Aulic Council. The Bohemian and Hungarian Chancelleries remained independent of the Court Chancellery, which in 1556 became an imperial rather than Austrian institution. Only in 1620 would a specifically Austrian Chancellery be established. Most significantly, Ferdinand's government was always reliant on the various provincial estates to provide

Illustration 11. 'Allegory on the House of Austria'. School of
Bartholomäus Spranger, 1580s. Austria is the central figure on
a rock; at her feet are Europe (on a bull) and Africa (on an
antelope). The four men trying to tear down the left obelisk
are the French king, a Turk, a Jew and an American Indian.
The inscription at the base of the obelisk is: Immota manebit
(She will not be moved).

additional tax revenues for the expensive Turkish and Hungarian
wars. These noble-dominated assemblies were prepared to do this
(as the peasants paid the taxes), but at the price of Ferdinand leaving them in control of local government, and tolerating Lutheranism
throughout his lands.

Luther's message had spread rapidly in the Austrian lands in the
1520s, especially in the towns and among the nobility. Noble sons
flocked to the northern German universities, where the new theology was taught. The Habsburg authorities tried initially to suppress
Protestantism, and in 1524 Kaspar Tauber was executed in Vienna
for heresy. Yet the Lutheran tide could not be stopped. Even the
Anabaptists managed to establish a community in Moravia, where,
as the Moravian Brethren, they remained until the seventeenth
century.

The renewed Turkish threat further helped the Protestant cause. When Ferdinand called on the Estates General of Austrian and Bohemian provinces in 1541 for help against the Turks, it responded by demanding religious concessions. In the late 1540s Ferdinand, riding Charles V's success, reasserted royal power, especially in Bohemia. Nevertheless, Protestantism kept spreading, even to Slovenian Carniola. Monasteries rapidly lost personnel as monks and nuns left their orders in the wake of the Protestant message.

Ferdinand's response was complex. As 'advocatus ecclesiae' he was supposed to defend the Catholic Church, and fidelity to Mother Church had been a feature of Habsburg myth. Yet Ferdinand, like his brother, retained the ideal of a united Church, and wanted accommodation *within* the Church, rather than schism or coerced uniformity. Unlike their Spanish cousins, the Austrian Habsburgs of the sixteenth century did not wholeheartedly back the militant drive for Catholic uniformity begun at Trent.

Ferdinand was more willing than Charles V to compromise to achieve the Augsburg Religious Peace of 1555, and although this settlement allowed the territorial ruler to impose his religion on his subjects, this did not happen in the Habsburg lands. Instead Ferdinand tolerated the communion in two kinds demanded by Utraquists[3] and Lutherans. In 1562, Emperor Ferdinand advocated a reconciliatory policy at the Council of Trent, but his *Reformationslibell* was rejected.

Ferdinand presided from the 1550s over a Catholic counter-offensive in the Habsburg lands, but it was based more on persuasion than force, centred on the Jesuits and Peter Canisius, founder of Prague's Clementinum. Ferdinand did not welcome the general militancy of the new Catholic establishment that emerged from Trent in 1563, and the hardening of doctrinal disputes which it signalled. The inability to reach an inclusive religious settlement before his death in 1564 was his greatest disappointment.

Ferdinand provided in 1554 for the division of his lands amongst his sons on his death. While his eldest son, Maximilian II, succeeded to the imperial, Bohemian and Hungarian thrones, as well

---

[3] Utraquists, the mainly Czech followers of Jan Hus, were so-called because they demanded communion in *both* the bread *and* the wine.

as inheriting the Austrian twin duchies, his other sons, Ferdinand and Charles, were given 'Upper Austria' (Tyrol and Further Austria) and Inner Austria respectively. Habsburg Austria thus returned to the complexities of divided rule, and the usual deleterious consequences further debilitated the Austrian Habsburgs' response to the Turkish threat and the internal religious crisis. The immensely powerful Spanish branch of the dynasty still had an influence on the Austrian branch that was sometimes supportive, but could also complicate and undercut Austrian policy. The 'Black Legend' that developed about the tyrannical and fanatical king of Spain, out to eradicate Protestant 'freedom', made Austrian Habsburg attempts at accommodation with *their* Protestant subjects that much harder.

Maximilian II was interested in such an accommodation. As a young man he had been attracted to the moderate Lutheran thought of Melanchthon and his Philippist followers, who had tried to reunite the reformers and the Catholic Church. This was very near to the stance of Maximilian, who reputedly confided to the papal nuncio: 'I am neither Catholic nor Protestant, I am Christian.'[4] Maximilian II did not become Protestant once he became emperor, as some had thought (or feared) he would, but he rejected the aggressive tactics of the Counter Reformation. He practised a relatively tolerant policy towards his Protestant subjects, resulting in the *Assekuration* of 1571, legalizing Protestantism among the noble orders in Lower Austria. He made similar concessions in Bohemia, where the vast majority was Protestant.

Maximilian's readiness to compromise was partly a result of his need for revenue to fight in the renewed conflict in Hungary, where by 1568 Transylvania had become a virtually independent princedom. The relative peace after 1568 allowed Maximilian to indulge in his fruitless campaign for the Polish crown, but the continuing Turkish threat meant that extra money was still needed for reinforcing the frontier, and the largely Protestant estates held the purse strings.

The nearer the Turkish threat was, the more it deterred implementation of the Counter Reformation. Ferdinand of Tyrol, far from the Turkish threat and with a still largely Catholic populace, could

[4] Bérenger, *A History of the Habsburg Empire*, p. 222.

impose a fairly aggressive Counter Reformation. His equally zealous brother, Charles of Inner Austria, the territory most exposed to
Turkish raids, had to concede the *Religionspazifikation* of 1572, giving the nobility broad religious freedom. Charles, however, founded
a Jesuit college in Graz in the same year. How long the Catholic
enthusiasts among the Habsburgs could be held back by the estates
and the moderation of the Austrian family head was becoming an
open question.

Maximilian II was succeeded by his eldest son, Rudolf II, in 1576.
Following a practice designed to ensure the inheritance of the Habsburgs' elective crowns, Rudolf had already been elected king of Hungary and Bohemia, and 'king of the Romans'. He had been raised
at the Spanish Habsburg court of Philip II, but he seems to have
remained more in the Austrian tradition of Charles V's universalism.
Hence he was prepared to countenance contemporary confessional
pluralism in the hope of future reunion, although he was reluctant to
grant official recognition of Protestant rights in the Austrian duchies
or Bohemia.

Bohemia clearly attracted him, for he moved the capital of his
assorted lands to Prague. This may have been partly owing to
Lutheran excesses in Vienna (riding horses in St Stephen's), but also
because Prague was at the centre of his richest province, and far
from the Turks. Rudolf established an elaborate court, ushering in
a Golden Age for Golden Prague. He became one of the greatest
patrons of the arts among the Habsburgs, and it was Rudolf II who
commissioned the crown of the House of Habsburg (with which
no Habsburg was ever crowned). He also evinced a great interest
in the sciences, both esoteric and natural, in an era when the difference between the two was unclear. Rudolf invited two of the
era's greatest astronomers, Tycho Brahe and Johannes Kepler, to
Prague, but he also indulged his interests by inviting astrologers and
alchemists.

Rudolf had a vaunted notion of the prestige of the imperial
title, and the Habsburgs' right to be at the head of the world's
monarchs, but he was not that interested in actually governing. He
therefore delegated the rule of many of his lands to his brothers,
and that is where complications began. The brothers Habsburg –
Ernst, Matthias, Maximilian and Albrecht – had, like Rudolf, been

Illustration 12. Crown of the House of Austria. Jan
Vermeyen, 1602. Commissioned by Rudolf II, no Habsburg
was ever crowned with it.

educated in Spain. In 1578 they each received a portion of the family
inheritance, and they were eventually found jobs within the family
enterprise. Maximilian became master of the Teutonic Order, and
then regent of Inner Austria, later Tyrol; Ernst was a regent in Lower
and Inner Austria, and then governor for Philip II in the Netherlands until 1595; Albrecht, at first a cardinal, later married Philip
II's daughter and became joint-ruler of the southern Netherlands in
1598. One brother, Matthias, proved very difficult to accommodate.

By 1595 he was in charge of both Upper and Lower Austria, but this was to prove not enough.

The decentralized character of Rudolf II's rule explains how religious policies in the Austrian Habsburgs' lands varied so much. While Rudolf himself was moderate in his early years, his uncle in Tyrol, Ferdinand, was implementing the Counter Reformation in full. In Upper Austria the Counter Reformation was not very active. What weakened Protestant hegemony here was the divisive effect of the peasant revolt, and a theological split within Lutheran ranks. Lower Austria saw a more concerted and successful effort at Counter Reformation directed by the cleric Melchior Khlesl. Protestant preachers were expelled from Vienna, and peaceful reconversion efforts in many cities swung the balance there in the Catholics' favour.

In Inner Austria the confrontation of 1578 between Charles and the estates over new religious concessions, the *Brucker Pazifikation*, had sparked a Catholic counter-attack. Relatively modest at first, the campaign of Counter Reformation began in earnest once Charles's son, Ferdinand II, came of age in 1595. Princely 'reformation commissions', with military escorts, began re-Catholicizing parishes by force. While the nobility were left alone, the campaign slowly changed the religious character of the region, coming in 1600 to the provincial capitals, Graz and Klagenfurt. What made this decisive, intransigent policy particularly significant was that Ferdinand was the likely heir to all Austrian Habsburg territories.

Ferdinand's campaign was all the more remarkable for the fact that it took place in the teeth of the Turkish threat. Turkish raids had continued after 1568, and full-scale warfare resumed in 1593. The campaign began promisingly, with the occupation of Transylvania in 1598, but a crass attempt to impose a Counter Reformation there led in 1604 to revolt, and war not only with the Turks but with the Hungarians as well. The peace settlement in late 1606 saw Transylvania become a virtually independent bastion of Protestantism, and the Habsburgs also made major concessions to the Hungarian estates, including religious liberty, in order to have the dynasty's right to rule restituted; the Turks recognized the emperor as an equal for the first time, and the yearly tribute to them became a one-time 'gift'. Yet the dreams of reconquest with which the Austrians had started resulted in only a marginal redrawing of the frontier in Hungary, with, if anything, Turkish gains.

Habsburg recriminations about the war's disappointing outcome were aimed largely at Rudolf II's alleged incompetence as emperor. Rudolf had indeed become more erratic in his decision-making, and had already responded to criticism in 1605 by giving Matthias responsibility for the war and negotiating peace. Rudolf found the resulting peace unsatisfactory and secretly dissociated himself from it, but in a clandestine meeting of the archdukes on 25 April 1606 arranged by Khlesl, it had already been agreed that Matthias would replace Rudolf as head of the family.

The resulting 'quarrel' (*Zwist*) in the House of Habsburg upset the fine balance in the Habsburg lands between dynasty and estates. It created ironic alliances: Matthias, a supporter of the Counter Reformation efforts of Khlesl, now had to seek support from the estates in Hungary, Moravia and the two Austrian duchies, whose leaders were almost all Protestant. The meeting of the Austrian and Hungarian estates at Pressburg in February 1608, which supported Matthias, was boycotted by the Catholic clergy and nobility. Rudolf, in turn, who had imposed the pro-Catholic 'Spanish party' on Bohemia in 1600, was saved from immediate defeat by the Bohemian estates. The great beneficiaries of this crisis were the estates and the Protestants, who could now auction their support: the two Habsburgs were forced into a competition of concession that culminated in Rudolf's Letter of Majesty (*Majestätsbrief*) of 9 July 1609, guaranteeing religious liberty in Bohemia for 'Utraquists', in reality all Protestants.

There was now open war between Rudolf and Matthias, with the latter clearly in the ascendant. Rudolf looked to his cousin, Leopold V, bishop of Passau and Strasbourg, for rescue, but Leopold's attempt to aid Rudolf with an attack on Prague by his *Passauer Kriegsvolk*, an unruly mercenary army, only led to the Bohemian estates turning to Matthias, who was crowned king of Bohemia in May 1611. Rudolf II, left in the Hradschin, Prague's massive royal citadel, with only his imperial title, died on 20 January 1612.

Matthias was elected emperor in June 1612. He soon re-established his residence in Vienna, but re-establishing Habsburg power was harder. Domestically, the estates and the Protestant interest had greatly increased their power and privileges. Matthias failed to assert Habsburg power in Transylvania, and the Treaty of Vienna with Turkey in 1615 saw few gains – but it did extend the peace for twenty crucial years.

With crises over Donauwörth in 1607 and the succession of Jülich and Cleves in 1609, the Empire was entering a serious crisis over the religious balance of power, and by 1609 a Protestant Union faced off against a Catholic League. Neither side was much interested when at Regensburg in 1613 Khlesl proposed a *Komposition*, a compromise. Khlesl was made bishop of Vienna in 1614 and cardinal in 1615, but his moderation was no longer in fashion, especially not with the heir apparent, Ferdinand II of Inner Austria.

It was in Bohemia that matters came to a head, politically, religiously and nationally. In 1615 the Bohemian diet passed anti-German legislation, which Matthias was forced to accept. The prospect of the intransigent Ferdinand II as emperor and king sharpened the conflict. Ferdinand II was duly elected and crowned as Bohemian king in June 1617, but over strong opposition from the estates' radical faction, which soon after gained ascendancy. The argument over religious rights escalated until, on 23 May 1618, furious estates representatives threw the two leading royal officials and their secretary from a window in the Hradschin. None was seriously hurt, and they escaped, but the defenestration of Prague was the signal for war.

Initial attempts by Matthias at compromise were foiled by Ferdinand, now formally king of both Bohemia and Hungary. He had Khlesl secretly arrested and locked up in Ambras Castle in Tyrol. Matthias now found himself, as his brother Rudolf before him, powerless to oppose his usurping successor. The war party of Ferdinand II, supported by the Spanish relations, was already in charge, when Matthias died on 20 March 1619.

The Thirty Years War exacted a huge demographic and economic price on Central Europe, especially in Germany. Although the Bohemian crownlands, especially Silesia, were also badly affected, the Austrian lands were largely spared devastation. Yet the war did have a profound effect on the Habsburg project. In the rollercoaster of the war's fortunes the Habsburgs' ambitions of political hegemony and religious conformity at times appeared close to realization, but, ultimately, their over-reaching and the superior military power of France and Sweden deflated Habsburg pretensions in

Europe and the Empire. At the same time, the war increased the Habsburgs' ability to realize those pretensions within their Central European territories.

The implications of war in 1619 were as little understood as those in 1914. Initially, it was not even clear that the Bohemian crisis was anything but a domestic dispute. The Bohemian estates' election of Frederick V of the Palatinate, leader of the Protestant Union, as Bohemian king elicited no rallying to the cause by the Protestant powers. Ferdinand II was elected emperor in August 1619 by a unanimous vote of the electoral princes, Frederick V of the Palatinate included. In March 1620 Protestant Saxony allied with Ferdinand II, and a non-aggression pact with the Protestant Union in July left the Catholic League, led by Maximilian of Bavaria, free to help Ferdinand II against the Bohemians.

Ferdinand needed Bavarian help, for the Bohemian rebellion was only part of a general estates rebellion across the Habsburg lands. Both the Upper Austrian and Lower Austrian estates, with Georg Erasmus von Tschernembl a leading figure, joined the Bohemian cause in the summer of 1619, along with the estates of Moravia, Silesia and Lusatia, and that winter the Transylvanian prince, Gabriel Bethlen, occupied most of Royal Hungary. Ferdinand II was able to deter a Bohemian attack on Vienna in 1619, and to reject the 'Storm Petition' of the Lower Austrian estates, but his internal position was weak. He was so desperate for external help that he mortgaged Habsburg lands reconquered by Bavaria (Upper Austria) and Saxony (Lusatia). He also welcomed help, and direction, from his Spanish cousins. The ensuing war was as much about the Spanish Habsburgs' attempt at European hegemony, as it was about the Austrian Habsburgs' position in their provinces and the Empire.

This external help, combined with rebel disorder, resulted in dramatic Habsburg success. Upper Austria was conquered, and then combined Catholic–imperial forces under Jean Tserklaes de Tilly, a Walloon, overran the Bohemian army in half an hour at the Battle of the White Mountain on 8 November 1620. Ferdinand II showed little 'Habsburg clemency'. Twenty-four of the rebel leaders were executed on one day, 21 June 1621, in Prague, and many more were expropriated and forced into exile. Their lands were parcelled out to reward loyalists and foreign collaborators. All the privileges wrung by the estates were deemed forfeit. The Counter Reformation was introduced in its most brutal form; by the 'Renewed Provincial Ordinance' (*Verneuerte Landesordnung*) of 1627, the Bohemian crown was made hereditary to the Habsburgs, and the powers of the diet reduced to a bare, ornamental minimum. The events of 1620 crushed Bohemian resistance. Czech culture and literature virtually disappeared, as German became the governing language; Bohemia now became the main engine of Austrian Habsburg absolutist power.

Then Ferdinand II, urged on by his Spanish and Bavarian allies, expanded the war to the Empire. His ruthless campaign against Frederick V and the Palatinate rallied the Protestant forces, and turned a domestic crisis into an Empire-wide war. The Dutch United Provinces and then Denmark intervened for the Protestant cause. With other campaigns in Hungary, the Swiss Grisons and Mantua – to secure the overland route from Madrid to Brussels via Milan for Spanish armies – the war now ranged over much of Central Europe. Although France was also becoming involved, the Spanish and imperial forces, the latter led by their new 'capo', Albrecht of Wallenstein, still dominated, and by 1629 Ferdinand II appeared the master of the Empire.

Even the mortgaging of Upper Austria to Bavaria had worked to Habsburg advantage. The duchy's new Bavarian rulers had combined a campaign of re-Catholicization and a crushing tax burden (to recoup Bavarian expenses) with exceptional cruelty, epitomized by the 'Frankenburg lottery' (*Frankenburger Würfelspiel*), in which peasant leaders were forced to play dice to decide who would be executed. This led to a peasants' revolt in 1626. The Mühlviertel was one of the centres of the uprising, and Leonfelden was the site of one of the revolt's major battles that summer, on 30 August. A joint Bavarian–imperial army put down the revolt and savage repression followed. When the province was returned to Austrian control in 1628, the resistance had been crushed, and the populace almost thankful to return to Habsburg rule, despite the imposition of both Counter Reformation Catholicism and absolutism. In Lower Austria alone of his Austrian lands was Ferdinand II prepared to tolerate Protestantism, but only among loyal nobles. Elsewhere Protestantism was banned, its adherents given the stark choice of conversion or emigration.

Ferdinand II, flush with victory, now over-reached. His Edict of Restitution of 1629 tried to return the Empire to the religious position of 1555. This assertion of imperial power was too much not only for the Protestant powers, but also for his allies. At the Electors' Meeting (*Kurfürstentag*) in 1630, they reined in Habsburg power, and forced Ferdinand II to sack Wallenstein. By then the Swedish army of Gustavus Adolphus II had already landed at Stralsund.

German Protestants were initially hesitant in their embrace of the Swedish entry into the war, backed as it was by Catholic France and with Sweden clearly having designs on the German Baltic coast. Any hesitancy disappeared, however, after the disastrous burning to the ground of Magdeburg in April 1631 by Tilly's imperial troops. In less than a year, Gustavus Adolphus II had imposed Swedish military hegemony in most of Germany, with Prague and Bavaria under Swedish occupation.

With even the Austrian lands threatened, Ferdinand II turned once more to Wallenstein, who, now 'supremo', salvaged the military situation. Even after Gustavus Adolphus's death at Lützen in 1632, however, the Swedish war effort continued, with France an ever larger factor, and Wallenstein became virtually an independent factor in the war. The eventual result was, on Ferdinand's oral command, Wallenstein's murder in February 1634. The loyal imperial generals were happy to divide up his wealth and vast estates among themselves, but the manner of Wallenstein's death was a serious blow to Habsburg authority, for it seemed to confirm the turpitude of the imperial house.

The year 1634 saw a string of imperial victories, and victory at Nördlingen would have sealed an advantageous peace for the Habsburgs, had the war not become by now much more than merely a German affair. France declared war on Spain on 19 May 1635, and the war entered its final and, for the Habsburgs, disastrous phase. By the end of 1636 northern Germany was once more under Swedish domination. When Ferdinand II died on 15 February 1637, his more pragmatic successor, Ferdinand III, was left with having to salvage the Habsburg enterprise from the wreckage left by his father's extremism.

The Habsburg, Catholic and imperial forces were rolled back. Alsace was taken by France in 1639; Swedish armies roamed into central Germany and Bohemia, and then in 1642 into Silesia and Moravia. Appeals by the Austrian Habsburgs to their once so powerful Spanish cousins were now futile. Pressed by the French, with its supply lines along the Rhine cut off, and with Catalonia and Portugal in revolt, Spain was collapsing as a military power.

The Austrian Habsburgs and Bavaria were on their own. Fortifications hastily put up on the northern border of the Austrian lands, remains of which can still be seen outside Bad Leonfelden, were ineffective. Swedish armies roamed through Bohemia, and in 1645 one invaded Lower Austria, occupying Krems. It might have joined up with a Transylvanian army to take Vienna, had the sultan not forbidden further Transylvanian advance. Bavaria was occupied in 1646; in 1647 a Swedish army took Bregenz; another Swedish army took the Hradschin at Prague in the summer of 1648, despoiling it of Rudolf II's fabled collections. In the autumn of 1648 peace was finally signed between the emperor and his French and Swedish adversaries at Münster and Osnabrück respectively. War between France and Spain went on until 1659, but the Peace of Westphalia ended hostilities in Central Europe.

Peace was made on French and Swedish terms. Actual territorial losses incurred by the Austrian Habsburgs were not that great, largely involving territories in Alsace ceded to France. Lusatia, mortgaged to Saxony, was ceded outright. Austria's Bavarian ally even managed to retain the Upper Palatinate and the seventh electoral vote. More serious for the Habsburgs was the diminution of the Empire and of their role in it. Switzerland and the United Provinces left the Empire entirely, and the remaining estates members now became fully independent political actors: they changed, in effect, from estates to states. The Empire was reduced constitutionally to a loose states federation, linked merely by the elective office of the emperor, the diet and the two law courts. The war to realize imperial power ended up eviscerating imperial power. Even worse for the imperial Habsburg house, Westphalia saw the strengthening of rival centres of power both in and next to the Empire. France, Sweden and Denmark now could meddle at will in imperial matters, and Bavaria, Saxony and Brandenburg gained territory.

On the European stage, the Habsburg ascendancy had been supplanted by French Bourbon hegemony, and in the Empire Habsburg power much diminished. Domestically, however, the war was a triumph for Habsburg absolutism and Counter Reformation Catholicism. The destruction of estates power and Protestantism in the Bohemian and Austrian lands was confirmed. Only in parts of Silesia and among the Lower Austrian nobility was Protestantism still tolerated. Large numbers, estimated at almost 200,000 from Bohemia and 100,000 from the Austrian hereditary lands, emigrated rather than convert. Most remaining Protestant nobles eventually converted to Catholicism, and (with the exception of Hungary) the Habsburg lands became a model of Baroque Catholic uniformity. Pretensions to universal monarchy were now forfeit, but the Habsburg world view of divine election and religious conformity was now realizable on Habsburg territory in ways it had not been even under Charles V: the establishment of the Habsburg Monarchy, with its trinity of dynasty, Church and aristocracy, could now take hold in earnest.

The impact of this new regime on Austrian history was to be profound. Many former Protestants in the Austrian hereditary lands became 'crypto-Protestants', making formal obeisance to the Catholic faith, but retaining if not a formal Protestant faith then a very strong scepticism or downright hostility concerning Catholic doctrine. This 'crypto-Protestant' tradition has been seen as continuing, both in popular religion and in high, intellectual culture, into the modern era, contributing strongly to the Austrian and Viennese penchant for distrusting any equation between appearance and inner reality, outward conformity and inner conviction. On the other side of the coin, 'Austria' became a byword among Protestants abroad, and later the disciples of Enlightenment and liberals, for the forced conformity to the superstitious religion of Baroque Catholicism.

This identification could go very deep. When he was choosing a motto for *The Interpretation of Dreams* in 1899, Sigmund Freud initially chose 'Flavit et dissipati sunt' (He blew and they were dispersed). Although eventually replaced by a quote from the *Aeneid*, this quotation appears apt for Freud's 'talking cure'. There is, however, one word missing from the original, which appeared on a commemorative coin, minted to celebrate the English victory over

Illustration 13. Armada medallion: 'Flavit et dissipati sunt'.
Gerard van Bylaer, 1588. Note the Hebrew letters at the top.

the Spanish Armada in 1588. On the coin, the Latin words appear
around a depiction of Philip II's navy being destroyed in a gale;
above this appears the word for God in Hebrew letters. It is the
Hebrew God's breath that is depicted. Freud's psychoanalysis can
be seen thus as yet another episode in the fight for spiritual freedom,
seen in the Protestant, English and Jewish traditions, against the
oppressive forces of Philip II, Spain, Catholicism, the Habsburgs –
and Austria.[5]

---

[5] W. J. McGrath, *Freud's Discovery of Psychoanalysis: the Politics of Hysteria*
(Ithaca, 1986), pp. 172–3.

THE ESTABLISHMENT OF THE HABSBURG
MONARCHY, 1648–1740

The century following the Thirty Years War saw another vast transformation in the fortunes of the Habsburgs and their Central European territories. The war's immediate aftermath saw both economic and demographic recovery, and consolidation of the new political, religious and cultural hegemony we know as Austrian Baroque. This domestic consolidation was followed by great success abroad, especially on the south-eastern frontier, which led by 1714 to the establishment of the Habsburg Monarchy as a great power in the European state system. Yet the foundations of the Monarchy's power and authority were shaky, its reliance on traditional notions of imperial and religious legitimation anachronistic in the light of the emerging concept of the rational state.

The Austrian Habsburgs were to find it hard to adapt to the age of Enlightenment because of their very success in tailoring their mission to the age of the Baroque. The style of 'Baroque' had actually appeared north of the Alps before the imposition of Counter Reformation Habsburg power, in non-Habsburg Salzburg. Under the patronage of a line of cultured archbishops, Wolf Dietrich, Marcus Sitticus and Paris Lodron, the city was transformed into the 'German Rome'. Italian architects led the building of such masterpieces as the cathedral (1628) and the archbishops' summer residence, Hellbrunn (1613–19), with its famous water games. Hellbrunn was also the site of the first performance of Italian opera north of the Alps, in 1618.

Salzburg maintained neutrality throughout the Thirty Years War, and the success of Baroque as a style and a culture in Central Europe was not ineluctably tied to Habsburg triumphalism in its subjugated territories. Yet that was the role it was given in those territories, and it proved very well suited. On the 'mala strana' (narrow bank) in Prague, the new dominant class of magnates, from both old and some very 'new' families (ex-adventurers and contractors who had been given expropriated estates), built Baroque palaces that embodied their exalted position in the new order. The basis of this new order was the imposition on the peasantry of a 'second serfdom', especially in conquered Bohemia, and the rise of the high aristocracy and the institutions of the Counter Reformation Church at the expense of the lesser nobility. An immense reservoir of resources was thus amassed to lavish on palaces, churches, and other expressions in stone and plaster of the glorious, divinely sanctioned order of the Habsburgs – aristocracy and Church.

The Baroque assumed that its celebration of God's order on earth would act as a sustaining factor of the political order, and this approach had strong roots in Habsburg tradition. Austrian Baroque can be defined as Italian art put in the service of promoting Habsburg power in Central Europe. The result was a new hybrid of Italianate, German and Central European culture that still marks the former Habsburg lands.

For all its achievement, the culture of the new Habsburg dispensation was one anchored in superstition and confessional intolerance. The persistence in the belief in magic, in alchemy and hermetic knowledge marked out the Habsburg lands as an anachronistic oddity. Admittedly, Newton himself dabbled in alchemy, and an age beset by recurrent plague and epidemic was prone to search for supernatural explanation, but the Counter Reformation emphasis on Christian white magic, the supernatural intervention by saints and the self-sufficiency of Catholic doctrine made Habsburg Central Europe tangential to the 'Age of Reason'.

It was during this period that the various Christian cults received their greatest development – whether the Habsburgs' favourite, the cult of the Eucharist, as embodied in the annual *Fronleichnam* (Corpus Christi) procession, in which Francis Joseph was still participating in the early twentieth century, or the cult of the Virgin Mary. In 1676, Leopold I visited the shrine of the Virgin at Mariazell, and made her the *generalissima* of his imperial army.

Confessional intolerance was common to the era, also in Britain and France. Yet Habsburg intolerance possessed a particularly retrogressive quality. The imposition of religious uniformity in the Bohemian and Austrian lands went surprisingly smoothly, although quite how deep the transformation was among the populace is debatable; once the various reform commissions had obtained formal, outward conformity to Catholicism, the pastoral responsibilities for vast swathes of the population were again neglected. In Hungary, however, the attempts to impose Catholic uniformity never fully succeeded, and burdened Habsburg–Hungarian relations.

Illustration 14. Mariazell, Styria. Pilgrimage centre and
major symbol of 'pietas austriaca', Habsburg piety.

At its worst the darker side of Austrian Baroque produced a foul
blend of obscurantism and xenophobia. In 1670, Leopold I banished Vienna's Jewish community, partly at the behest of Viennese
merchants, but partly to satisfy the Catholic zealotry of his Spanish
wife. Perhaps the most powerful literary exponent of the Austrian
Baroque was Abraham a Sancta Clara, court preacher in Vienna

Austreibung der Juden im Jahre 1670

Illustration 15. 'March of the Jews from Vienna and other places in 1670'.

from 1677. Born Johann Ulrich Megerle in Swabia, he became famous for his outlandish and burlesque sermons, in which witty use of language distracted from the incoherence of the message. Praised as models of inspirational oratory, these sermons were full of moralizing, bluster and deep insecurity, expressed in vehement attacks on Protestants, Turks and Jews.

The strange mixture of confidence and insecurity that typified Austrian Baroque culture partly arose from the precariousness and incoherence of the Habsburgs' position in the larger world. The gap between Austrian Baroque ideology and material reality was immense: on the European stage the Habsburg emperor was almost always dependent after Westphalia on Protestant allies to defend his position against *Catholic* France.

France was the dominant power in Europe after Westphalia. On Ferdinand III's death in 1657, his son, Leopold, only achieved election as emperor in 1658 by bowing to French pressure and agreeing to a Capitulation that forbade the Austrian Habsburgs to aid their Spanish cousins. Even a Catholic triumph such as the abdication of Queen Christina of Sweden in 1654 and her conversion – in a ceremony performed in the Court Chapel at Innsbruck – could result in a war won by Austria, but a peace in 1660 won for Sweden by French diplomacy.

Initially Leopold I resisted the logical conclusion of French dominance. Instead of joining with Protestant powers in opposing Louis XIV's aggression in the War of Devolution of 1667–8, Leopold took the path of appeasement. Yet the French attack on the United Provinces in 1672 compelled Leopold to resist. The Dutch War of 1672–9 saw the fervently Catholic emperor allied with Calvinists and Lutherans against his cousin and fellow Catholic, Louis XIV, for the simple reason that the alternative was complete French dominance. As it was, the Peace of Nijmegen of 1679 ushered in an era of French expansion through the 'reunions' of territories on France's eastern border, culminating with Strasburg in 1681.

Habsburg influence in the west was compromised by Habsburg policies to the east, most notably in Royal Hungary and Transylvania. In 1664 an imperial army, formed at Leopold's request to beat back the Turks, won a decisive victory at Saint Gotthard in Styria. Leopold, however, concerned at the French threat in the west, agreed to a peace so disadvantageous that it drove the Hungarian leadership into a fury, and eventual revolt. The initial resistance of a Catholic 'magnates' plot' was ineffective, soon discovered and the ringleaders executed in 1671. It was when Leopold, in reaction, imposed an absolutist regime and a large-scale campaign of Counter Reformation that a rebellion in the northern counties began in 1672, soon changing into a full-scale civil war between the Protestant '*kuruc*' (crusaders) and the Catholic loyalist '*labanc*' (pedestrians).

In 1681, Leopold made large concessions to the Hungarian leadership, with restoration of Protestant rights foremost. Yet the *kuruc* revolt continued, supported by the Ottoman Grand Vizier, Kara Mustapha, who in turn was being encouraged by the French to attack Austria. The background to the siege of Vienna of 1683 was thus a Hungarian liberation movement combined with French diplomacy. The *kuruc* campaign in 1682 remained limited to Hungary, but Kara Mustapha decided to exploit the ensuing Habsburg vulnerabilities by sending a large army finally to conquer this bastion of Christendom that had eluded the Turks since the sixteenth century.

The Turkish advance on Vienna in 1682–3 proved to be a god-send for Leopold and the Habsburgs. Despite French delaying tactics, most of the states of the Empire and Central Europe rallied to the emperor's side. Pope Innocent XI and most of the Italian states, Spain and Portugal provided money. The Habsburg army, under Charles, duke of Lorraine, initially retreated to the north bank of the Danube, leaving a well-garrisoned Vienna to face the Turks. The city was besieged from mid-July. With the garrison commanded by Count Ernst Rüdiger von Starhemberg, and the townsfolk led by Mayor Andreas Liebenberg, Vienna withstood Turkish attempts to breach the walls, while a large army, with contingents from the Empire in addition to Habsburg and Polish forces, gathered. This army attacked from the Kahlenberg on 12 September 1683, destroyed the Turkish army, and pressed home the victory in a sustained counter-attack.

Legend has it that the relief of the second siege of Vienna brought about two great culinary institutions, the coffeehouse and the croissant or *Kipfel*, a crescent-shaped breakfast pastry that was first baked in Vienna to celebrate the victory over the Muslim Turks, and which Marie Antoinette subsequently brought to France. Breakfast pastries in Paris are still called *viennoiseries*.

The relief's real effect on Austrian history was transformative. Before 1683 the defence of the Habsburg position in the Empire against French encroachment had been the first priority. Now the collapse of the Turkish threat and the march of the Habsburg armies deep into the south-eastern borderlands quite changed the dynamic of Habsburg power. Charles, duke of Lorraine, embodied this change. With France having occupied his lands, he had entered Habsburg service to fight on the Rhine; but now he was achieving glorious victories on the Danube

The success was spectacular. With French neutrality secured by recognition of the 'reunions', the armies of the Holy League swept onward. Poland dropped out in 1685 as a result of French pressure, but was replaced by Brandenburg. Ofen fell in 1686 and in 1688 Belgrade was taken.

The War of the League of Augsburg brought the offensive in the east to a temporary halt in 1689, and the mishandling of relations with the region's Serbian and Albanian populations also hampered

Illustration 16. 'Siege and Relief of Vienna 1683'.

the campaign. In 1690 Belgrade was lost, upwards of 30,000 Serbs retreating with the Habsburg armies to be resettled eventually in southern Hungary. Habsburg fortunes reached a new crescendo when in 1697 Prince Eugene of Savoy, another Western European who began in the French orbit but who made his career in the 'Wild East', became the new commander-in-chief. His crushing victory at Zenta on 11 September 1697 sealed the humiliation of the once mighty Turkish army.

The Peace of Carlowitz of 1699 provided enormous gains for the Austrian Habsburgs. All of the kingdom of Hungary, except for a small strip of Slavonia and the Banat of Temesvar, was now Austrian, as was Transylvania. The war in the west, with Leopold allied to the leader of Protestantism and England's 'Glorious Revolution', William of Orange, had also brought Habsburg gains in 1697, but these were dwarfed by the success in the east.

The military success against the Turks (and the *kuruc*) also greatly strengthened Leopold's position within Hungary. After a rather brutal regime was initially imposed in the newly acquired lands, Leopold, learning from past mistakes, sought accommodation with the Hungarian leadership. At the Pressburg diet in 1687 he agreed to uphold the Hungarian constitution and respect Protestant rights. In return the diet agreed to make the Hungarian throne hereditary in the male line of the House of Habsburg, and surrendered the right of resistance. In 1690 Leopold also recognized the traditional constitution of Transylvania, and in December 1691 he issued the *Diploma Leopoldianum*, a constitution that guaranteed the religious and national rights of the traditional groups in the diet (although not those of the Orthodox Romanians). By 1699 Leopold's moderation had secured his acceptance in both Transylvania and Hungary, and the undisputed right of the Habsburgs to rule a vastly expanded empire.

Meanwhile the Spanish Habsburgs, lacking a male heir for Charles II, was facing the ultimate dynastic nightmare: extinction. The question of the Spanish succession dominated European politics at the end of the seventeenth century. When Charles II died in 1700, there were only two serious candidates for the succession: either an Austrian Habsburg or a French Bourbon. Until the last days it appeared that Charles II had chosen Leopold's second son, Charles of Austria, as his sole heir, but in his very last will Charles was persuaded to bequeath his empire to Philip of Anjou, Louis XIV's grandson. Louis XIV offered a partition of the Spanish territories, but on terms unacceptable to Leopold. The outcome was the War of the Spanish Succession.

From 1701 until 1714, France faced most of the rest of Europe and, despite humiliating setbacks, was still able to hold on to Spain and much of its empire for the Bourbons. Yet the war also saw Habsburg Austria become the lynchpin of the new balance of power in Europe, and the full fruition of the alliance between Protestant England and the Catholic emperor. This reached its apogee in the series of Allied victories at Blenheim (1704), Ramillies (1706), Oudenarde (1708) and Malplaquet (1709), in which Marlborough's 'English' victories were made possible by support from Eugene's Austrian army. The war had fronts not only in the Netherlands, but also Italy, the Rhine, Spain itself, the colonial territories, and even Hungary, with a resurgence of the *kuruc* rebellion. The possibility of yet another, northern front was avoided by Joseph I's promising Charles XII of Sweden to respect the rights of Silesian Protestants at Altranstädt in 1707.

In 1703 there was a severe crisis for Austria, resulting from a Bavarian attack and a Hungarian uprising, but once Blenheim removed Bavaria from the war in 1704, the campaign went so well that the prospect of a vast expansion of Habsburg power opened up, even the restoration of the dual Spanish–Austrian Habsburg hegemony. By 1709 Louis XIV was prepared to sue for a disadvantageous peace. Yet the Allies, having won the war, could not win the peace, and in England, the peace party of the Tories won elections. Even worse, on 17 April 1711, Joseph I, emperor since Leopold's death in 1705, died of smallpox, leaving Charles as heir.

Charles was elected emperor in 1711, and his position was strengthened by the peaceful ending of the *kuruc* insurrection that year, but having the same Habsburg on the imperial and the Spanish throne contradicted the nascent balance of power policy of the maritime powers, England and the United Provinces. Charles VI, still stubbornly dreaming of the Spanish throne, was deserted by his allies, who made peace with the French at Utrecht in 1713. After battling on for a while, Charles VI signed a less advantageous peace at Rastatt in 1714.

Charles and the Habsburgs still had made large gains. 'Austria' had tacitly to accept the loss of Spain itself and the Spanish overseas empire, but it acquired most of the rest of Spain's European empire: large chunks of Italy, including Milan, Mantua, Mirandola, Sardinia and Naples; and the Spanish Netherlands. The prosperous and strategically significant northern Italian territories were a genuine prize, Naples less so. The acquisition of the Netherlands was problematic from the start, for it came with onerous concessions to the Dutch, including the closure of the Scheldt to commercial traffic, which condemned Antwerp to economic limbo. Even before it was acquired, Eugene had attempted to swap the Spanish Netherlands for Bavaria. Nevertheless, the combined effect of Rastatt and Carlowitz made Habsburg Austria a great power on the European stage.

Military and political success was accompanied by an economic expansion which favoured the largest landholders, such as the Liechtensteins and Esterhazys. Estate capitalism in the core lands of Bohemia and Austria created more onerous burdens on the peasantry, but it left the high aristocracy with large revenues. Meanwhile, in the reconquered lands of Hungary, depopulated by decades of war, large-scale colonization, especially by Germans and Serbs, transformed the landscape and the region's ethnic composition, redounding once again to the benefit of the feudal lords-turned-entrepreneurs who had been granted the land. The Habsburg ruling elite and the Habsburg house itself had much to celebrate, and now the wherewithal to do so. The result was the High Baroque, whose more concrete expressions still dominate the Austrian landscape.

The face of Vienna was transformed after 1683, as magnates commissioned new palaces, both within the city walls and without. The epitome of this rebuilding was the double summer palace of Prince Eugene himself. Designed by Lucas von Hildebrandt and completed by 1723, the Upper and Lower Belvedere remains one of Austria's most treasured architectural sites; a close competitor is the Karlskirche, designed by Johann Bernhard Fischer von Erlach, and built between 1716 and 1739. These two buildings symbolized

Illustration 17. Donauschwaben Memorial, Graz. German colonists, known collectively as Danube Swabians, settled large tracts of the reconquered fertile Danube valley in the eighteenth century. They stayed until 1944, when forced to flee to, among other places, Graz.

the power of both the aristocracy and the Church, but also confirmed the glory of the dynasty, which employed the aristocrat and was patron of the Church (albeit Charles's Jewish financier, Samson Wertheimer, provided the funds for building it). As it became the ubiquitous style of the Austrian Habsburg lands, the Baroque naturalized. Fischer, a pupil of Bernini, had the most prestige, being given the initial commission for Schönbrunn; Hildebrandt oversaw the Baroque rebuilding of Stift Göttweig; but it was the third star of Austrian architecture, Jakob Prandtauer, who designed the most emblematic and dominant Baroque edifice, the monastery at Melk, which to this day majestically looms over the Danube valley at the entrance to the Wachau, leaving no doubt as to where the power and the glory lie.

Illustration 18. Austrian Baroque: Upper Belvedere Palace,
Vienna (1723). Note the roofs in the shape of Turkish
campaign tents.

The High Baroque spread far and wide over the Austrian lands,
a potent symbol of Habsburg power, and the culture penetrated
deep into the populace. Leonfelden also received its modest share
of Baroque culture. The miraculous cure of a carpenter in 1686 by
the waters of the village spring led to the latter becoming a site of
pilgrimage, complete with an image of the Virgin Mary from Mariazell. On this site first a small wooden chapel was erected; then in
1761 a larger stone chapel, built in a Baroque style; the Bründlkirche
received its final, enlarged form in 1790. By then, however, Baroque
had become anachronistic. Even as the Habsburg High Baroque
flourished after 1714, the flaws in its political, ideological and financial foundations had been clear to see.

In 1703 a Bavarian attack found Leopold unable to pay for
the defence of the Austrian heartlands. For decades the Austrian
Habsburgs' revenues had been quite insufficient for the huge outlays necessary for almost unending war. The difference had been
met by financiers, most notably Samuel Oppenheimer, Leopold's

'court banker' from 1680 to 1703. Oppenheimer had acted as both financier and military contractor; hence it was a Jew, resident in a city from which Jews had been expelled, who largely financed and provisioned the war that saved Christendom from the infidel Turk. On Oppenheimer's death in May 1703 the Habsburg regime cancelled the huge debt owed him and declared his bank bankrupt. This predictably boomeranged, effectively bankrupting the regime as well. The crisis was overcome by reorganization of the finances, loans from magnates and subsidies from the maritime powers. The Habsburgs eventually found another Jewish financier, Samson Wertheimer, Oppenheimer's nephew, but the Habsburgs' financial situation remained fragile.

Charles VI knew fiscal reform was necessary, but this would have disrupted the comity of aristocratic and clerical interests on which Habsburg power depended. The Bohemian and Hungarian diets, which still held the purse strings, were relatively forthcoming after 1714, and the direct control by Vienna of the Hungarian Military Border and Transylvania also led to increased revenue. Yet the overall fiscal basis of the Monarchy, and hence its financial status, remained inadequate. After Count Gundaccar Starhemberg left the Hofkammer in 1715, reforming zeal in finances lapsed. Compared with Hanoverian England, where the modern financial system was being developed, Austrian finances looked both antiquated and corrupt.

Charles VI's inability to confront the vested interests of the Monarchy was compounded by a crisis in the Austrian succession. This stemmed from the continuing dynastic, even feudal, nature of the Monarchy. The Habsburg lands were, in legal terms, still only a personal union. As late as 1665 the Austrian Habsburg lands had not had a common ruler, Tyrol being ruled by another branch of the family. Various attempts had been made to strengthen the bonds between the various territories, but the situation had never been fully regulated. Hungary only become hereditable in the Habsburg male line in 1687. As in Britain, where the Act of Union of 1707 regulated a long-standing personal union, there was a perceived need to establish a proper legal basis for the *de facto* union of the Habsburg lands.

The secret 'pact of mutual succession' of 1703 between Leopold I and his sons, Joseph and Charles, strengthened the principle of primogeniture, in the male line and then also in the female line; but it left unclear whether, in the event of no male heir, the eldest daughter of the elder or younger brother should inherit. To clarify this – in favour of his prospective children – Charles VI made the secret succession pact public on 19 April 1713, but then appended a brief statement which made the Habsburg lands indivisible and inseparable, *'indivisibiliter ac inseparabiliter'* and, in the event of his having no male heirs, inheritable first by his daughters and only then through Joseph's.

This Pragmatic Sanction was a very modest document, but it provided the subsequent legal basis for the permanent union of the Monarchy's lands. It changed the status of the Habsburg Monarchy from a regime based on divine right and dynastic inheritance to a single entity in law. To be legitimate, however, this legal document required recognition. Securing this legitimacy was then complicated by the fact that there turned out to be no male heir. In 1716 Charles VI's son died only a few months after birth, and Charles's two surviving children were girls, Maria Theresa (1717) and Maria Anna (1718). It was the securing of Maria Theresa's right to succeed to the whole Monarchy to which Charles dedicated the rest of his reign.

Securing assent from the compliant estates of the Bohemian and hereditary Austrian lands proved easy, and the Croatian and Transylvanian diets also voted for recognition. The most important and hardest case was Hungary, but the renewed Habsburg success against the Turks and mutual circumspection on the Hungarian and Habsburg sides led to the Hungarian estates giving their unanimous approval in 1722. The Pragmatic Sanction formally became the law of the united lands on 6 December 1723. Securing its recognition by the European powers now became a main aim of Habsburg foreign policy, and, as in domestic policy, led Charles to concessions he would otherwise not have made.

The Monarchy began in a strong position after 1714. Renewed war against the Ottomans in 1716 led to the Peace of Passarowitz of 1718, which saw more gains for Austria, especially the fertile Banat of Temesvár, as well as Belgrade and northern Bosnia. In the west, Austrian diplomacy and the British alliance procured Spanish acceptance in 1720 of the Habsburg acquisitions in Italy. Then things began to go wrong.

The core problem was Charles VI's plan to make the Austrian Netherlands prosperous and hence a net contributor to the Habsburg cause. His patronage of the Ostend Company in 1722 was an expansion of Austrian colonial trade policy. In 1719 the Second Oriental Trade Company, based in Trieste and Fiume, had been founded, and Austrian 'factories' established in India and China. The British and Dutch, however, wanted Austria as a continental balancing power, not as a commercial rival on the Channel. The result in the 1720s was a diplomatic debacle for Austria that resulted in the loss of Parma, Piacenza and Tuscany to the sons of Elizabeth Farnese, the Spanish queen, as well as the dissolution of the Ostend Company.

In the 1730s Charles VI continued canvassing recognition for the Pragmatic Sanction by Europe's powers, yet Austria's diplomatic position had not been well served by alienating the former maritime allies. Charles made the situation worse when he betrothed his heir, Maria Theresa, to Francis Stephen of Lorraine, rewarding a stalwart ally but deeply antagonizing Lorraine's neighbour, France. When war started again in Europe in 1733, ostensibly over the Polish succession, it was a disaster for the poorly prepared Austrian army. Peace in 1738 saw more Austrian losses in Italy, with the partial compensation that Tuscany was given to Francis Stephen of Lorraine; but this was only compensation for the loss of Lorraine and Bar (eventually to France in 1766). France did recognize the Pragmatic Sanction.

Habsburg fortunes were no better in the east. The Second Turkish War, 1737–9, was a military and diplomatic disaster, resulting in the loss of Belgrade and most Austrian gains from Passarowitz, though the Banat was retained. The loss of prestige from these setbacks was almost worse than the territorial loss. All the main European powers and domestic institutions had recognized the Pragmatic Sanction by the time of Charles VI's death in 1740, but the perceived (and real) weakness of the Habsburg Monarchy made its effectiveness questionable in the ruthless dynastic state politics of mid-eighteenth-century Europe. Maria Theresa may have had legitimacy on her side, but Charles left his daughter very exposed, were that legitimacy not to prove binding.

The Baroque Habsburg Monarchy had lost its élan by 1740, and its mystique. Its Counter Reformation culture appeared outmoded compared with the revolution in thought, now known as the Enlightenment, that was sweeping the salons and coffee houses of lands to the north and west. Christian Wolff, the father of the German Enlightenment, had been born a Habsburg subject in Silesia, but he had been forced to make his career abroad, as the Habsburg establishment actively discouraged Enlightened thinking.

Baroque culture, and the accompanying political, military and social arrangements, had served Austria well until the 1720s. Yet things had changed by 1740. In 1685 the expulsion by the archbishop of Salzburg of 1,000 crypto-Protestants from Defreggental had not caused much comment, but when 22,000 suspected crypto-Protestants were expelled from Salzburg's Pinzgau and Pongau in 1731, this was no longer regarded as civilized behaviour, nor was this self-inflicted loss of human resources seen to be rational. The Habsburg authorities also expelled some 1,200 Protestants from the Salzkammergut at around the same time, but avoided losing population by sending the 'Landler' into internal exile in Transylvania, where freedom of religion was still allowed.

Habsburg religious policy continued to be extremely intolerant, and often inhumane. In 1726 and 1727 Charles VI instituted the cruel Familiants Laws (*Familiantengesetze*) for the Bohemian lands, which capped the Jewish population there by denying any but the eldest sons in Jewish families the right to marry. More stringent measures preferred by Charles VI were not passed, however, because of the negative economic consequences. Despite Baroque appearances, there was a growing awareness in the Monarchy of the need to adapt to the rationalist developments in economic and social policy emanating largely from Western Europe.

Mercantilist thought in its German form of cameralism had influenced Austrian policy for many decades. Its three most famous theorists in Austria, Johann Joachim Becher, Philipp Wilhelm von Hörnigk and Wilhelm von Schröder, all Protestants from the Reich who converted to Catholicism, had begun publishing policy prescriptions from the 1660s. These largely followed Colbert's policies in France, discouraging luxury imports, encouraging domestic

Illustration 19. Austrian Baroque: Minorite Church in Eger, Hungary (1758–73).

luxury industries, establishing overseas trade companies, generally trying to increase the net inflow of bullion. The cameralists particularly stressed the benefits of a prosperous peasantry, as a means to increase the human resources (population) necessary for military strength and economic self-sufficiency.

Some of this was implemented. The Linzer Wollzeugfabrik, founded in 1672, employed more than four thousand workers by 1725, making it one of the largest factories in Europe. Trade companies were founded, as were companies in many luxury industries. Yet trade companies were sacrificed for foreign policy, ordinances protecting the peasantry from undue exploitation were passed but not enforced, so as not to antagonize the aristocracy. Hörnigk's *Österreich über alles, wann es nur will,* from 1684, reveals the main problem in its very title: 'Austria above all, if only it wanted to be'. The Habsburg lands might have the resources to become a major power as Hörnigk urged, but before 1740 it was unclear that its ruling trinity of dynasty, aristocracy and Church – which was what 'Austria' really meant – wanted to do so.

The cameralist vision for Austria cut across the Baroque, transcendent culture and authority on which the Habsburg dispensation depended. The emphasis on *natural* resources and on the need to encourage *popular* well-being was quite at odds with Habsburg assertion of *divine* authority and reliance on *elite* consensus. To follow the new thinking, Habsburg Austria would have to transform itself from a dynasty with a God-given mission to rule the Christian Empire, into a rational, coherent power-producing state. It might no longer rule 'over all' in the spirit of AEIOU, but it could remain a major power in the European states system. Yet adapting to this new model was complicated for the Habsburgs, with their involvement in the twin traditional institutions of universal authority, the Holy Roman Empire and the Roman Catholic Church. It would mean a complete change in the quality, justification and character of Habsburg power. In 1740 it was unclear whether 'Austria' would go through with this radical change; but Frederick II of Prussia forced the choice upon it.

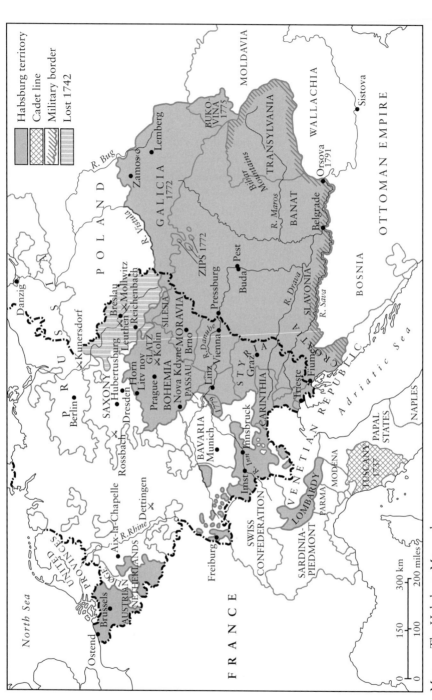

Map 4. The Habsburg Monarchy, 1792

3

Countering reform, 1740–1866

On 16 December 1740, Prussian troops invaded Silesia, and despite two major wars the Prussians stayed. The loss of Silesia ushered in a period of profound change for the Habsburg (now formally the Habsburg-Lorraine) dynasty and their territories. The Pragmatic Sanction having proved unable to preserve the integrity of the Habsburg lands, the problem now for Maria Theresa and her advisers was how to protect the Habsburg interest in the era of power politics embodied by Prussia.

The immediate goal was to regain Silesia and crush Prussia. When this proved impossible, the Habsburgs faced the existential task of adapting their regime and the basis of their authority for survival in the age of Enlightenment, an age of administrative rationalization, increasing state power and rationalist challenging of tradition.

Over the next century and more the Habsburg dynasty responded to this challenge of modernity by first adapting its institutions and outlook to the new circumstances, then reacting against the radicalization of those circumstances, and finally attempting to pull off the trick of both adapting to modern economic and social circumstances while denying the political change that went with these.

This process, with its theme, counter-theme and resolution, appears analogous to the sonata form associated with the contemporary musical revolution in Vienna. Yet it was actually much more like the sonata form's philosophical counterpart, the Hegelian dialectic, for harmonious resolution was lacking. Even with a discordant resolution, at another battle with the Prussians in the Bohemian lands, at

Königgrätz on 3 July 1866, the era of Progress continued to develop and change in ways which were to prove inimical to the dynasty's – and the Monarchy's – interests.

In the period 1740 to 1866 the Habsburg Monarchy was unsuccessful in handling the challenges of modernity. Yet it survived, and in the very failure to preserve Habsburg power a dramatic transformation in Austrian culture and society occurred, as also in the very understanding of what it meant to be 'Austrian'.

THE ENLIGHTENED STATE, 1740–1792

For half a century Habsburg rulers tried reform to regain the dynastic footing lost in 1740, when the very existence of the Habsburg Monarchy was jeopardized by the collapse of consensus on the Pragmatic Sanction. The chief instigator of this crisis was Frederick II of Prussia. He exploited the protest of Charles Albert of Bavaria at Maria Theresa's succession by in effect blackmailing the Habsburgs, then invading Silesia when his 'offer' was rejected. His victory over the Austrians at Mollwitz in 1741 was the signal for much of the rest of Europe to indulge in a feeding frenzy on Habsburg territory. The signatures and promises proved worthless without a strong army to enforce them. Even in Bohemia and Upper Austria, the noble estates were quite prepared to recognize Charles Albert, when he conquered the territories in 1741. The one great exception was, ironically, Hungary: the support of the Hungarian diet for Maria Theresa in the autumn of 1741 was crucial in restoring a sense of legitimacy and purpose to the Habsburg cause.

Soon after, the Habsburgs' authority received one of its worst setbacks. Charles Albert was elected and crowned Holy Roman Emperor in February 1742, the only non-Habsburg to enjoy the office during the period from 1440 to the Empire's end in 1806. Yet 1742 was also the year in which Austria, boosted by British subsidies, regrouped and took the fight to the enemy. The War of the Austrian Succession was complex, erratic and patchy, including not one but two 'Silesian Wars' between Austria and Prussia, the first ending in 1742 and the second ending on Christmas Day 1745. The wars in the Netherlands and Italy, as well as the Franco-British colonial war, only ended in 1748.

Considering the dire straits of 1740, Austria came out of the war in relatively good shape. The death of Charles Albert in 1745 and the subsequent election of Francis Stephen of Lorraine, Maria Theresa's husband, as emperor restored to Habsburg control their traditional base of authority. Territorial losses in Italy were small. The vital Hungarian support, on the basis of the Pragmatic Sanction, might also be seen as some vindication of Charles VI's policy. Nevertheless, Prussia retained almost all of Silesia and the Bohemian county of Glatz, with Austria retaining only three counties in Upper Silesia.

This was a body blow to the Habsburg Monarchy, with large repercussions for its future. The Monarchy lost in Silesia one of its wealthiest and most industrialized provinces as well as one with a large – and largely German-speaking – populace. The Monarchy also lost one of its main trading arteries, the Oder, as well as a large buffer zone for its heartland. Above all the stealing of Silesia was a challenge to Habsburg prestige that Maria Theresa was determined to reverse, even if it meant radical reform.

In many respects Maria Theresa represented more Austria's Baroque past than the era of Enlightened reform that she introduced. She was a zealous Catholic, despite her mother having been Protestant, and she held many of the prejudices of Baroque Catholicism, including an intolerance to Protestantism among her subjects and a visceral antisemitism. The internal exiling of crypto-Protestants from the hereditary lands to Transylvania continued, including 2,600 from Upper Austria in the 1750s.

Maria Theresa was prepared to tolerate Protestant businessmen and financiers, such as Swiss-born Johann Fries, even in Vienna, but this stemmed from her urge to be freed from her father's 'usurious' Jewish financiers. Jewish financiers such as Diego d'Aguilar were still significant sources of credit for the Habsburg enterprise, but Maria Theresa's anti-Jewish prejudice led her in 1744 to order the expulsion of the Jews from Prague and eventually all Bohemian crownlands, for alleged treason. The expulsion order was rescinded in 1748 after interventions by various powers including the British, but not before inflicting severe disruption on Prague Jewry. Maria Theresa herself remained unrepentant about her hatred of Jews: 'I know of no greater plague than this race, which on account of its deceit, usury, and hoarding of money is driving my subjects to beggary.'[1]

Yet Maria Theresa also showed a remarkable flexibility and openness to novel approaches when it came to adapting the Habsburg Monarchy to its new challenges. She was prepared to do almost anything to restore the prestige and power of her House, including practising amateur dramatics before the Hungarian diet in 1741, pleading for help with her four-month-old son, Joseph, in her arms. She was also prepared to listen to low-born advisers such as Johann Christoph Bartenstein and Friedrich Wilhelm Haugwitz (both converts from Lutheranism), who persuaded her that her 'House' must change its administrative and financial structures radically to survive.

The first wave of reform was led by Haugwitz. As governor of the remaining Austrian Silesian province, Haugwitz had set about emulating the success of the new Prussian administration in Silesia. The promising results led in 1749 to his appointment as head of the Directory (*Directorium in publicis und cameralibus*), the new central administrative agency, and his 'project' was intended to replicate his Silesian success on a Monarchy-wide scale. The new system, with institutions down to the level of the District Office (*Kreisamt*), represented a radical centralization. Where before the Habsburgs had left the internal arrangements for funding largely to their noble and clerical allies, now a class of central government officials, 10,000 strong by 1760, was to supervise estate activity, with the threat of intervention if revenues proved insufficient.

The Haugwitzian reforms had limitations. Unlike in Prussia, the estates were not fully circumvented, Haugwitz preferring to achieve increased provincial 'contributions' by agreement rather than coercion, and bureaucratic oversight remained sketchy. Lombardy, the (Austrian) Netherlands and Hungary were almost entirely untouched by the reforms, which were concentrated on the hereditary lands and Bohemian crownlands. Nevertheless, with Leopold Daun's reforms providing an improved army, Haugwitz's reforms provided Maria Theresa with the resources to relaunch the campaign for Silesia.

[1] Charles Ingrao, *The Habsburg Monarchy, 1618–1815* (Cambridge, 1994), p. 192.

The diplomatic terrain had also been transformed by the 'Diplomatic Revolution'. Dissatisfied with her British ally, Maria Theresa was persuaded by Wenzel Anton Count Kaunitz, the rising star of Austrian diplomacy and state chancellor from 1753, that Austria should reverse its traditional foreign policy and ally with France. As the largest continental power, France was no longer powerful enough to be a threat, but could still be decisive in overpowering Prussia. The resulting First Treaty of Versailles of May 1756 between France and Austria represented a *bouleversement* of European politics. Frederick II's pre-emptive invasion of Saxony in August 1756 then helped Kaunitz convince the French to turn a defensive alliance into an offensive one in May 1757, which was joined by Sweden and Russia, and most of the Empire's states as well. With only a few minor Protestant states and British subsidies on Frederick II's side, it seemed Austria would be reclaiming Silesia in a matter of months.

Thus started the Seven Years War. Despite the much improved situation of Maria Theresa's Monarchy, its over-cautious armies still failed to achieve decisive victory against Prussia. Berlin was occupied twice, and at times Frederick II became more like a fugitive than a monarch, but he and his forces survived. Meanwhile France suffered crushing defeats by the British overseas, and its enthusiasm for its Austrian ally waned. Events in Russia in 1762 also worked against Austria, with the new tsar, Peter III, allying with Prussia. His assassination ended that Austrian nightmare, but Catherine II's opting for neutrality still meant that the Austrian game was up.

The war ended with huge French colonial losses to the British. France's Austrian ally fared better, the Peace of Hubertusburg of 1763 confirming the territorial *status quo ante*. Considering what Austria had brought to the conflict, however, this was a terrible disappointment. The Habsburgs were once more a major force, but all the recasting of their enterprise had not produced the desired result: Silesia was still Prussian.

This failure led to another rethinking of how to run the Monarchy. The Directory in 1761 was recast as a United Austrian and Bohemian Chancellery, with a separate, independent judiciary, and separate financial bodies. As head of the new Council of State (*Staatsrat*), responsible for internal policy of all Habsburg lands, and also state chancellor (foreign minister), Kaunitz was now the dominant figure in Maria Theresa's government and remained so for the rest of the reign. His ascendancy brought a qualitative change in Austrian policy.

Kaunitz pursued a policy of what might be called aristocratic Enlightenment. Ever the diplomat, Kaunitz relied more on persuasion in dealing with the estates, and some of Haugwitz's centralization was pruned back in favour of estates officials. Yet the centralized character of the Haugwitzian system remained, and the central administration's growing institutional strength was behind Kaunitz's success in negotiating large revenue increases. By 1780 state revenue had reached 50 million florins, and in 1775 the Monarchy achieved the first balanced budget in its history.

While the aristocracy regained some power at regional and local levels, they were increasingly overshadowed at the centre by non-noble or recently ennobled officials. With a new state-oriented ethos, this nascent bureaucracy began a radical overhaul of the Monarchy, especially concerning religion, education and the agrarian economy. By intervening forcefully in the relationship of the populace with both the Church and the nobility, the Theresian regime transformed the tenor of relations between the Habsburg dynasty and its subjects. No longer content to let its domestic allies teach and rule the populace, it now decided that reason of state required a new, direct link between state and society.

There had been antecedents for this shift in policy. The maternalism of the self-styled 'general and first mother' to all her lands, and her sense of God-given responsibility for 'my House', left Maria Theresa open to arguments about the welfare of her subjects, the peasantry included.[2] Cameralist thought, especially *Populationistik*, also prescribed increasing population for augmenting state power. Given that the peasantry comprised most of the populace and the tax base (nobles being largely exempt), easing peasant burdens appeared the key to increasing prosperity, population – and revenue. This necessitated, however, a radical intervention in peasant–lord relations: commissioning of thorough land survey, and regulating and reducing peasant obligations such as the *robot*, the mandatory

---

[2] P. G. M. Dickson, *Finance and Government under Maria Theresa, 1740–1780* (Oxford, 1987), vol. II, p. 4; vol. I, p. 325.

labour owed by the peasant to the lord. Tentative moves to protect the peasantry along these lines were made already in the 1750s.

The ground was also shifting in religious and cultural affairs. Maria Theresa's devout and intolerant Catholicism was counterbalanced by practicality and a proprietary sense when it came to relations between Church and secular government in her own lands. The religious dispensation of the High Baroque, moreover, was being undermined from within by Reform Catholicism. Led by such thinkers as Lodovico Antonio Muratori, this emphasized the role of reason and knowledge in human affairs, and decried the excessive waste of secular resources to religious ritual and 'superstition' exemplified by the Jesuits. There were many reform strands within the Church, but the cumulative effect led to a consensus in Austria – and eventually throughout Europe – that the Jesuit influence over religious, intellectual and cultural life had to be curtailed, and the 'unproductive' forms of religious life (such as contemplative orders and the excessive number of holidays) reduced. It is indicative that the archbishops of Vienna in this period, Trautson and Migazzi, were initially active allies of reform.

The secularization of cultural affairs began with Gerhard van Swieten, Maria Theresa's Dutch physician, reforming Vienna University from 1749, and the Censorship Commission taking over from the Jesuits in 1751. Educational institutions were also established to prepare officials for the future state bureaucracy. The Theresianum was founded in 1746 to educate nobles' sons; a military school was founded in Wiener Neustadt in 1751, an Oriental Academy for training the diplomatic service in 1754.

By the 1760s the already established reform movement was ready to advance further towards Enlightenment. The team of advisers around Kaunitz and Maria Theresa, including van Swieten, the political and legal theorist Karl von Martini and the polymath (and convert from Judaism) Joseph Sonnenfels, now thought less in traditional dynastic terms, and much more of the interests of the state and of its populace, and of the rational policies needed to secure those interests, unencumbered by tradition.

The members of the Educational Commission (*Studienhofkommission*) established in 1760 came to style themselves the 'Party of Enlightenment', for they were convinced of the need to replace Jesuit control of education with a broader-based 'enlightening' system. It was, however, the dissolution of the Jesuit Order by Clement XIV in 1773 that forced Maria Theresa to follow the Party of Enlightenment. The Habsburg authorities confiscated Jesuit property and used the proceeds to establish a universal system of education in 1774, with compulsory elementary education, a greatly expanded secondary education system and 'normal schools' to train teachers. The new, secular and compulsory education system met resistance in many sectors, not least from nobles and peasants who wanted the children to work in the fields, yet overall the effort was very successful, with more than six thousand schools functioning by 1780.

The deviser of this scheme was the Catholic abbot of Sagan monastery, in Prussian Silesia, Ignaz Felbiger; as with administrative reform, Prussia provided much of the inspiration for both the form and the spirit of the new educational system, which was informed with Protestant Pietism. Maria Theresa might want the new schools to teach Catholic orthodoxy, but the curriculum emphasized social responsibility, social discipline, the work ethic – and the use of reason by pupils to understand their subject rather than rote learning. The new system was a dramatic break with the previous forms of social control, which had emphasized through visual splendour the need for unquestioning obedience among the illiterate populace. Conservative complaints about the new curriculum's impiousness were only half wrong. The resulting spread of literacy was to create new challenges in the relations between ruler and ruled, especially as the new compulsory elementary education was conducted in the vernacular (national) languages.

The other radical change came in agrarian policy. Cameralism had already urged government intervention to maximize the land's resources, to increase economic and hence military power. The government followed such principles in its industrial policy. After the loss of Silesia, it instituted subsidies and trade barriers to encourage the transfer of the Silesian textile industry to northern Bohemia, and it similarly encouraged other industrial enterprises, especially at the luxury end. As part of this effort, guild privileges were cut back and internal duties on trade either reformed or, in the Austrian-Bohemian lands in 1775, abolished. The trend to remove restraints on trade and particularist privileges to enhance state power was not new in industrial policy. What was new was serious government intervention along these lines on the land.

The key issue in agrarian policy was how to reduce or at least regulate noble privileges. The need for peasant well-being had been prominent in cameralist thought, and Enlightened Physiocratic theory had elaborated this notion. Many Habsburgs had passed ordinances demanding noble restraint concerning the peasantry, but these had been intentionally ineffectual. Maria Theresa had initially also resisted meddling in such matters, but the perceived need for economic power and the emergence of a functioning bureaucracy now made intervention in peasant–lord relations desirable, and feasible.

Widespread peasant unrest, brought on by the effects of war, the famine of 1770–2 and noble abuse of manorial rights, made such intervention much easier. While in Hungary the counties were still left to (not) implement regulations, *robot* patents limiting labour dues in Bohemia, Moravia and the hereditary lands were enforced by local state officials armed with new land surveys. The utility of labour dues was itself being questioned. From 1775 a pilot project directed by Franz Anton Raab on two crown estates in Bohemia replaced the *robot* system with one based on cash rents, with such success that the scheme was expanded in 1777. The Raab system now showed what could be done, if old privileges were replaced by a new order.

The person on whom hopes for even more radical change were concentrated was Joseph II, elevated by Maria Theresa to be co-regent in 1765 on the death of Francis Stephen. Educated by moderate reformers such as Bartenstein, Joseph II nevertheless became an ardent advocate of Enlightenment – in its étatist, Central European form. His role model (and main enemy) was Frederick II of Prussia.

As co-regent he was allowed most influence in foreign policy. The team of Joseph II and Kaunitz played the game of rationalist *Realpolitik* with Frederick II and Catherine II of Russia. Despite Maria Theresa's objections that it was a 'violation of every standard of sanctity and justice', her son and chancellor together persuaded her to go along with the First Partition of Poland in 1772, which brought with it Galicia and 2.6 million new subjects. In 1775 the Bukovina was acquired peacefully from the Turks, to help integrate

Habsburg territories. Similar considerations of territorial integrity, and a rationalist willingness to ignore traditional circumstances, led to another attempt to swap Bavaria for the Austrian Netherlands. Frederick II's alarm at this prospect led to the War of the Bavarian Succession of 1778–9. The 'Potato War' or 'Plum Rumble' set back Austrian financial improvement and ended with Austria gaining only the Inn Quarter.

In domestic affairs, it was clear where Joseph's sympathies lay. Joseph had long been a convinced Enlightened absolutist, both as Enlightener and absolutist. His Catholic faith was a form of radical reform Catholicism, especially concerning state control over religion. He also followed the Enlightened idealization of 'the people', having the two major royal parks in Vienna, the Prater and the Augarten, opened to the public in 1766 and 1775 respectively. The Augarten's main entrance was adorned with the motto: 'This place of recreation has been dedicated to the People by one who esteems them.'[3] Joseph II displayed his humanitarianism by helping persuade Maria Theresa to abolish torture in 1776. Largely shut out by his mother from actual decision-making before 1780, he devoted much of his time to roaming his future realms incognito, often under the alias of Count Falkenstein, to get to know the people's true condition. He even condescended on occasion to push a plough, a gesture that created the legend among the peasantry of Joseph, the people's emperor.

The devotion to the people and the state was sincere. As his Pastoral Letter (*Hirtenbrief*) to Habsburg officials of 1783 shows, he felt it his duty and his privilege to be the first servant of the state, sacrificing his own interest to that of the public good. Unusually, he genuinely believed in the idea of the social contract between the monarch and his subjects. It was in this spirit that Sonnenfels could proclaim that the Habsburg subjects were now 'citizens' (*Bürger*).

The Enlightened approach to the state that later was to be called Josephism (or Josephinism) had already made its mark before Joseph II became sole ruler. Vienna in 1780 was the capital of an empire of 247,000 square miles and a population of roughly 26 million, almost as much as that of France. Vienna itself already had a

[3] T. C. W. Blanning, *Joseph II* (London, 1994), p. 65.

Illustration 20. Austrian Rococo: Admont Monastery
Library (1776).

population of 200,000 (with Prague at 80,000), and was benefiting
from the region's industrial and economic expansion. Yet Vienna
was more than just the Habsburg capital: it had become the centre
of Enlightened hopes in all of Germany and Central Europe.

The relatively open atmosphere of the city during the co-regency
led to greater intellectual and cultural vitality. The medical school
was establishing a good reputation; and the world of literature, or
at least the press, was expanding. In the world of German drama,
Sonnenfels restyled the Burgtheater, opened in 1741, as the 'German
National Theatre' in 1776, and made it an ideological weapon in his
Enlightened fight against the traditional, popular comic Hanswurst
theatre that he saw as part of the Baroque past.

Both Maria Theresa and Joseph II imposed economies on court
life, but remained generous patrons of the arts, and so did the high
aristocracy and the Catholic religious establishment. Architecture
continued to flourish. The Rococo style, exemplified in the splendid
interiors of Schönbrunn and the exquisite library of the Benedictine
monastery of Admont, provided a lighter version of Baroque. The
era saw a change from an emphasis on representational grandeur to

one of more modest, if refined taste. Joseph II's change of residence from the grand but remote Schönbrunn to the less splendid but central Hofburg exemplified this.

Musical life came to the fore, with the operas of Christoph Willibald Gluck presenting a German form to rival the Italian. Vienna became the centre of the new music in the German lands. Joseph Haydn, born in Rohrau in Lower Austria, started as a Vienna choirboy and acquired his musical training in the city before becoming the master of music of the Esterhazys in Eisenstadt. Haydn only moved to Vienna in 1790, but he kept in touch with developments there, and in the 1770s had mutually productive contacts with Wolfgang Amadeus Mozart. Mozart, a native of non-Habsburg Salzburg, had been the *Wunderkind* of German music since the 1760s. After falling out with his patron, the Prince Archbishop of Salzburg, Mozart moved to Vienna in March 1781. Once in the Habsburg capital, he set about establishing himself, with varied success, as the leading composer of his age. He eventually became court composer in 1787, and all the time he was composing one work of genius after another, right up to his tragically early death in 1791.

The atmosphere in Vienna and the Habsburg Monarchy on the accession of Joseph in 1780 was one of optimism and expectation of further reform. Joseph II was not going to disappoint. Held back for so long by his mother, he launched a cascade of reforms, all along Enlightened lines, and some with large liberalizing effects.

One of Joseph II's first acts as sole ruler was to put censorship under the liberal control of Gottfried van Swieten, thus effectively bringing freedom of expression to the Habsburg lands. The number of publications rose exponentially. The Toleration Edicts of 1781 also greatly expanded freedom of religion for the main Protestant sects and the Orthodox Church.

The Toleration Edicts for the Jews (for Bohemia in 1781, Moravia in 1782, Hungary in 1783 and Galicia in 1789) were less sweeping. The Familiants Laws remained, as did prohibitions on residence in most of the hereditary lands. Some of the most humiliating taxes and restrictions on Jews were removed, however, and Jews granted greater economic and educational opportunities. In return, the Monarchy's Jewish communities had to surrender much of their communal and cultural autonomy, with Jewish children compelled

Illustration 21. Enlightened propaganda: Joseph II's religious reform – and the beneficial consequences: a) 'Sie fingen eine grosse Menge . . .'; b) 'Ein jeglicher Baum . . .' C. J. Mettenleiter.

to attend German-speaking schools teaching secular subjects. The edicts were nevertheless hailed by many *maskilim* (followers of the Jewish Enlightenment) as a great advance, and earned for Joseph II the ironic soubriquet of 'Emperor of the Jews' from conservative opponents.

Joseph's aim in his Jewish policy had been 'to make the totality of Jewry harmless, but the individual useful'. Utility also guided Joseph in his wholesale restructuring of the Catholic religious establishment, which represented a radicalization of the changes introduced under Maria Theresa. Monasteries that served no useful purpose, which amounted in Joseph's eyes to more than seven hundred, roughly one-third of all monasteries in the Habsburg lands, were dissolved. The funds from the dissolution were used to overhaul and expand the secular clergy. The network of parishes was redrawn, and new churches built to guarantee that no one was too far from a church. Professional standards and training were imposed on the clergy, who were now to be paid a regular state salary. To aid enforcement, Joseph also asserted the monarch's control over the Church hierarchy at the expense of the papacy.

Joseph was intent on imposing a new, 'rational' approach in society. Religious fraternities were dissolved, processions, pilgrimages, many holidays were abolished. The expensive funeral rite was also ended, with the dead to be buried in sacks not coffins, because this was cheaper and would aid decomposition of the bodies. Religious institutions were replaced by useful, secular correlates. In Vienna, the Allgemeines Krankenhaus (General Hospital) opened in 1784 as the largest and most modern medical centre in the world. On the local level the changes were less grand, but still significant. In 1783 money from dissolved religious fraternities and societies was put into a fund to build and expand schools. In Leonfelden this fund paid for expansion of the schoolhouse in 1785, while proceeds from the sale of the dissolved town hospice, the Bürgerspital, in 1786 went into the fund. Similarly, the Spitalskirche, which had been the hospice church, and the town's Protestant centre in the seventeenth century, was secularized and sold off to the townspeople, becoming the town hall in 1787.

The legal system was also reformed. Justice and administration were separated and the judicial system professionalized, curtailing patrimonial jurisdiction. The first part of the new Civil Code (*Allgemeines bürgerliches Gesetzbuch, ABGB*) was published in 1786, and the new Criminal Code in 1787. Not only did this code reflect the more humanitarian approach inspired by Cesare Beccaria, it also, radically, proclaimed equality before the law – for noble and commoner alike.

The destruction of 'unnatural' legal barriers, distinctions and privileges was also evident in economic policy. Admittedly, part of Joseph's prescription for promoting industry in his lands was to impose prohibitive tariffs on many goods in 1784; but behind this tariff wall policy was aimed at removing artificial barriers to enterprise, such as guilds, and allowing the individual entrepreneur to create wealth. The same approach prompted the reduction of industry subsidies, and the opening of new trades and industries to Jews.

Agrarian reform shared the new thinking: freeing the individual peasant would encourage production and hence strengthen the state.

Personal serfdom was abolished in Bohemia on 1 November 1781. The two Austrian archduchies already were free of serfdom, but abolition patents followed for Inner Austria and Galicia in 1782, and the Hungarian lands in 1785. Peasants were further given the right to buy hereditary tenure, and a directive of 1783 gave peasants (except in Galicia) the right to commute *robot* through payments in cash or crops: a *de facto* abolition of compulsory *robot*.

The initial phase of Joseph's sole reign was a resounding success. There was resistance from religious conservatives, and much of traditional religious life continued despite being officially abolished. There was also grumbling from many nobles, but government policy was designed to shelter the material interests of the nobility, so opposition was muted.

Joseph's staunchest support in his lands came from the small but influential community of the Enlightened. Secret brotherhoods such as the Illuminati and the Freemasons gained many powerful and prominent members. Both Mozart and Haydn belonged to Masonic lodges; the dissatisfaction with the *ancien régime* and optimism about the future prevalent in these organizations is obvious in the operas which Mozart co-wrote with Lorenzo da Ponte, a Jewish convert and former Jesuit, especially *Le nozze di Figaro* (1786) and *Don Giovanni* (1787).

The opera that Mozart wrote with Emanuel Schikaneder in 1791, *Die Zauberflöte*, has at its core a model of the Masonic version of Enlightened society, complete with deistic ritual and belief in the superiority of universal humanity over traditional social hierarchy: 'Is he a prince?'; 'More, he is a human being.' There is further the notion that it is for the wise and the virtuous (Sarastro) to bring mankind out of the clutches of the Queen of the Night into the realm of light, by force if necessary. The weaknesses of Papageno, the commoner, are indulged, not vindicated.

This was close to the Josephist ideal, perhaps too close. With Joseph in charge, this was no longer Kaunitz's aristocratic Enlightenment, but rather very much *autocratic* Enlightenment. Joseph thought himself an absolute monarch and meant to rule as such. Even the supportive Freemasons were distrusted as outside his control. Joseph II tried to remould not only the government of his subjects but also their behaviour. In Maria Theresa's last decade there had been approximately a hundred decrees issued every year; under Joseph the average was almost seven hundred per year.

Joseph, the idealist, had none of his mother's sense of the possible, and he was convinced that, being well-intended and faithful to reason, he knew what was best for the people. Joseph's ideal was a *Beamtenstaat*, in which a loyal, rational officialdom would both police the populace, and also provide them with the 'policy' (synonymous at the time with police) that would protect their welfare. Government might be *for* the people, but it was to be performed *by* the officials, and was definitely the government *of* Joseph II. This model was a very poor fit with the actual Habsburg *ancien régime*.

Joseph's astounding early success unfortunately encouraged him to attempt the impossible. The Jewish community was one thing – it could be made 'harmless' by gutting its autonomy because it was *already* harmless, powerless to resist state policy. Other bases of particularist power – the noble estates, the Church and the 'political nations' of outlying provinces – were much tougher. Moreover, Joseph's reform success encouraged demands for even more radical reform: the relaxation of censorship unleashed a torrent of opinions – and criticisms. When the reform process threatened to escape *his* control, Joseph clamped down hard, suppressing revolts, using the new police force, formed in 1782 under Johann Anton Count Pergen, as informers, and reintroducing strict censorship. There was to be revolution, but only from above.

Joseph II thought to recast the Habsburg Monarchy as a unitary, rational state by over-riding traditional local institutions such as the estates and provincial diets. He centralized the government of the core Austro-Bohemian lands and Galicia under the United Court Office (*Vereinigte Hofstelle*) in 1782, and ordered the amalgamation of various provincial administrations. The crownlands, now provinces, were divided into rationally defined districts, the Hungarian counties abolished in 1785.

Joseph's approach to Hungary was particularly radical. Whereas his mother had treated Hungary very circumspectly, Joseph was determined not to let Hungary block state-wide reform. Never summoning a diet (and thus never crowned king), he intended to rule Hungary by Reason alone. In 1784 he directed that German replace Latin as the administrative language in Hungary, because it made administrative sense; tradition and national sensibilities were irrelevant.

Joseph displayed a similarly rationalist contempt for tradition when it came to the other outlying provinces, the Holy Roman Empire and foreign policy generally. He replaced Kaunitz's relatively subtle cajoling of local elites by a policy of imposition. In Tyrol he imposed military conscription; in Milan and Mantua local institutions were abolished. In the Holy Roman Empire, he tried to use his imperial prerogatives to further only Habsburg state interests, with little if any regard for shoring up the imperial office, which still retained considerable informal power.

His handling of Belgium, the Austrian Netherlands, showed Joseph at his most blundering. When the Dutch refused his demands to open the Scheldt, Joseph tried again in 1785 to swap Belgium for Bavaria. When Frederick II assembled a League of German Princes, the Fürstenbund, to block this deal, Joseph then decided to make Belgium useful. In 1787 he imposed a new administrative system there, abolishing ancient local institutions and liberties, even Brabant's 1355 constitution, the *Joyeuse Entrée*. Such a frontal attack on local privileges might be possible in the Austrian-Bohemian lands, but in Belgium it produced first a revolt, and then, in 1789, a revolution.

Joseph's first reaction to the Belgian revolt was to reassert control, reimposing censorship and relying ever more on Pergen's police force. From 1788 the emperor was also suffering from tuberculosis. Yet he was determined to press on. In 1784 he had commissioned a comprehensive land registry (*Kataster*) to use as the basis for radical future tax reform. In February 1789, before the registry's completion, the Land Tax Reform was issued. This truly revolutionary measure provided for a radical reduction in the taxes paid by peasants to their lord from rustical lands, and dues from dominical lands appeared to be next, threatening even larger reductions in noble income. Even the usually docile Austro-Bohemian nobility protested against the new law, and in Hungary the combination of tax reform and the assault on local institutions provoked a noble revolt. The peasants themselves refused to pay their taxes, thinking that an even better deal was imminent. The law was formally implemented in November 1789, but it never functioned, a victim of the catastrophic finale of Joseph II's reign.

On top of the Belgian and Hungarian crises, clumsy foreign policy had led Austria into war against the Turks in 1788, in which Joseph II, commanding in the field, contracted the tuberculosis that would soon kill him. In 1789, the tide of war turned in Austria's favour, but by then King Frederick William II, new king of Prussia, seeing Joseph's predicament, had formed an alliance with Turkey, Belgian rebels and Magyar nobles, and was preparing to invade Bohemia. Beset with crisis on crisis, and in the last stages of tuberculosis, Joseph made a dramatic volte-face. On 28 January 1790 he recalled almost all reforms imposed on Hungary, and suspended the land tax decree for all his lands. Joseph II died on 20 February 1790.

His successor, Leopold II, was a more moderate figure than his brother. As Grand Duke of Tuscany since 1765, he also had tried to introduce enlightened reform, but more gradually and tactfully. He had even tried to introduce elements of constitutional government. His response to the crisis of 1790 was retrenchment, but not at any price. He rescinded the new tax law; and recast the legislation on *robot* in the landlords' favour. Leopold also returned the power to collect taxes to the respective provincial estates. With the nobility in the core lands placated, Leopold settled with Prussia in July, which in turn ensured his election as Holy Roman Emperor in September. Peace was then made with Turkey. This left Leopold the Belgian and Hungarian rebellions, both of which he defeated by a deft playing of internal divisions among the rebels. Tyrol was placated by the restoration of freedom from military conscription. Concessions to tradition were also made in religious life, with some monasteries restored and some of the banned religious practices again allowed.

Overall, however, it is remarkable what Leopold achieved. The position of the Habsburg Monarchy had been restored, and most reforms preserved, especially in religion and education. There were even advances: Leopold reliberalized the press, reined back the police, and replaced Pergen with Sonnenfels, who cut back on social control and re-emphasized the welfare side of Joseph's original concept.

By now, however, domestic reform was overshadowed by events in France, to which there was a family link: Leopold's sister, the beleaguered queen of France, Marie Antoinette, yet one more instance of the Habsburg tradition of cementing alliances by marriage. Joseph II, predictably, had greeted the initial French Revolution in 1789 as confirmation of his principles. Leopold II might have been prepared to compromise with the revolutionary French authorities even in 1792. Yet the promise of Leopold II's reign was cut short by his unexpected death on 1 March 1792. With his son, Francis II, a new era began, in which not reform, but responding to the forces unleashed by the French Revolution became the Habsburgs' imperative.

Joseph II, on his deathbed, ordered his epitaph to read: 'Here lies a prince whose intentions were pure, but who had the misfortune to see all his plans collapse.' Characteristically, this was too radical a claim. Building on the achievements of his mother's reign, Joseph's reforms had instituted immense changes: for the first time the Habsburg Monarchy possessed a functioning bureaucracy, whose numbers had increased by the 1790s to approximately 14,000. The relation between the state and its citizens/subjects had changed profoundly, as had the image of the monarch, now seen as a fount of reform and defender of 'the people'. This sense of the authorities and the state as a positive agent of change and as a bulwark of popular welfare became very deeply ingrained. The reliance on the welfare state is still particularly strong in Austrian political culture. Joseph II became the 'good Habsburg' for many progressive elements in Habsburg society, whether as the agrarian reformer and pusher of ploughs, or as a liberal German centralizer. Josephism, emphasizing state control and rationalism, remained strong in both the bureaucracy and Catholic hierarchy.

Joseph II's legacy went beyond the borders of the Habsburg Monarchy. Beethoven's *Fidelio* is one of the great hymns to human freedom. Beethoven, usually thought of as the archetypal German composer, spent much of his creative life in Vienna. Even his youth in Bonn was lived under a Habsburg elector of Cologne, Maximilian Franz, Joseph II's youngest brother. Beethoven became resident in Vienna in 1792, and *Fidelio* was written and premiered there in 1805. The thematic material was probably initially suggested by none other than Emanuel Schikaneder, the writer of *Die Zauberflöte*.

The links between the world of Joseph II and Beethoven go much deeper. When Beethoven was still in Bonn he was commissioned by the Lesegesellschaft, a successor to the Order of Illuminati, to write a *Cantata on the Death of Joseph II*. The music for one part of the cantata for the dead Joseph, 'Da steigen die Menschen an's Licht', a suitable theme, was included by Beethoven in *Fidelio*, as the music for 'Welch' ein Augenblick'. This is the penultimate chorus in the opera, a moment of pious celebration of deliverance from the tyranny of local despotism by the grace of an Enlightened monarch.

THE LEGITIMATE EMPIRE, 1792–1848

Edmund Burke perceptively recognized in his *Reflections on the Revolution in France* how French revolutionary Cartesian rationalism, rejection of the past and insistence on centralist national uniformity provided a radical challenge to the empirical, evolutionary and precedent-based character of British liberty; revolutionary France posed an even greater threat to the Habsburg Monarchy. This was at heart a dynastic enterprise, ruling various territories populated by many ethnic groups. A modern nation-state based on popular sovereignty such as revolutionary France was not just another rival power, but Austria's ideological nemesis.

The French revolutionary threat effectively ended any hope of resuming Austria's own attempt at reform from above. The traumatic experience of the French revolutionary and Napoleonic wars led Austria eventually to abandon its attempt at basing its authority on its modernity, utility and ability to serve the people, and to retreat instead to the base from which it had, almost a century before, ventured forth, the claim of legitimacy. This served reasonably well for some decades, but, in an age of nationalism, liberalism and progress – the values embodied in the French Revolution – it was ultimately an inadequate basis on which to justify a supra-national dynastic empire, however 'legitimate' it might be.

Initially the impact of the French Revolution on Austria appeared minor. Domestically, Joseph II's reforms, for all their incompleteness, acted as a sort of inoculation to more radical change, and the events in Paris after 1789 had not prevented Leopold II envisaging further reform. When his son, Francis II, succeeded him, many thought that he would continue moderate reform, especially in agrarian policy. Francis soon took a more conservative course; but the Josephist bureaucracy was still in place, and two of the great, progressive legal reforms in Austrian history occurred under Francis: Sonnenfels's Criminal Code of 1803 and the General Civil Law Code (*Allgemeines bürgerliches Gesetzbuch, ABGB*) of 1811. In religious policy as well, Francis might be conservative, but he retained Josephist state control of the Church, along with much of the Josephist religious establishment.

Francis seems genuinely to have believed in the rule of law, and although he reinstalled Pergen as chief of police he initially held back from cracking down on dissent. This changed with the discovery of the 'Jacobin plot' in the summer of 1794. The resulting Jacobin Trials (named after the radical French revolutionary party) resulted in the execution of nine, including Franz Hebenstreit and the Hungarian radical Ignaz von Martinovics, as well as imprisonment for thirty-one others. The plot caused momentary alarm in ruling circles, and has been seen as evidence of a revolutionary potential in Austria, but there was actually little radical pressure on the Habsburg authorities. Even the Austrian Jacobins were more frustrated Josephists than true revolutionaries. Most resistance to the Josephist regime had been conservative; once Francis's rightward adjustments satisfied the ruling classes, there was no major domestic threat to Habsburg rule.

The external threat from the French Revolution had initially appeared equally innocuous, Austria threatened most by the loss of the French ally against Prussia and Russia. As conditions in France veered ever leftward, Leopold II had joined Prussia in the Pillnitz Declaration of 27 August 1791, and had allied with Prussia on 7 February 1792, but it was the French who declared war on Austria on 20 April 1792. By then Francis was Habsburg ruler, but there was no particular air of crisis. It was thought the campaign against the French would be a cakewalk, and order quickly restored. Both Prussia and Russia were more interested in gaining additional territory in Poland, and Austria was again planning to swap Belgium for Bavaria.

The campaign in France was a momentous disaster. The French forces defeated the Allied army at Valmy on 20 September 1792. The French National Convention abolished the monarchy the next day, and the revolutionary forces went on the offensive, occupying both Belgium and the whole left bank of the Rhine. On 21 January 1793, Louis XVI was executed. Two days later, on 23 January, Russia and

Prussia concluded the Second Partition of Poland; but Austria took no part, and had opposed it, because by now it recognized the dire threat posed by France.

In March 1793, Austria led the First Coalition of many European powers (but neither Prussia nor Russia) against the French. The campaign's initial success was reversed by the revolutionary authorities in Paris instituting the *levée en masse* in August 1793. The armies of the *ancien régime* states had never encountered the new, mass citizen armies of the French, and the result was a dramatic advance of the Revolution. While the execution of Marie Antoinette on 16 October 1793 appalled the ruling elites of the *ancien régime*, French military success was even more alarming. By the end of 1794 the French had regained the entire left bank of the Rhine and conquered the Dutch United Provinces. Prussia and Russia, and Austria this time, responded with the Third Partition of Poland of October 1795, but the cynical étatism behind this final despoliation of one of Europe's major historic states was completely anachronistic in light of French advances.

The Peace of Campo Formio (*recte* Campoformido) in 1797 saw unprecedented territorial gains for revolutionary France, but it proved a mere truce. Further French aggression led to the War of the Second Coalition in 1799, and further disaster for Austria, with Vienna coming under direct threat after the French victories at Marengo and Hohenlinden in 1800. The Treaty of Lunéville of 9 February 1801 saw a further decline in the Habsburg position. Salzburg gained a Habsburg ruler for the first time, but this was only because of the eviction of that ruler from Tuscany, as France took over the entire Italian peninsula. Lunéville also spelled doom for Habsburg control of the Holy Roman Empire, for it necessitated a recasting of the Empire's territories under French tutelage that resulted in 1803 in the first ever Protestant majority in the College of Electors.

Lunéville was a humiliation, but Austria's situation only worsened as its traditional bases of power and authority were destroyed by the modern version of French *gloire*. In May 1804 Napoleon Bonaparte had himself declared emperor of the French. This was a clear challenge to the Habsburgs, traditionally the imperial doyen of European monarchs. The Holy Roman Empire itself, reduced and

Illustration 22. Francis I, Emperor of Austria. Friedrich
Amerling, 1832.

recast, no longer looked guaranteed to elect Habsburgs, and its very survival appeared questionable. Such considerations led to Francis II declaring himself Francis I, first 'hereditary emperor of Austria' on 11 August 1804.

The new title was an odd basis on which to found an 'empire'. The imperial title did not in fact create a new, unified Austrian Empire. It applied to all lands ruled by 'Austria', defined as the House of Habsburg, but there was also an assurance that none of the existing constitutions and rights of those lands would be affected. The proclamation did not speak of an Austrian state, but rather of Austrian *states*. The imperial title was of dubious legal standing and ignored traditional institutions. Symbolically, however, it relied heavily for its legitimacy on the Holy Roman Empire. The new imperial arms showed the Austrian arms crowned by the Roman imperial crown, the new imperial colours, black and yellow, were the same as the imperial black and gold, and even the new Austrian imperial eagle was the double-headed eagle of the Holy Roman Empire. The hereditary Austrian Empire was thus in its heraldry a virtual simulacrum of the elective Holy Roman Empire, which still, at this point, existed, Francis being both Francis II and Francis I.

The new Empire had its own crown, the house crown commissioned by Rudolf II, but this 'Austrian' crown was never used by an Austrian emperor. When Napoleon Bonaparte crowned himself emperor on 2 December, Francis I responded by declaring himself Austrian emperor in an official ceremony on 7 December, but there was no coronation. The adoption of the title was really an admission of defeat, and the end of the traditional world picture on which Habsburg power and authority had rested.

The War of the Third Coalition of 1805 saw British victory at Trafalgar on 21 October; on the European mainland the war dramatically confirmed French dominance. Napoleon entered Vienna, where the populace greeted him more as a celebrity than as the enemy. When Beethoven's *Fidelio* was premiered on 20 November the sparse audience was mainly composed of French officers of the occupation. Napoleon then ended the war with his crushing victory at Austerlitz on 2 December 1805.

At the resulting Peace of Pressburg, Austria gained Salzburg (from a junior branch of the Habsburgs), but suffered massive losses of territory, including Tyrol and Vorarlberg (to Bavaria) and

Habsburg Swabia (to Württemberg). Napoleon recast Germany into the Confederation of the Rhine in July 1806, effectively supplanting the Holy Roman Empire. Francis II/I reacted to this *fait accompli* by formally abdicating as Holy Roman Emperor on 6 August, and declaring the Empire dissolved. In 1806 France crushed Prussia at the battles of Jena and Auerstädt. This was no particular comfort for Austria, however, as it tried to find its way in the new Napoleonic Europe, bereft of most of the traditional, imperial institutions that had been at the heart of Austrian authority.

No longer fully independent, Austria was forced to do French bidding, in 1808 joining the Continental System – Napoleon's economic blockade of Britain. This imposed policy had mixed economic results for Austria. The textile industry was actually boosted by wartime demand (for uniforms) and protection from British competition. The huge fiscal deficits inflicted by the war – for much of the period expenditures were roughly double revenues – led to a price inflation that impoverished urban populations; but many peasants enjoyed higher real incomes as a result of increased demand for army provisions.

Culturally, as well, this was an ambivalent era. Suppression of dissent by a traumatized regime made Austrian intellectual life increasingly sterile. Francis insisted on the rule of law and due process, most of the time, but he also instituted a 'Recensorship Commission' in 1803. Yet Vienna was also the city where Beethoven was composing his great works, including the Eroica Symphony, performed in 1805, and the Fifth and Sixth, performed together in December 1808.

Nor did the reformist spirit of Josephism seem entirely defeated by the Franciscan reaction: after 1805 the new foreign minister, Count Johann Philipp Stadion, persuaded Francis I to try a new sort of Josephist populism. Its inspiration came from Spain, where Napoleon's occupation had sparked a national revolt. Stadion concluded that the French had to be beaten at their own game: the one effective antidote to Napoleon would be to rouse the Austrian 'nation' to throw off the French yoke.

Quite what was meant by the Austrian 'nation' was never spelled out, nor how 'Austria' related to 'Germany'. Stadion himself was Swabian, and his main propagandist, Friedrich von Gentz, Silesian. Among the writers gathered in Vienna to rouse public opinion was the German Romantic Friedrich Schlegel. While much was made of the common history of all Habsburg subjects, most propaganda was aimed at the Monarchy's German-speakers, and it was among them that the Austrian 'national idea' most resonated. Stadion himself, when he claimed – in French – that 'we have constituted ourselves into a nation', seems to have had a patriotic and *not* nationalist idea of the 'nation' in mind. Nevertheless, many Germans, including Austrian Germans and even Archduke Johann, viewed Stadion's 'national' uprising as one in which Austria would serve as counter-revolutionary leader of the *German* nation.

The government established historical museums in the provinces to bolster the patriotic pride of the various constituent nationalities of 'Austria'; yet the main expression of this Austrian 'national' mobilization, the citizens' militia of the Landwehr, was heavily concentrated in the German-speaking hereditary lands. The Poles of Galicia were seen as too pro-French, there was a lukewarm response in Bohemia, and the Hungarian diet rejected the idea of a Landwehr.

It is even unclear whether Stadion's policy was really Josephist. The two leading archdukes, Johann and Charles, were Josephist reformers. Charles instituted large-scale, progressive reforms in the army, and Johann both led the campaign to set up the Landwehr and was a leader of the 'national' propaganda effort. Aided by Joseph von Hormayr, he was also behind efforts to incite revolt in Tyrol against the Bavarian occupiers. The regime consciously used the Josephist heritage as part of its appeal to the masses. The statue of Joseph II, now in the Josephsplatz in Vienna, was put there in 1807, as part of the rallying to the 'national' cause. Yet, while the archdukes wanted further Josephist centralization, Stadion's policy, influenced by his Romantic, conservative advisers, was to decentralize power and appeal to the traditional powers in the Monarchy, the estates.

Stadion's plan never went much further than some changes in the central administration, army reform, the Landwehr and a large-scale propaganda campaign. There was never the thoroughness that marked the Stein–Hardenberg reforms in Prussia, even though Stadion's policy was similar in its inspiration. There was no serious attempt to reform the agrarian economy, reduce police power or involve larger numbers of the populace in state affairs. The campaign to 'nationalize' Austria went off at half-cock.

That said, the initial efforts were effective in rousing public opinion to resist the French. The army reforms and the creation of the Landwehr meant that by early 1809 there were potentially more than 700,000 troops available to defend the Monarchy from French attack, and more than 300,000 available for campaigns beyond Austria's borders. Unfortunately, these efforts were vitiated by the decision for war being made too early, in February 1809, before the reforms were completed. Attempts at a fourth coalition also came to naught. When Austria declared war on 9 April, it thus stood alone against Napoleon and his many German allies, including Bavaria.

The Tyrolean rebellion, designed by Johann and Hormayr to coincide with the Austrian war effort, was led by Andreas Hofer to remarkable success against overwhelming odds. Hofer's campaign against Bavarian and French forces, and the four Tyrolean victories at Bergisel over the spring and summer of 1809, have become part of Tyrolean (and Austrian) legend. By the fourth Bergisel battle in August, however, the Tyroleans were fighting without Austrian support, and by the fifth on 1 November, when the French and Bavarians finally won, Austria had already made peace. The most Austria could do by then was to plead for amnesty for the rebels, and it was a mere spectator when Hofer's ill-advised further resistance led to his execution in Mantua on 20 February 1810.

This 'betrayal' of Tyrol occurred because, yet again, the French had trounced the Austrians in the main campaign. The Austrian effort was an honourable failure: Archduke Charles's inflicting on Napoleon his first major defeat, at Aspern-Essling on 21–24 May 1809, is often cited as a great moral victory. Yet by then Napoleon had already reoccupied Vienna, residing there for 158 days, and his victory at Wagram in July left Austria now at his mercy. The Treaty of Schönbrunn of 14 October reduced Austria to only a middling power and virtual French satellite. Napoleon could have carved Austria up entirely, only relenting because Talleyrand had convinced him after Austerlitz that Austria was 'absolutely indispensable for the future well-being of the civilized world'.[4] Instead he just carved off substantial limbs, leaving Austria a landlocked torso, imposed a

---

4 Ingrao, *The Habsburg Monarchy*, p. 237.

large indemnity, and limited Austrian forces, so that Austria would never again threaten French hegemony.

Francis I blamed the reform project for the debacle of 1809. His brothers, the archdukes, were removed from all responsible positions, and Stadion was replaced by Clemens Wenzel Lothar Count Metternich. Metternich, from an enlightened Rhenish family, believed in (enlightened absolutist) reform, but obedience to his master, the emperor, came first. He combined domestic repression with a sophisticated diplomatic campaign whose initial aim was to reconcile the French. The nascent patriotism of the Stadion experiment was cast aside. The Landwehr was disbanded; when Hormayr and Johann were discovered plotting another Tyrolean uprising, Hormayr was arrested and Johann interned and eventually banished to Styria. Despite Francis's disgust at the humiliation, his daughter, Marie Louise, great-niece of Marie Antoinette, was married to Emperor Napoleon on 11 March 1810.

On 20 March 1811, Marie Louise gave birth to a son, cementing the new French alliance; this appeared fortunate, for on 20 February the Austrian state, overwhelmed by the costs of war, French occupation and war indemnity, had effectively declared bankruptcy. The Austrian Empire by 1811 was a defeated, bankrupt French satellite. When Napoleon decided to attack Russia, Austria had little option but to become a full ally in March 1812, and to provide its own army of 30,000 troops under Prince Karl Philipp zu Schwarzenberg as part of Napoleon's 'Grand Army' that summer.

The disaster of the 1812 Russian campaign for Napoleon's forces completely changed the balance of power in Europe, and the outlook for Austria; but Metternich was extremely circumspect in taking advantage of the new situation. While Prussia joined the Russian 'war of liberation' in March 1813, Metternich offered Austria's 'armed mediation' *between* the parties, and Austria only joined the Fourth Coalition in August. Even after the 'Battle of the Nations' at Leipzig on 14–18 October, at which Austria contributed the largest Allied contingent, Metternich continued to protect the French position, partly out of dynastic considerations. Napoleon's refusal of all compromise, however, led to France's total defeat in May 1814.

Austria, completely vanquished by 1812, had, by good fortune and Metternich's diplomacy, ended up on the winning side, as its apparent leader. The conference to put Europe together again after decades of revolutionary upheaval was held at Vienna, starting in September. Even though the Austrians presided over the Congress of Vienna, it was clear that Russia and Prussia had actually won the war, with British and Spanish help. When Napoleon returned from Elba in his hundred days' encore, it was British and Prussian armies that defeated him at Waterloo on 18 June 1815. Austria had contributed, it is true, a large army of 568,000 men to the campaigns of 1813 and 1814, but it had come in late, with poorly supplied and trained troops. Metternich was hence negotiating from weakness, and was constantly reliant on British support and the persuasiveness of his concept of the balance of power.

The Congress of Vienna concluded on 9 June 1815 (nine days *before* Waterloo). The greatest territorial gains – compared with 1792 – were made by Russia and Prussia (and Britain overseas). Austrian gains were comparatively modest. This reflected relative Austrian weakness, but also Metternich's more strategic and diplomatic thinking. The swapping of Belgium and Habsburg territories in Swabia and the Breisgau for Venice, Salzburg, Brixen and Trent meant that the Habsburg Monarchy was now a solid, contiguous territorial block, as once desired by Joseph II. Possession of Lombardy-Venetia and Habsburg princes in Tuscany and Modena meant that Austria would again dominate Italy. In Germany, although the Holy Roman Empire was not resurrected, Austria became president of the new German Confederation, even though Prussia was still larger than before. Metternich also arranged, by assuring lenience for France, the balance of power that was his diplomatic ideal. Complementing this, an alliance system was to be the basis of a Concert of Europe, where the great powers were to meet periodically at congresses to settle outstanding concerns. The Monarchy was hence provided a reasonably advantageous and secure position from which it could recover after the traumatic years of war.

What the Congress of Vienna did not achieve for Austria was a return to the traditional structures and loyalties of the *ancien régime* that had constituted so much of Habsburg authority, or a way for Austria to regain legitimacy and authority under the post-revolutionary dispensation. The former was impossible, and the latter was something only the Austrian authorities could do for themselves. Yet Francis I was simply unwilling to adjust to the new, modern world taking shape, and Metternich was unwilling to risk his job. Instead he tried to buttress Habsburg authority by invoking the spirit of a conservative Romanticism that ranged the forces of religion and order against the spirit of 1789 and revolution – wherever it might occur. The Holy Alliance of 1815 between Russia, Prussia, Austria and eventually most other European states became the symbol of Metternich's 'System' – the attempt to extinguish any move against the 'legitimate' order as revolutionary contagion. Metternich was not so much the 'coachman of Europe' as its fireman, putting out 'revolution' wherever he could.

Britain, Metternich's strongest backer at Vienna, was alienated by this repressive interventionism, and eventually withdrew its support, undermining Metternich's cherished balance of power. The turn to reaction was also pernicious for the image of Austria, again symbolic of repressive backwardness, and for the character of domestic policy and politics. In a Europe of rapid economic and social change, the embrace of stasis in Restored Austria almost guaranteed the System's eventual collapse.

Despite the success of 1813–15, Austria never really recovered from the disaster of 1809–11. In foreign affairs the series of congresses, Aix-la-Chapelle in 1818, Troppau in 1820, Laibach in 1821 and Verona in 1822, began encouragingly enough with the full reintegration of France into the European power system in the Quintuple Alliance of 1818, but increasingly degenerated into a forum for the suppression of change, initially in Italy and Spain. Metternich did not mind this 'triumph of the Holy Alliance over the Quadruple Alliance', for it confirmed his policy of 'legitimacy', and appeared to leave him in control of all Europe. Yet the Greek revolt of 1821 showed his power over European affairs to be hollow. Russia, as the major Orthodox power, had a strong interest in defending Greek rights in the Ottoman Empire, and the widespread Romantic fashion of philhellenism produced enthusiastic public support for the Greek national cause in most of Europe. Against this, Metternich's arguments for legitimacy and the balance of power were unpersuasive, especially after the revolt's ruthless suppression by Mehemet Ali. In 1827 Russia, France and Britain intervened, and in 1830 Greece – as a nation-state – became independent.

By then Metternich's System was fraying severely. Britain had used its sea power to allow South America's breaking away from Spain

and Portugal, and enabled a liberal regime in Portugal. Metternich
was more successful in Central Europe. He rallied the German states
to his reactionary programme, getting them to clamp down on the
German nationalism formerly encouraged in the 'wars of liberation'.
The student Wartburg Festival of 1817 and the assassination in 1819
of August Kotzebue elicited the Karlsbad Decrees of August 1819,
which curtailed free speech and attempted to suppress the German
nationalism rife in German universities. The Vienna Final Act of
1820 empowered the German princes against the constitutional systems still allowed by the 1815 settlement. Yet German nationalism
still grew, in more covert and antagonistic forms.

In 1830, France had another revolution and became a liberal
constitutional monarchy, while Belgium, with British protection,
became independent. While liberal and national revolts in Italy and
Poland were successfully crushed, Austria was increasingly cast as
the main enemy of Progress. Metternich could still rely on Russia, and the quarrels between the Western powers over the Eastern
Question worked to his benefit. Yet the Eastern Question indirectly
provoked in 1840 a great upsurge in German nationalist sentiment,
most famously expressed in 'The Watch on the Rhine', exposing
the futility of Metternich's efforts at suppressing German nationalism. Meanwhile the creation in 1834 of the Prussian-led German
Zollverein (customs union) was creating a German national unit –
without Austria.

Nationalism and liberalism were on the rise throughout Europe,
including within the Austrian Empire, but there was little response
from the Austrian state. Francis I, after his experience of the revolutionary wars, would not challenge the status quo in Habsburg
society: the most absolute Habsburg monarch was also the most
ineffectual.

There was some reform, especially in the financial arena. The
National Bank was founded in 1816 to restore Austria's creditwor-
thiness after the bankruptcy of 1811. In fiscal policy, however, the
authorities left the vested interests of Habsburg society relatively
undisturbed. Taxation was still largely administered and appor-
tioned on the provincial level; the aristocracy paid a small fraction
of taxation and the tax burden across the Empire remained highly
uneven – with Hungary's contribution to imperial revenues being

disproportionately minute. The army was thus chronically under-funded, and without a well-funded army Metternich's diplomacy often amounted to little more than a glorified shell game.

There was little significant administrative reform. In 1817 Galicia received a diet, but Metternich's proposal for a comprehensive over-haul of the Monarchy's structures was stuck in a drawer by Francis I. There was no significant land reform, and *robot* and patrimonial jurisdiction remained features of most of Habsburg agrarian society. The peasants felt aggrieved at this betrayal of Josephism, while the nobility resented the impositions of an expanding bureaucracy. With the state's fiscal problems starving the private economy of credit, the agrarian sector grew only sluggishly, and fell behind population growth.

'Bureaucratic absolutism' pleased neither peasant nor noble, but it proved capable of suppressing political discontent. There was an extensive security apparatus, headed by Count Joseph Sedlnitzky but under Metternich's personal control, which clamped down on any-thing untoward, including religious fervour. Although Metternich encouraged a rapprochement with the papacy as part of the author-itarian alliance between throne and altar, he was only interested in religion's function as a support for authority, and kept the statist structures, and culture, of the Josephist Church in place. The influ-ence in Austria of Clemens Maria Hofbauer's circle, with their Romantic, exalted version of Catholicism, was limited. Bernhard Bolzano, with his radical interpretation of Catholicism, could be condemned by the papacy, and persecuted by the authorities, and yet gain the protection of forces *within* the Church in Bohemia.

Metternich's Austria continued to be a Josephist state in many respects. The bureaucracy kept on expanding, even if the status and pay of officials declined. The education system also kept expanding, extending to girls as well as boys. Yet what was being taught, and what people were allowed to read and say, was severely restricted, at least officially. The teaching of Kantian philosophy was proscribed, because of its perceived threat to religious belief. German idealism in general was eyed suspiciously by a state that required its 'citizens' to obey first and think later, if at all.

Francis I stated to an educator in 1821: 'There are new ideas around, that I cannot, and shall never, approve of. Stay away from these and keep to what you know, for I do not need scholars, but rather honest citizens. Your duty is to educate youth to be such. Whoever serves me must teach as I order; anyone who cannot do this, or who comes with new ideas, can leave, or I will arrange it for him.'[5] Given such views from the top, it is not surprising that intellectual life in the Monarchy lagged behind that to the north and west. Censorship was actually full of loopholes, allowing much 'banned' literature to be circulated, albeit illegally, but it still weighed heavily. The mix of repression and incompetence had a deadening effect on civic life, a sense of political and intellectual stasis.

The death of Francis I in 1835 caused the Austrian state to function with even less sense of purpose and direction. Out of deference to legitimacy, Francis's eldest son, Ferdinand, succeeded to the throne, despite being mentally and physically incapable of such a responsibility. Metternich initially tried to secure for himself sole control over policy, but Archduke Johann's intervention foiled this plan, and a 'Privy State Conference', headed by Archduke Ludwig, was established to run the government. This body was ruled by the conflict between two of its members, Metternich and Count Franz Anton Kolowrat-Liebsteinsky, the head of domestic policy from 1826, and the net result was stasis. In the *Vormärz*, the thirteen years 'before March' 1848, policy consisted of resistance to change at the provincial level, and arguments about how the increasingly strapped state was to pay for this.

Political life did take place in the Monarchy, especially in Hungary, but Metternich's police state discouraged any politics but its own. The dominant spirit of Restoration Austria was political quietism. In the 1810s and 1820s this was almost a welcome respite from recent tumults, and there was a sense of relief in the cultural world. Reactionary though Metternich's Austria might appear, that hymn to human freedom, Beethoven's Ninth Symphony, received its world premiere in Vienna in 1824. The Gesellschaft der Musikfreunde (the Musikverein) was founded in 1812. Franz Schubert (1797–1828) wrote all his mature work in this period, with its exquisite combination of elegance and deep emotion.

The more modest, subjective tone of Schubert's art was typical of the emphasis on privacy and domesticity in this 'Biedermeier' era. Another name for it is the 'Backhendlzeit', the time of fried chicken,

---

5 Helmut Rumpler, *Eine Chance für Mitteleuropa* (Vienna, 1997), p. 212.

which captures well the return to the simple pleasures in life, away from the concerns of high politics and ideology. Painters such as Ferdinand Georg Waldmüller and Josef Danhauser concentrated on portraiture and bucolic scenes from country life and prosperous bourgeois society. In the spirit of carefree escapism and hedonistic pleasure, this was also the era in which the waltz became a mainstay of Austrian life.

In literature several great Austrian German writers emerged in this era. First among them was Franz Grillparzer (1791–1872), who, with his combination of sardonic critique, dynastic loyalty and worldly resignation, is seen as the paragon of Habsburg Austrian character. Adalbert Stifter (1805–68), born in Oberplan, Bohemia, just a few miles across the border from Leonfelden, also began his career in this period. Ferdinand Raimund and Johann Nestroy have proved to be the greatest popular playwrights of the period, the former employing fairytale allegory, the latter indulging in biting and sophisticated satire, as well as considerable ad-libbing, which confused the censors.

Starting in the 1830s, Austrian German literature began to be much more critical of the Metternichian regime. Charles Sealsfield (Carl Postl) had written a broadside against the System in *Austria As It Is*, published in 1828 but abroad, and it was banned in Austria. Many Austrian liberals and writers went abroad, or at least into the other German states, where they were relatively safe from Metternich's police. In 1841, a Jewish liberal journalist, Ignaz Kuranda, started a periodical in Brussels, the *Grenzboten*, to be smuggled into Austria to propagate the German liberal agenda. Writers in and outside of Austria became bolder and more critical. Even aristocrats, such as Viktor von Andrian-Werburg, wrote very critically of Austrian conditions. Writers of an older generation, such as Grillparzer, also became more biting. By the time Eduard von Bauernfeld's play *Grossjährig* (Of Age) was performed in 1846, its scarcely veiled call to let the public off the leash of the paternalistic Austrian state had become conventional social wisdom.

The reason for this shift from acceptance to impatience was that Austria's economy, culture and society had changed, regardless of the regime's reactionary stance. Economic change was especially marked. The Monarchy, especially the north-western quadrant nearest the German and Atlantic markets, experienced the first concerted wave of industrialization during the first half of the nineteenth century. The state bankruptcy of 1811, followed by the inevitable dislocations at war's end, led to a severe economic depression, of longer duration than to the north-west. From the end of the 1820s the economy recovered and grew at a respectable rate thereafter, not catching up with the West, but keeping up with the Zollverein economy. Growth was, however, very patchy by region and sector. The textiles sector was the fastest growing, and the Bohemian lands were the leading regions of growth. In comparison, Hungary experienced only a low level of industrialization.

Technological advances drove much of the economic growth. Expansion of the textile industry relied on the steam engine and mechanization; the fast growth of the iron industry in Bohemia and Moravia, especially the development of the Vitkovice works by Salomon Rothschild in the 1830s, depended on new technologies imported from England. Communications were revolutionized by the development of steam-powered transport: the steamboat and the railway. The Danube Steamship Company started operations in 1831, and in 1832 Austria's – and continental Europe's – first railway began operating between Budweis (the Moldau) and Linz (the Danube), passing just a few miles to the east of Leonfelden. This railway was horse-drawn, and was never much of a success. The real railway age arrived with the opening of the Kaiser Ferdinand Nordbahn in 1838. Financed by Salomon Rothschild, it connected Vienna with Olmütz to the north, and Rothschild's iron works at Vitkovice. Other routes from Vienna, to the south and west, were also begun during this period, and in 1841 the government took control of the growing network.

That a Rothschild was a pioneer in two of the Monarchy's most important sectors, railways and iron, points to the key role of Jewish entrepreneurs in Austrian economic expansion. One area where Josephism survived quite well was in the government's industrial and commercial policy, which was quite progressive. The authorities were keen on fostering useful, technical knowledge: many of Austria's most prestigious technical institutes, such as the Viennese Polytechnikum (the later Technische Hochschule), were founded in this period. Technical progress and economic enterprise were

welcome – as long as they did not threaten the state. In an economy where credit and financial expertise were relatively scarce, and
the government in chronic need of financing, capital investment
was welcome from Jews, especially those who demonstrated political loyalty. The Rothschilds in particular were favoured by a state
grateful for having been repeatedly bailed out during the war and
its aftermath. Jewish entrepreneurs thus became major investors in
industry and commerce, especially in leading growth sectors such
as cotton. A wealthy and influential Jewish financial and industrial
elite formed, with several titled families.

Meanwhile, Jews in Bohemia were still operating under humiliating restrictions, and residence for Jews in Vienna, with the exception
of those specifically 'tolerated', was still officially banned. Despite
this, Vienna had become by 1848 a major Jewish commercial centre,
with an actual Jewish population in the thousands. The authorities,
mindful of the commercial benefit, tolerated the illegal presence, but
corrupt officials in the notorious Judenamt often milked the system
by coercing bribes from 'illegal' Jews.

Relations between the Austrian state and other ethnic groups
often had anomalous outcomes. While this was an era of political
quietism, it was also when nationalism came of age, partly encouraged by government policies. While the government suppressed
political life, it allowed 'cultural' life, including 'research' into the
history of the Monarchy's various 'nations'. The unwillingness to
confront the estates meant these developments often occurred under
official auspices. František Palacký, as head of the diet-funded
Bohemian Museum, transformed an institution of Bohemian provincial patriotism into a bastion of language-based Czech nationalism.

Among the Monarchy's 'historic nations', nationally conscious
ruling classes with a recognized high culture, such as the Italians,
Magyars and Poles, there was already a well-developed sense of historic 'rights'. Cultural nationalism easily combined with political
nationalism amongst intellectuals and aristocrats. Austrian alienation of local elites by overly centralist policies further encouraged
nationalism in both Lombardy-Venetia and Galicia. Yet nationalism's reach, in Galicia at least, was still limited, as shown by the
brutal counter-revolt of the peasantry in 1846 against a nationalist uprising of the Polish nobility. In Hungary, Metternich closed

down political life by ruling from 1811 to 1825 without the diet, but the Magyar linguistic and cultural renaissance continued. Once fiscal exigency forced Francis I to recall the diet in 1825, its sessions became the arena for a Magyar nationalist reform movement, with *Magyar* cultural nationalism now informing the political drive for *Hungarian* rights.

The state responded ambivalently to this surge of nationalist sentiment in the Monarchy. Metternich was not averse to trying to play one ethnicity off against another, which explains the occasional encouragement of cultural nationalism among the 'nations without history', such as Slovenes or Slovaks, so called because they were seen as peasant nations without their own ruling class or established high culture. As these new national movements developed, however, he increasingly saw them as a threat, and started emphasizing the Monarchy's German nature, for the state's coherence relied on German as a *lingua franca*, not only in the administration but also in the main commercial centres north of the Alps, Prague and Buda-Pest included.

The use of German as a language of administration, scholarship and commerce increased greatly during this period. German Enlightened and Romantic thought, especially the work of Johann Gottfried Herder, was also very influential in the growth of nationalism. Had the Monarchy's political life been more open after 1815, however, German might have become the common, supra-national language of political debate, encouraging empire-wide identification and hence mitigating cultural nationalism's divisive tendencies.

This never happened, because Metternich's main target after 1815 had been 'revolution', understood in its liberal form. As the centre of liberal political activity was among the German-speaking urban middle classes, it had therefore been their political life that had been most suppressed. Yet the absence of a unifying, *supra*-national, state-wide, civic political culture at the imperial centre left the way clear for the partial nationalist solutions that were to cripple the Monarchy. The regime itself engineered the ethnicization of Austrian politics.

Civil society did develop in *Vormärz* Vienna. A form of surrogate politics was practised in cultural and business associations, most notably in the Juridisch-politische Leseverein (Legal-political

Reading Association), founded in 1841. It was from this world of associations, literary salons, coffee-house groups and personal and business networks that the call voiced by Bauernfeld for the government to let society enter its majority arose. Yet this Vienna-centred, Austrian civil society, restrained so long by the regime, was never that strong and reached only so far – to the *bürgerlich* (quasi-bourgeois) elements in the German-speaking regions and towns.[6]

Without a strong, unifying *Austrian* civil society at the imperial centre, regional civil societies, and hence political life, developed separately, combining liberalism with nationalism. The liberal idea of popular sovereignty fused with nationalism's emphasis on loyalty to a particular people in a particular area. Political debate outside of the regime became focused not on the popular sovereignty of the Monarchy's citizenry, but rather on the national sovereignty of the various national groups. The nation, and not the state, had by 1848 become the main focus of loyalty for the political nations of Austria.

In itself this was not fatal for the Austrian state, as it represented the supra-national principle, the apparently indispensable umpire above the nationalities. Yet the state's rulers offered little more in the way of justifying their authority apart from the anachronistic appeal to divine and historic dynastic right. Stadion's attempt at a *national* Austrian identity was abandoned in 1809, and the post-1815 regime never formulated a convincing reason for the populace to support the Monarchy. When told that a person requesting an audience was a patriot, Francis I is reputed to have asked: 'But is he a patriot for me?' There is no recorded answer.

The only effective answer that Metternich's 'System' had come up with was that there was no alternative, for the authorities prevented any; the state should be trusted to provide security and an adequate standard of living, while keeping up with economic modernization. Yet by the late 1840s this rather utilitarian basis of authority no longer held true. The emergence of civil societies was evidence of the loosening of the state's grip. The Monarchy's fiscal problems continued, especially considering the large sums needed for the expansion

[6] There is no good translation of the words 'Bürger' and 'bürgerlich': a 'Bürger' can be both bourgeois and citizen, but the term also extends to petty bourgeois categories of traditional urban trades and handicrafts. On this point see John W. Boyer, *Political Radicalism in Late Imperial Vienna, 1848–1897* (Chicago, 1981).

Illustration 23. The Imperial Eagle: battle flag of an Austrian infantry regiment, by 1836 regulation. The black double-headed eagle on a 'Habsburg' yellow ground replicates the symbol and black and gold colours of the Holy Roman Empire.

of the now state-run railways. With population growth outrunning agrarian economic growth, the industrial areas and cities, especially Vienna, were flooded with people desperately looking for a living wage. Poor harvests and the failure of the potato crop in the mid-1840s increased pressure on the authorities.

Such conditions were far from unique to Austria. The revolution of 1848 occurred in most of Western and Central Europe, as a transition crisis of industrialization. The crisis was particularly severe in the Monarchy, because it struck at a regime that neither could fulfil its side of the implicit bargain of prosperity for domestic peace, nor really still believed that it could. The concept of Austria as a supra-national necessity would prove remarkably resilient, but Metternich's method of preserving empires by self-asserted legitimacy did not.

The 'people', or their self-appointed leaders, felt they had come of age. Whether all those years of being treated as minors, in separate nurseries, had compromised their ability to act responsibly and collaboratively was a question to be answered in the next decades. That it remained unanswered was to haunt the Monarchy's remaining years.

THE CHALLENGE OF PROGRESS, 1848–1866

On 13 March 1848 a band of students and their sympathizers marched on the Lower Austrian diet in the Herrengasse to present a reform petition. Protest turned to revolution when troops fired on the crowd, killing five and setting off mass rioting. By nightfall Metternich had been dismissed and on the 15th a constitution promised. The 'Springtime of the Peoples' of 1848 had breached Metternich's reaction. The Habsburg authorities had to devise a way of matching the spirit of progress. They were only half successful.

The March revolution in Vienna did not appear out of thin air. Within the Habsburg Monarchy unrest had been building, with riots in Milan in January and an ever more assertive Hungarian diet. There had been a run on the Viennese banks, the 'Bank Hullabaloo', owing to doubts about Habsburg solvency. When the news of another revolution in Paris, on 24 February, spread eastwards, it found a receptive audience in Central Europe. One chain of events spread through western Germany, but another such chain saw the regime's fall in Vienna sparking off secondary, 'national' revolutions in the rest of the Monarchy. Louis Kossuth's call in Pest on 3 March for radical reform of the whole Monarchy had been a further catalyst for the Viennese revolution, which in turn sparked revolution in Hungary and most other parts of the Monarchy, while also buttressing the revolutions in Germany.

Within days, most of reactionary Europe seemed transformed into a collection of freely self-governing, constitutional states, not by physical force but rather by the power of ideas. In retrospect the revolution was mainly a result of a failure of will and ideological bankruptcy on the part of the ruling powers. At the time it seemed that the revolution had inevitably succeeded because of ideas such as 'the people's will' and 'freedom'.

Ideas, or ideology, had indeed anticipated and partly created reality. Aided by advances in communications, and the precedents of two , now three, French Revolutions, the revolts spread like wildfire, and the principles of bourgeois liberalism and popular nationalism informed the insurgency even where, as in Vienna and Pest, there was neither much of a bourgeoisie nor much of a *popular* nation.

There was a feeling of euphoric optimism, with almost all groups anticipating their own emancipation as part of a general liberation of humanity. Rabbi Isaak Noah Mannheimer pleaded on 15 March, at the burial of the victims of 13 March, for Jews' full human rights now that the emancipation of all Austrians was nigh. The memoirs of the Polish revolutionary Florian Ziemialkowski describe a celebration of the nations in Vienna in April, in which the Polish flag was placed next to the black-red-gold German tricolor and the 'blue-white-green Hungarian tricolor': 'we all lived as if in a beautiful dream'.[7]

The problem was how to convert the dream into action, and that was complicated, even in flag terms. Where were the flags of the Monarchy's many other peoples? And where was the Austrian flag, or should there be one? From the start it was unclear whether the revolution in Vienna was Austrian-Habsburg or German. German nationalism was very strong among the more radical revolutionaries. On 1 April the German black-red-gold tricolor was hoisted on St Stephen's steeple. The next day the flag was carried to the statue of the 'German' emperor, Joseph II, and was flown above the Hofburg. Vienna and the Monarchy's German-speaking regions participated fully in both elections to the German Frankfurt parliament, and that parliament chose a Habsburg, Archduke Johann, as the 'imperial regent' of Germany. Yet it remained unclear how much of the Habsburg Monarchy to include in new, constitutional Germany. Should Hungary be let go? Should Galicia form part of a reconstituted Poland?

Some Viennese revolutionaries were prepared to countenance such national 'liberations', but there were also many opposed. It

---

7 *Neue Freie Presse*, 13 March 1898, p. 3.

soon became clear too that the leaders of the 'nations without history' were not prepared to rely on the largesse of their 'historic' counterparts. The Czech leader, Palacký, refused an invitation to the Frankfurt parliament because he did not regard Bohemia as part of 'Germany' and instead saw Austria as best for Czechs. It was in this letter of 11 April that Palacký stated: 'Truly, if the Austrian Empire did not already exist, one would have to hurry to create it, in the interests of Europe, in the interests of humanity.'[8] Palacký's Austro-Slavism relied on the insight that Czechs were better off being ruled from Vienna in a state in which Slavs were a majority than from Frankfurt in a German nation-state.

The feeling was mutual on the Austrian German side. When Prince Alfred Windischgrätz suppressed the revolution in Prague in June and dispersed the Slav Congress, the general response in Vienna was not fear at the Habsburg interest's military resurgence, but rather satisfaction at the retrograde Czechs' comeuppance. The liberal and national revolutions collapsed in 1848 through being at cross-purposes with each other and themselves. This year attested not to the weakness of the Habsburg Monarchy, but to its surprising tenacity. Its national diversity and particularist patchwork made any coherent insurgent ideology almost impossible, leading to vast conflicts of interests and opinions that beset national relations *within* the Monarchy, to say nothing of relations with Germans and Italians outside. Once the Habsburg authorities regained their equilibrium it proved relatively easy to exploit these divisions to reassert power.

Control of the military was the key. Grillparzer wrote of Count Joseph Radetzky, leader of the Austrian army in Italy in 1848: 'In deinem Lager ist Österreich' (Austria is to be found in your camp). Radetzky's victory at Custozza in July, coupled with the fall of Prague, restored the Habsburg dynastic interest as a major factor in the political swirl, and as a rallying point for 'order'. In a sea of competing national interests, the loyalty of the army assured the 'Austrian' Habsburg interest of renewed power, but how this 'Austrian' interest used that power in relation to the revolution remained open.

---

[8] Rumpler, *Eine Chance für Mitteleuropa*, p. 294.

Illustration 24. Revolution: the opening of the Reichstag in the Viennese Court Riding School by Archduke Johann, 22 July 1848.

In Vienna the periodic upsurge of radical unrest, based on the alliance of students and the lower middle and working classes, led to a revolt on 15 May, prompting the imperial family to flee to Innsbruck, and another revolt on 26 May, which resulted in a Security Committee taking control of the city. The committee's leader, Adolf Fischhof, who as a Jewish assistant doctor had been a leader of the

Illustration 25. Reaction: storming of the Burgtor,
31 October 1848.

revolution on 13 March, proved relatively moderate, and by July
the moderate liberals had reasserted control.

On 22 July the *Austrian* parliament, the Reichstag, met in Vienna.
Elected on the basis of universal male suffrage, its 383 deputies represented all the Monarchy, except Hungary: almost half, 190, were
Slav, and one-quarter were peasants. The parliament debated many
issues, and on 7 September passed one major piece of legislation:
the full emancipation of the peasantry. This great achievement of
the revolution had the ironic consequence of neutralizing the peasantry as a factor when it came to the simmering conflict between
the forces of revolution and monarchical 'order'.

Matters boiled over when the Ban of Croatia, Josip Jellačić, led his
army into Hungary on 11 September. The complex play of forces in
Austria, and in Vienna in particular, now resulted in the destruction
of the revolution by the resurgent Habsburg interest. The threat
of being sent to fight the Hungarians led on 6 October to mutiny
and a radical uprising in Vienna. The court again fled, to Olmütz,
as did a significant minority of the Reichstag deputies to nearby
Brünn. Within weeks, on 31 October, this second revolution was

crushed by troops under Windischgrätz and Jellačić. Several of the October revolution's leaders, among them Wenzel Messenhauser and Hermann Jellinek, were executed.

The triumphant Habsburg court, while intent on putting down the Hungarian rebellion, still appeared committed to the process of Austrian state renewal. The parliament reconvened at Kremsier on 22 November and continued deliberating a new constitution. The new prime minister, Prince Felix zu Schwarzenberg, seemingly wanted to co-operate with the popular forces unleashed by the revolution. When on 2 December Ferdinand was made to abdicate and was replaced by his eighteen-year-old nephew, Francis Joseph, this was seen as Habsburg recognition of the need for modernization. The very name of the new emperor combined the traditionalism of Francis I with the supposed liberalism of Joseph II. Yet advocates of constitutional change were to be disappointed. Too much in the spirit of the real Joseph II, Francis Joseph was intent on modernization, but with absolutism.

The goal of the revamped Habsburg interest was to reassert Habsburg power. Once the regime felt itself militarily secure, troops dispersed the Kremsier parliament by force on 7 March, and Francis Joseph imposed a 'decreed' (*oktroyiert*) constitution. This dismissal of the elected parliament, and the rejection of the constitution that the deputies were about to pass on 15 March, were probably Francis Joseph's most tragic mistakes.

The Kremsier Constitution, apart from guaranteeing the usual liberal freedoms, had been an artful compromise between centralists (largely German speakers) and federalists (largely Slavs). In the constitution power was shared on *three* levels: central government, the historic provinces and districts (*Kreise*) within those provinces that were to be divided along ethnic lines. At the same time it proclaimed the equal rights of all nationalities in the Empire as well as the equality of all citizens before the law. This was about as subtle a way of solving the nationality problem as possible, and it had the legitimacy of being produced by popularly elected deputies. Its destruction by the restored Habsburg power left the question of the nationalities not properly addressed for another two decades, by which time attitudes had hardened and any such compromise was nigh impossible.

Kremsier would have made Austria a parliamentary system, with strong limitations on imperial power. The deputies had also refused to include Hungary and Lombardy-Venetia in their plans, whereas the new emperor's motto was *Viribus unitis* – with *united* powers, for his main priority was to preserve the Empire's unity. On those terms Kremsier was unacceptable to the new regime. There was, admittedly, the more moderate 'decreed' constitution offered in Kremsier's stead, but it had no popular backing, and was never put into effect. It was initially suspended owing to the continuing crisis, and when that was over the regime was well on its way to becoming a purely absolutist regime.

The major proponent of keeping the 'decreed' constitution was Schwarzenberg, who, in his world-weary Byronic cynicism, thought the constitution a useful cover, and its system of ministerial government useful leverage for ensuring his power as prime minister. Francis Joseph himself became convinced by 1850 of the need to abolish the constitution and impose absolutism, and in 1851, advised and encouraged by Karl Kübeck, he did so, starting with the setting up of a Reichsrat in March, and culminating in the Sylvester Patent, promulgated on New Year's Eve 1851.

By then the regime had experienced a spectacular restoration of power, secured by military success and the ruthless diplomacy of Schwarzenberg. Radetzky had confirmed Habsburg hegemony in Italy in 1849, and Venice had surrendered in August. The Hungarian rebellion had also ended in August 1849, with the surrender of General Arthur Görgei – to the intervening Russian army. The Russians were there at Austrian invitation. The unlikely success of the Hungarian rebels in early 1849 had led to the humiliation of Francis Joseph asking Tsar Nicholas I for military help in May. The result was twofold: an ominous diplomatic debt of Austria to Russia; and a particularly vindictive and bloody Austrian occupation of Hungary that deeply alienated Magyar opinion.

The only piece of Habsburg power still needing to be restored was in Germany. The Frankfurt parliament had lost much of its meaning when the Prussian king, Frederick William IV, had refused to become constitutional monarch of a united Germany in April 1849, and what remained of the assembly was forcibly dispersed in June. When, however, a monarchic version of German unity was arranged at Erfurt in February 1850, Prussia had happily agreed to be Germany's leader. Schwarzenberg was nevertheless able to strong-arm the Prussians into giving up this form of German union at the *Punktation* of Olmütz in November 1850. When more negotiations to create a German union including Austria broke down in 1851, the end result was the restoration of the German Confederation, with Austria retaining the presidency.

With Habsburg power restored, Francis Joseph now ruled as Schwarzenberg had advised, disregarding traditional centres of power, abolishing the provincial noble estates, and relying solely on the power of his bureaucracy, police force and army to impose his imperial will. This was to be radical absolutism, without any Baroque niceties, but it was also to be a modern form with a modernizing imperative, *neo*-absolutism.

It was said during the neo-absolutist era that Francis Joseph ruled with four armies: one that marched (the military), one that sat (the bureaucracy), one that knelt (the clergy) and one that crawled (informers). This was fairly accurate. Instead of traditional authority, the dynasty relied on force over its subjects to maximize Habsburg power. Neo-absolutism amounted to another attempt to build Joseph II's rational state, but without the enlightened idealism. It would restore Habsburg power by providing order, efficiency and prosperity, and hence still any hankerings of the populace for a say in government. Tradition and precedent would be replaced by economic and hence financial power as bases of authority; moreover, a modern administration and army would allow the Monarchy to assert itself against Europe's other modernizing great powers. The key goal was ultimately one of foreign, not domestic policy: having the Monarchy provide enough military power to maintain it as a great power in the European state system. Neo-absolutism, in other words, was the culmination of the drive begun in 1740 to rationalize the Monarchy in order to maintain Habsburg prestige and power.

When Schwarzenberg died in April 1852, domestic policy found a most capable substitute in Alexander Bach, former revolutionary and now minister of the interior. The foundation of neo-absolutism's domestic agenda was the acceptance of the emancipation of the peasantry and the legal equality of all subjects before the law, with the concomitant abolition of noble tax privileges, patrimonial jurisdiction and feudal dues. Neo-absolutism replaced these feudal arrangements with an efficient, centralized bureaucratic apparatus, hierarchically ordered down to the district level, which extended the administrative power of Vienna to all reaches of the Monarchy, including Hungary. For the first (and last) time, all of the Monarchy was ruled directly from Vienna by a German-speaking officialdom.

Bach's system offered a vision of Austria as a land in which everyone was equal – in their subordination to the emperor (and bureaucracy). Yet this picture had ironic consequences, and was deceptive. Croatia, whose support had been vital in 1848, was under military rule just as Hungary was. The policy of equal treatment seemed to 'reward' loyalty as much (or as little) as it did betrayal. Similarly, the Sylvester Patent might proclaim the legal equality of citizens, but it specifically negated Kremsier's guarantees of equal rights for the nationalities, and the imposition of German-speaking bureaucrats clearly favoured Germans.

Religious policy also undermined the idea of legal equality. Francis Joseph was later to be seen as the most philosemitic emperor, and his granting of equal rights to Jews (under the 'decreed' constitution) highlighted. Yet Francis Joseph had refused to confirm Jewish emancipation in the Sylvester Patent. For much of the 1850s, therefore, Jews lacked basic rights such as the right to own land, or in some provinces the right of residence.

Francis Joseph's denial of Jewish emancipation in 1851 was probably a result of his deeply conservative Catholic faith, which also explains why the one traditional institution whose position was actually greatly strengthened in this period was the Catholic Church. The Concordat of 1855 with the papacy, signed on Francis Joseph's birthday, returned most control over the Catholic Church in Austria to Rome, as well as control over primary education and marriage. This, with its surrender of the opinion-forming pulpit, was a striking cession of power. It also severely compromised the regime's claims to be a progressive, modern force. Liberals could now rally around opposition to this triumph of 'clericalism'.

Secondary and higher education was also controlled by an enthusiastic supporter of the Concordat, Count Leo Thun. Yet neo-absolutist exigency, and the social and cultural reality of Central

Europe, led Austrian education in a quite different direction. The drive to close the large gap between secondary education standards in the Monarchy and those in Prussia and other German states, together with the dearth of qualified teachers in the Monarchy, resulted in the Austrian authorities recruiting many teachers from non-Habsburg Germany. Most of these new teachers were Catholic, but most held liberal and even German nationalist convictions. The culturally conservative neo-absolutist regime thus ended up ensuring the German liberal dominance of Austrian higher education.

A similar dynamic was at work in the economic sphere. The regime, with Karl von Bruck as its main economic and financial policymaker, adopted a *laissez-faire* policy towards commerce and industry, which swept away the privileged position of many vested interests. Railway construction was deregulated in 1854, and the *Gewerbeordnung* (Industrial Code) of 1859 virtually abolished guilds. Credit availability was enhanced by the state-supported Credit-Anstalt, organized by the Rothschilds and their allies. Economic liberalization and a prudent fiscal policy enabled respectable growth in the 1850s, with crucial strategic gains in such areas as the railway network. Yet the main beneficiaries of this prosperity were the urban professionals and middle class, who supported the government's liberal adversaries. The fact that much of the capital financing this growth (and the regime) came largely from Jews, most notably the Rothschild group, also sat uneasily with the young emperor's initial opposition to full Jewish emancipation.

Jewish entrepreneurs were also prominent in the prestige project of neo-absolutism: Vienna's Ringstrasse. Resulting from the decision in 1857, *à la* Haussmann, to tear down the walls of the old city centre both to be 'modern' and to facilitate the putting down of popular unrest (an exercise ground and two barracks were in the original plans), the Ringstrasse project was converted by its main financial backers into a project whose political symbolism was at best ambivalent, so that after 1860 the Ringstrasse was easily seen as the epitome of *liberal* progress and idealism.

The fact that neo-absolutism strengthened the regime's liberal critics was not its greatest flaw. That was to be found in defence and foreign policy. Despite its many reforms, the regime never did have the confidence in its own authority to impose the level of taxation needed to be a serious great power. Yet state revenues would have sufficed, had the military not been so inefficient and foreign policy not so incompetently led.

The army, personally directed by Francis Joseph, was not successfully reformed, had large domestic commitments and was immensely expensive. In the Crimean crisis in 1854 even 'armed neutrality' meant that Austria's military budget for the year was spent in the first three months. The prohibitive cost of mobilizations in a still fragile financial situation made the army more a liability than an asset.

Metternich had faced a similar Austrian military fragility, but he had been careful, especially after 1833, to keep Russia as an ally. Schwarzenberg was not so wedded to the Russian card, but he had the ruthless guile necessary for post-1848 international diplomacy. His death in 1852 was not catastrophic for neo-absolutism's domestic agenda, but it proved so for foreign policy.

His successor, Count Karl Buol-Schauenstein, proved unsuited to the new world of *Realpolitik*. Francis Joseph's second-guessing and frustrating of his own foreign minister's policies did not help. The sequence of events that was to transform Europe by 1871 was precipitated by Nicholas I, the paragon of reaction. Having saved Europe from revolution, Nicholas sought compensation – at Turkish expense. He even invited Francis Joseph to share in the prospective gains, but Francis Joseph declined. Although distressed at the ingratitude to his former patron, he accepted Buol's argument that Turkey's preservation was in Austrian interests, and, as the emperor remarked, 'One must above all be an Austrian.'[9]

Russia went ahead anyway, and in the ensuing Crimean War Austria managed to tack and trim long enough in her neutrality to avoid fighting Russia while still ending up on the winning side of Britain and France. The war ended in 1856 in Russian humiliation. Austria's pro-Western neutrality, and role as mediatory power, appeared a success. In the longer term it was disastrous, for Austria's fence-sitting deeply alienated its former main ally, Russia, while earning it scant respect in Britain or France.

[9] Steven Beller, *Francis Joseph* (Harlow, 1996), p. 65.

Napoleon III was soon conspiring with Count Camillo Cavour, prime minister of Sardinia-Piedmont, in 1858 to expel Austria from Italy. Francis Joseph and Buol obligingly fell into the trap set for them by declaring war on Piedmont in April 1859. This allowed France to come to Piedmont's orchestrated defence. The ensuing Franco-Austrian War saw two major battles, Magenta and Solferino, the bloodiness of which inspired the establishment of the Red Cross. Both battles were lost narrowly by Austria. A regime with a large fund of authority and financial credit can survive a couple of lost battles; Francis Joseph's neo-absolutist regime collapsed. There was a run on the banks even before the war started and defeat now destroyed any remaining confidence in the regime. Over the course of late 1859 and early 1860 almost all the main figures of the regime were fired.

The defeat left Francis Joseph without his richest province, Lombardy, with a nascent Italian nation-state to his south, and without any allies. (A Prussian offer of help had been conditioned on co-presidency of the German Confederation.) The 1859 debacle forced the emperor to abandon his cherished absolutism. With no public confidence in his governance, and with Hungary in turmoil, he had to find a different method of governing his still considerable Empire.

It was to be several years until the Monarchy regained its equilibrium. Domestic and foreign events were closely intertwined. The various representative and constitutional schemes tried, starting with the expanded Reichsrat on 31 May 1860, were responses to various external and internal interests, and in turn their creation or dissolution had domestic and foreign policy consequences.

Francis Joseph only reluctantly accepted the anathema of constitutionalism. He had no choice, given the financial crisis, and the group of Viennese bankers, many of them Jewish, who were the only realistic source of funds, and whose attitude was summed up by Anselm Rothschild in 1860 as 'no constitution, no money'. This was also the year of effective Jewish emancipation, when Jews achieved the right to own real property and freedom to change domicile. Given the 'spirit of the times' and the financial and political circumstances, there was really no alternative to some sort of liberal constitutionalism. Yet the emperor's continued conservative resistance compromised Habsburg attempts to lead Germany, where such liberal ideas were becoming commonplace. By 1866 the circle had truly closed, and Austria once more was stranded on the wrong side of Progress.

The first major recasting of the Monarchy was the October Diploma of 20 October 1860, a conservative, federalist solution, which would have restored traditional Hungarian autonomy, while structuring the rest of the Monarchy on similarly decentralized lines. It failed because of continued Magyar opposition, and because of the dissatisfaction of German liberals and their financial backers with the mock constitutionality of the new structure. Francis Joseph then turned to the German liberals, appointing Anton von Schmerling as prime minister. Schmerling's 'enabling legislation' for the October Diploma, the February Patent of 28 February 1861, completely recast the Diploma to produce a centralized and Germanocentric, but also much more parliamentary and constitutional, structure.

The February Constitution saw Kübeck's Reichsrat of 1851 transformed into an imperial parliament. Though still indirectly elected by the provincial diets – with an 'electoral geometry' ensuring an overwhelming German majority despite Germans comprising only a quarter of Austria's population – the new Reichsrat had most legislative competence, and controlled a centralized administration. The emperor retained his prerogative in military and foreign affairs, but the Reichsrat set the budget, including for the army. It was not quite constitutional, parliamentary government, but it was close, and liberals thought it could be improved over time. It was to be the basis for Austrian government until 1918.

'Schmerling's theatre' and the new German liberal predominance greatly enhanced Austria's standing in Germany, and a major goal of the prime minister was achieving Austrian leadership of a Great German 'empire of seventy million'. Given the concurrent crisis in Prussia over the 1862 Military Bill, it appeared that this gambit might work, a view confirmed by the goodwill evident at the Frankfurt Fürstentag of August 1863. Francis Joseph celebrated his birthday there on 18 August, surrounded by the other German monarchs under the black-red-gold banner of German liberal national unity. After disaster in Italy, perhaps Habsburg status in Germany could be enhanced by going along with moderate demands for liberalization and national unification.

There were problems with this German-oriented policy. The one monarch missing at Frankfurt was William I of Prussia, whose new minister-president, Otto von Bismarck, was not interested in Austrian leadership of Germany. Given Prussian dominance of northern Germany and the Zollverein, any new arrangement in Germany was very difficult without Prussian agreement. Within the Monarchy, the German liberal version of Austria antagonized all the other national groups. Magyars, Czechs and Poles all boycotted the new Reichsrat; in Hungary there was a national revolt, compromising Austria's new liberal image. Moreover, the problem of Hungary being outside the German Confederation confounded efforts to integrate the part of Austria inside the Confederation into the proposed Great Germany.

Francis Joseph's refusal to cede Venetia also continued Austria's diplomatic isolation. Finally, his further refusal to accept his role as a constitutional monarch completely undermined Schmerling's policy. It was Francis Joseph's conservative insistence on Prussian co-operation that deemed the Frankfurt meeting of 1863 a failure, despite its success in German public opinion. In 1864 he severely reprimanded Schmerling for a speech praising Austrian constitutionalism, yet that constitutionalism was a major part of the attraction of Austrian leadership for the German middle states.

In 1864 Francis Joseph again changed course, adopting a more conservative strategy. At home, bypassing Schmerling and his failed 'We can wait' policy, he began direct talks with the Magyar nobility. In early 1865 Ferenc Deák's 'dualist' Easter article appeared, and negotiations progressed so well that in the summer Francis Joseph sacked Schmerling and in September suspended the February Constitution, in anticipation of a Hungarian agreeement.

In foreign and German affairs, Francis Joseph and his new foreign minister, Count Johann Bernhard Rechberg, similarly changed tack by co-operating with Bismarck's Prussia. Yet this only led into the trap of Schleswig-Holstein, whereby Austrian collaboration in the 1864 invasion of the Danish-ruled provinces and their joint Austro-Prussian administration simply helped Prussia take leadership of the German national cause.

When in June 1866 the trap laid by Bismarck in Schleswig-Holstein was sprung and war started, most of the German states backed Austria. Yet Austria was completely isolated where it counted, among the great powers. The decisive problem was Francis Joseph's refusal to cede Venetia, despite British and French entreaties, and even an offer from Italy to purchase the territory. Francis Joseph's honour would not allow such mercenary deals, and he still envisaged reconquering Lombardy. As a result Austria faced Prussia alone in 1866. Italy allied with Prussia in April, and French neutrality was only secured by the treaty of 12 June and Austria's agreement to cede Venetia to Italy if Austria gained territory, probably Silesia, from Prussia. Austrian troops died in 1866 defending territory that Francis Joseph had promised to give up if Austria *won*.

On paper, even alone against Prussia and Italy, Austria should have won, and against Italy, with victories both on land, at Custozza, and at sea, with Wilhelm von Tegethoff's resounding victory at Lissa, it did. Even in the north, raw numbers pointed to Austrian victory. Yet the Austrian army under the command of Ludwig August von Benedek was strategically overwhelmed by the invading Prussians, and at Königgrätz (also known as Sadowa) it was crushed on 3 July.

Prussia won because it had successfully adapted to the modern industrial age, and Austria had not. The Prussian army was able to use the rail network, including the Austrian rail network, much more effectively. Crucially, the Prussian infantry had breech-loading rifles, while the Austrians still had front-loaders. The breech-loaders, though not as lethal, could be fired rapidly and the psychological impact of seeing troops mown down where they stood was immense and decisive. The Austrian army had rejected breech-loaders in 1851, because of the problems of instructing the poorly educated, ill-disciplined, polyglot ranks of the Austrian conscript army in the flexible tactics necessitated by breech-loaders. The technological gap was the result of an even more critical gap in the organizational and educational levels of the army, and by implication the state.

The Peace of Prague of 23 August 1866 was, on the face of it, relatively painless. Austria lost Venetia, but Bismarck claimed no territory for Prussia. His one major demand was that Austria accede to the formation of the North German Confederation and a South German Union, neither having linkage to Austria. The full import of this only emerged in 1871, after Prussia formed the German Empire, but the defeat of 1866 had clearly ended the contest begun in 1740 with a complete victory for Prussia. It also marked the effective end of the centuries-long Habsburg involvement in German affairs. German Austrians, even Grillparzer, had thought of themselves as Germans, but now Austria was no longer to be a part of Germany, politically defined, and this was to have profound effects on Austrian German identity.

The year 1866 marked the end of the project to reform the Habsburg dynastic agglomeration into a unitary state that could compete in the European states system. After 1866, Austria was never to regain its credibility as a great power of the first rank. It retained that status in diplomatic protocol, but the very way in which it regained its footing, as a Dual Monarchy and junior partner to Germany, ended its standing as the hegemonic power of Central Europe.

The project begun by Maria Theresa nevertheless transformed Austrian state and society. The condition of the educational system, civil society, the economic infrastructure and nascent political life, though trailing northern Germany and the West, was much more advanced than conditions to the south or east. The bureaucratic state and legal structure were relatively well developed. The citizen and the state were no longer separated formally by a feudal layer of patrimonial jurisdiction, and some regions, especially around Vienna and in Bohemia, were almost as modern as north-western Europe. The success of reform could be seen in the facts on the ground.

Yet there remained large and powerful pockets of backwardness and resistance to reform. The antagonism to liberalism and constitutionalism began with the emperor. The Monarchy remained a largely agrarian society, with modern formal structures but premodern social realities. Its adaptation to the modern world was far from complete. It remained to be seen how well the Monarchy could be recast, yet again, for its new, reduced role in European affairs. Defeated by German and Italian nationalism abroad, it now had to face similar nationalist problems at home, while still surviving in the international arena. The disaster of Königgrätz appeared to herald another advance of modern, liberal constitutionalism at the dynasty's expense. Appearances can deceive.

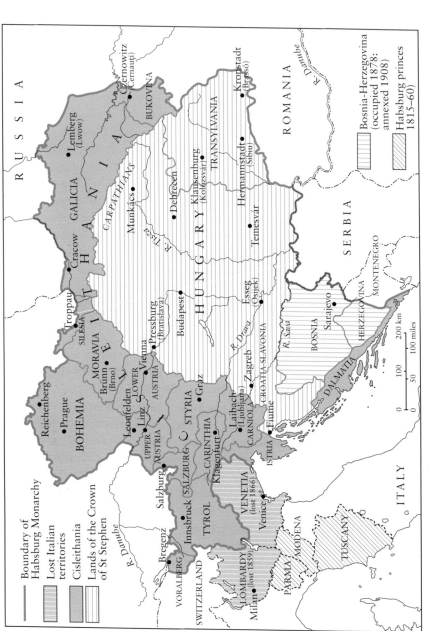

Map 1 The Habsburg Monarchy 1815–1918

4

Empire on notice, 1866–1918

After Königgrätz there remained a large Habsburg Monarchy, which soon became the Dual Monarchy of Austria-Hungary; just over fifty years later this disappeared, torn apart to create an apparently neat pattern of nation-states across the face of East Central Europe. The last half-century of the Monarchy has usually been seen as the inevitable decline and fall of a dynastic supra-national state unable to resist the tide of nationalism. Even at the time, the very impermanence of the Compromise of 1867, with its renegotiable clauses, strengthened the impression of the Monarchy as an 'empire on notice'.

Subsequent Austrian history is unthinkable without the experience of imperial collapse, but historians have recently begun emphasizing the staying power of the Monarchy, that its destruction after 1914 was not a tragic inevitability but rather prematurely ended a viable, even flourishing polity, and there were indeed positive aspects to this last phase. There were greater transformations – economic, technological, social, political, cultural and intellectual – in the Monarchy during these last decades than at any other time in its history.

Yet the Monarchy's modernization was particularly contested and problematic. Some societies are more adaptable to modernization than others, and the presence of pre-modern elements of a common identity greatly facilitated the emergence of modern nation-states; not so the Habsburg Monarchy. The agrarian and traditional sectors proved more powerful and intractable than in other societies; and the Monarchy's ethnic diversity vastly complicated attempts to provide a sense of common endeavour. In an age of fading traditional sources of authority, when the dominant surrogate for authority was the sovereignty of the people, the Habsburg Monarchy was at a considerable disadvantage. A dynastic enterprise which never acknowledged the sovereignty of the people, and whose emperor declared war in 1914 not on the people's authority but on his own, the Monarchy never did discover how to transform itself to survive in the modern world.

The Monarchy's history in this period was exceptionally complex, with a fabulous array of ideologies and sources of authority, old and new, competing as agents of loyalty. The resulting intellectual and cultural turmoil brought many imaginative responses from the Monarchy's populace. 'Vienna 1900' or 'fin de siècle Vienna' has become famous as a major centre of modern culture and thought that 'invented the twentieth century'. The Monarchy's multi-national experience has, in our age of pluralism, come to be seen in a new, positive light. Yet Austria-Hungary was also, in Karl Kraus's words, a 'proving ground for the world's destruction'.

The Monarchy in its last decades was Janus-faced. One face – with its cosmopolitan and pluralist high modern culture – pointed forward; the other, shadier face of the same society – with its ethnic strife, social and political oppression, authoritarianism, racism and rampant antisemitism – pointed backwards, or, if forward, to an anti-modern and radically illiberal future that was to reach its hideous realization in the death camps of Hitler's Third Reich. Both faces were part of the immense 'contribution' of Austrians to the twentieth century.

THE COMPROMISED MONARCHY, 1866–1879

After the catastrophic defeat by Prussia, Francis Joseph quickly made terms with the Magyar leadership. He was so relieved that Deák had not increased his demands that he agreed to them all. The result was the *Ausgleich*, or Compromise, of 1867, by which the Austrian Empire was transformed into the Dual Monarchy of Austria-Hungary.

This agreement was intended to turn the Habsburg Monarchy into a German–Magyar condominium, the Magyars ruling Hungary and the Austrian Germans ruling the rest of the Empire. Francis Joseph was to continue as a quasi-constitutional monarch in both halves, as king in Hungary and as 'emperor' in the rest of the Monarchy. Ironically, 'Austria' disappeared as an official name. While the Dual Monarchy as a whole was 'Austria-Hungary' and Hungary was officially Hungary, the non-Hungarian 'half' (which in population terms was more like 57 per cent of the whole) was not Austria, but rather 'the lands represented in the Reichsrat'. Informally this territory was called Austria, and semi-officially it was known as 'Cisleithania', the River Leitha being the border between Lower Austria and Hungary. Only in 1915 was Cisleithania officially allowed to be called 'Austria'.

The Compromise's neglect of the Monarchy's other ethnic groups was clear at the time. At the crucial Ministerial Council meeting on 1 February 1867, Count Richard Belcredi, a conservative federalist, asserted that the monarch should not rely on specific nationalities but be above them all, and certainly should not ignore the Monarchy's Slavs. The imperial chancellor, Baron Friedrich Beust, saw things differently: 'I am quite aware that the Slav peoples of the Monarchy will view the new policy with mistrust; but the government cannot always be fair to all the nations. Therefore we have to rely on the support of those with the most viability (*Lebenskraft*) . . . and those are the Germans and the Hungarians.' Francis Joseph's response to all this was characteristic, and fateful: 'It might be that the way suggested by Count Belcredi is the less objectionable, but that of Baron Beust ought more quickly to lead to the desired goal.'[1]

Francis Joseph was concerned primarily with dynastic power and prestige. His whole policy after 1866, including the Compromise, was aimed at vengeance on Prussia, and re-entering German affairs. Once that policy was nullified by Prussian victory in the Franco-Prussian War in 1870 and the establishment of the German Empire in 1871, however, the domestic considerations voiced by Belcredi

---

[1] Steven Beller, *Francis Joseph* (Harlow, 1996), p. 98.

reasserted themselves, and so Francis Joseph installed the conservative Hohenwart ministry to federalize Cisleithania.

The 'Fundamental Articles' of 1871 would have done so, most notably giving the Czechs more power in Bohemia. They failed because of Czech demands for yet more concessions, pressure from the new German government and protests by the Austrian German liberals. Crucially, the Magyar leadership saw the Articles as a breach of dualism and threatened to withdraw their support. To Francis Joseph, satisfying the Czechs and other federalists was not worth risking loss of power; therefore the Compromise of 1867 remained the basis of the Monarchy until 1918.

The basis of the Compromise was strangely asymmetrical. It was an agreement between the emperor and the Magyar leadership of the Hungarian diet. The Austrian German liberal leadership in Vienna was presented with a *fait accompli* which they perforce confirmed in the December Constitution of 1867. Francis Joseph never had an Austrian constitution imposed on him; officially at least, it was granted by his grace.

This asymmetry was the background to the problem over nomenclature – of Austria-Hungary and 'Cisleithania', but not Austria. It also lay behind the battles over the use of the terms 'k.k.', *kaiserlich-königlich* (imperial-royal), and 'k. und k.', *kaiserlich und königlich* (imperial and royal), for the Dual Monarchy's various joint institutions. The former suggested that there was still an overall empire, in which there was a Hungarian kingdom, whereas the latter suggested there were two separate state entities, an imperial Austria and a royal Hungary. The latter Hungarian view won out, characteristically.

Beyond these niceties, the Compromise consisted of two parts, the 'pragmatic' and the 'dualist'. The pragmatic part was based on the Pragmatic Sanction and was therefore, counter-intuitively, the permanent element, confirming the 'inseparable and indivisible' character of the Habsburg/Hungarian link. This involved establishing joint ministries of foreign affairs, war and finance. There were also to be meetings of delegations from the two parliaments, alternating between Vienna and Budapest, but the Magyars ensured these meetings would never constitute an imperial parliament. The joint affairs of the Monarchy were co-ordinated instead by a body that was never recognized formally, the Crown Council. An informal imperial cabinet, its composition varied, but usually included the joint ministers, the premiers of Cisleithania and Hungary, and the chief of the general staff, along with anyone else Francis Joseph chose to consult. Foreign policy and the conduct of war remained the emperor's prerogatives.

The dualist part consisted largely of economic and financial agreements that preserved the Monarchy's customs union, but were to be renegotiated every ten years. Also renewable every ten years were military arrangements: there remained a common, k.u.k. army and navy, although Cisleithania and Hungary also had their own military forces, the Landwehr and Honved. It was this dualist part that led to the Monarchy being called an 'empire on notice', for it left vital elements of common concern, such as tariff rates and defence funding, subject to long-drawn-out negotiations every decade that almost inevitably led to political brinkmanship. The common, k.u.k. army and the 'quota' that Hungary was to pay as a portion of common expenses, originally set at 30 per cent, proved notorious flashpoints.

It soon became clear that the Compromise gave Hungary a disproportionate influence over the Monarchy's affairs. An imbalance also developed concerning mutual influence within the respective halves. The Hungarian king, Francis Joseph, gave the Magyar leaders free rein within Hungary's borders, and prevented the Austrian emperor (himself) from intervening. The Magyars, on the other hand, had shown in 1871 that they had an effective veto on any major change in Cisleithania's constitutional structures, and they often used this to influence policy there. This was still frustratingly short of Hungarian national independence, however, and Magyar dissatisfaction with the Compromise was a recurring, and debilitating, theme of Austro-Hungarian politics.

The years immediately following the Compromise were nevertheless ones of liberal achievement in both halves of the Monarchy. In Cisleithania, the German liberal leadership, personified in the Bürgerministerium, proceeded to put in place a liberal state. The December Constitution of 1867, actually a set of 'Basic Laws', secured the basic liberties and norms of a constitutional state. A key provision was equality before the law for individuals regardless of religious confession, thus achieving full Jewish emancipation in Austria. The law on nationality rights was directly taken over from the 1848 Kremsier Constitution. The German liberals systematically implemented their agenda, based partly on the Josephist tradition, and partly on liberal models elsewhere in Europe; the Vormärz experience of nascent civil society was also influential, providing a home-grown aspect to Austrian liberalism.

The liberals established a true rule of law, making Austria a full Rechtsstaat for the first time, by establishing an independent judiciary, crowned by an Imperial Supreme Court, the Reichsgericht, in 1869. This was complemented in 1875 by an Administrative Court, the Verwaltungsgerichtshof, for appeals against the officialdom. The Army Act of 1868 also instituted significant military reforms, although Francis Joseph's resistance frustrated full modernization.

The German liberals had greater success reducing the power of the Church, with the Josephist legacy reinforcing liberal anti-clericalism. The May Laws of 1868 reversed the 1855 Concordat's concessions on marriage and education. One of the greatest liberal achievements was the establishment of eight years of free compulsory education for all children. The Concordat was abrogated by Francis Joseph himself in 1870, in response to the Declaration of Papal Infallibility, which was a challenge to *Habsburg* authority.

In the early years of liberal hegemony the economy, helped by *laissez-faire* economic policies, immense optimism and huge outlays of capital, chalked up very impressive rates of growth. These were the *Gründerjahre*, the years of the founders of many industrial, financial and commercial businesses. The development of the Ringstrasse in Vienna was both symbol and part-engine of this boom. That the main representational boulevard of the Monarchy's capital was lined with the 'palaces' of Jewish banking houses such as the Epsteins and Todescos spoke both to the success of Jewish entrepreneurs in the new economy, and to society's acceptance of this Jewish success, when the going was good.

In Hungary the Magyar liberal establishment introduced similarly progressive legislation, with a Compromise, the Nagodba, with Croatia in 1868, and Nationality and Education Laws. While

Illustration 26. Ringstrasse historicism: Parliament
(1873–83), Vienna. The home of the Reichsrat during the
Dual Monarchy, and of the Nationalrat and Bundesrat of the
First and Second Austrian Republics. Behind it is the
(neo-Gothic) central tower of the Rathaus (City Hall), seat of
Vienna's municipal government.

genuinely liberal in many respects, these two laws were also intended
to turn the kingdom of Hungary (where Magyars were only about
40 per cent of the population) into a Magyar-speaking nation-state.
Similarly in Cisleithania, where Germans comprised only 37 per cent
of the populace, few German liberals doubted that their modern
state would be German speaking.

This was based on illusions. German liberalism's dominance in
Cisleithania depended on Schmerling's 'electoral geometry' of 1861.
Until 1873 Reichsrat deputies were elected indirectly, as delegates
from the provincial diets. Each diet in turn had its own corporatist, curial franchise that allotted seats from various constituencies, some territorial but others institutional, such as the chambers
of commerce and the class of 'large landowners'. Even within the

territorial constituencies the franchise was limited to high-level tax-payers. Liberal control of the diets ensured liberal dominance of the Reichsrat. When the Reichsrat became directly elected in 1873, this curial structure was carried over into the new electoral system in order to give the liberals, representatives of the propertied and educated, German-speaking middle class, an insuperable advantage. Two-thirds of the seats in the Reichsrat of 1873 represented German constituencies.

National politics also helped the German liberals. They bought the support of the Polish deputies by giving Galicia and its Polish-dominated diet *de facto* autonomy. Although Poles were actually less than half the population, Galicia was run from 1868 as a Polish state in the making. The Czech deputies, meanwhile, boycotted the Reichsrat in 1863, and did so again in 1867, to protest against the denial of their national rights. The debacle of 1871 had merely confirmed their impotence, and their continued absence from the Reichsrat compounded the German liberal stranglehold on power.

There was, however, the emperor to contend with, for Francis Joseph was much more powerful than a normal constitutional monarch. Article 14 of the December Constitution allowed for emergency legislation by imperial decree when the Reichsrat was not in session. Crucially, there was no real ministerial responsibility to the Reichsrat. The ministers were responsible, but to Francis Joseph. The government of Cisleithania was his government: he chose his ministers and fired them. Foreign policy and the military were his domain, but so were Cisleithanian domestic affairs. To gain their fiscal support, he left this area to his liberal ministers, but he remained – formally and often practically – in charge. The Cisleithanian officialdom remained the imperial bureaucracy that it had been before 1867, loyal to its emperor.

Francis Joseph also retained the loyalty of the high aristocracy. This group had retreated from centre stage, but they were still immensely wealthy and politically powerful. They dominated the Reichsrat's upper chamber, the Herrenhaus, but less obviously the curia of the 'large landowners' occupied 85 of the 353 seats in the Reichsrat's elected lower house, even after 1873. At the liberal zenith, the majority of deputies in this curia were moderate liberals, '*verfassungstreu*', loyal to the constitution. Yet their liberalism was susceptible to persuasion, if challenged by their loyalty to the emperor. Liberal support in the less advanced rural communes was also fragile. Were the Poles to switch sides, and the Czechs return, the Reichsrat might look quite different.

The episode of 1870–1 had been a warning, and the subsequent liberal government was much more circumspect than its predecessor. Until 1873, however, with the economy booming and Vienna preparing to host the World Exhibition, things looked set fair. Then, on 9 May, the Stock Exchange crashed, and with it the liberals' optimistic world view. In retrospect the *Krach* was an inevitable correction after years of heady speculation, and it was part of a Europe-wide recession. The economy eventually recovered, but scores of businesses were ruined and the core liberal claim to endless prosperity through economic freedom severely compromised.

Johann Strauss Jr's waltz, 'On the Beautiful, Blue Danube' had appeared shortly after the military disaster of 1866 to provide distraction. Now the Viennese middle classes found consolation for their economic woes in Strauss's operetta, *Die Fledermaus*, which debuted in 1874. The words of one of its most famous arias were directly relevant: 'Glücklich ist, wer vergisst, was doch nicht zu ändern ist' (Happy is he who forgets about what can no longer be changed).

Even in the mid-1870s liberal hegemony, if embattled, seemed secure. Financial and corruption scandals further darkened liberalism's reputation, but there seemed little practical alternative. Opposition to the government came mainly from the ranks of the liberals themselves, with the more radical, socially oriented and nationalistic 'Young' taking on the establishment. This all changed when foreign policy took centre stage.

After 1871, Austro-Hungarian foreign policy concentrated on its one remaining sphere of interest in the Balkans, one of the poorest and most chaotic areas of Europe, with an unreconciled Russia as the main competing power. Count Gyula Andrássy, foreign minister from 1871, initially chose an assertive approach against Russia, but Bismarck's new international order made him reconsider, Austria-Hungary joining the Three Emperors' League with Germany and Russia in 1873. When the Bosnian revolt of 1875 reignited the

Eastern Question, co-operation continued. Only when the Russians forced virtual Turkish capitulation in 1878 did Austria-Hungary object, along with the *other* main player in the Eastern Question, Britain, and Germany offering to play honest broker.

At the Congress of Berlin of 1878 Austria-Hungary's main goal was to annex or occupy Bosnia-Herzegovina, the largely Serbo-Croat Ottoman provinces beyond the hills above Austrian Dalmatia. Francis Joseph preferred outright annexation, as part-compensation for the catastrophic losses he had incurred, but Andrássy persuaded him to accept occupation. This was because the Magyar Andrássy had no interest in integrating yet more South Slavs into the Monarchy, tipping the popular balance yet more against the Germans and Magyars. Moreover, if Hungary did not want Bosnia, it also did not want Cisleithania to have her, which would make dualism even more unbalanced. Accordingly, when Bosnia was occupied, it was governed neither by Hungary nor by Cisleithania, but under the anomalous auspices of the Joint Finance Ministry.

The German liberal leadership in Cisleithania was opposed to even the occupation of Bosnia as a profligate imperial adventure and an unwelcome addition of even more Slavs. Eduard Herbst also saw an opportunity to wrest foreign policy from the emperor and hence make Austria-Hungary, or at least Cisleithania, a real constitutional monarchy.

The attempt to assert parliamentary power over foreign policy was a catastrophic failure. In the political crisis of 1878–9 Francis Joseph did not back down; the Reichsrat ratified the occupation, but a majority of liberals voted against. Francis Joseph, viewing the liberals as having broken their bargain with him, appointed a new regime, under his boyhood friend Count Eduard Taaffe. Francis Joseph was now determined that Cisleithania be ruled on his terms, and Taaffe proved remarkably adept at fulfilling his wishes. At first Taaffe kept moderate liberals in his government, but he also persuaded the Czechs to re-enter Cisleithanian politics, gained Polish support, and leant on the nobility to back their emperor against the upstart liberals. In the 1879 election the previously overwhelming liberal majority in the Reichsrat disappeared.

The liberals had lost through the very electoral geometry that had once so helped them, with losses in the large landowners' curia being decisive. They still held almost half the seats, and many still assumed that the next round would see them back in power, if chastened. They were wrong. The liberals were never to enjoy a majority in the Reichsrat again, and the era of Taaffe's 'Iron Ring' would destroy any idea of Cisleithania as a German liberal state.

For once Otto von Bismarck was rattled by the upheaval in Cisleithanian politics, combined with Andrássy's resignation that autumn. To preclude Austria-Hungary becoming a pro-Slav, hostile power, Bismarck offered the outgoing Andrássy a defensive alliance that would buttress the Monarchy in relation to Russia and sustain German influence within the Monarchy. Francis Joseph had always wished for a conservative alliance between the two 'German' powers, if not quite on these terms, and the Magyar Andrássy welcomed German support against Russia. The treaty that began the Dual Alliance was signed on 7 October 1879. At the very moment that Germans lost power within Austria, the fate of Austria-Hungary was tied to Germany. Neither event seemed irreversible at the time, and there was to be much chopping and changing before 1914. As it turned out, though, the contradictory parameters for the rest of the Monarchy's existence had been set.

AUSTRIA TRANSFORMED, 1879–1908

On 12 August 1879, Taaffe formed his new ministry, supported by a ragbag of groups in the Reichsrat, including Czechs, Poles, German Clericals and German Conservatives, Slovenes, Croats and Romanians. This coalition of the previous 'outs' of Austrian politics, the 'Right', had fewer seats under its direct control (168) than the German liberals, the 'Left' (174), but neither side had a majority of the 353 seats, and therefore, having the emperor's support, Taaffe's 'Iron Ring' remained in power, until 1893.

The battles between the German liberal 'Left' and the 'Right' of the Iron Ring were waged against the backdrop of a complex and unstable situation in the Reichsrat, where ideological boundaries were confused, with moderate liberals still in Taaffe's cabinet until 1881 and liberal nationalists, such as the Old Czech party, supporting the Right. Taaffe took full advantage of this complexity and the emperor's backing: he employed the very precariousness of the government's position to put pressure on coalition members to moderate their demands and swallow their disagreements – otherwise the liberals would be back.

Taaffe's method of keeping everyone in a state of 'well-tempered dissatisfaction' worked very well. By the time he left power, the German liberals, once Austria's party of government, had been reduced to being one interest group among many in a much changed political landscape: more heterogeneous, and far more concerned with narrow national and group interests. This change from an *Honoratioren* style of principled politics to one where policy became a tradable commodity between interest groups was common to most of contemporary Europe; in Italy it was called *trasformismo*. While nowhere near as corrupt as that, Taaffe's rule did set Austrian politics on the road to the 'politics of the bazaar'. The heterogeneity of the national and group interests in Austria meant that Taaffe's *Fortwursteln*, 'muddling through', also made Austrian representative government almost impossibly complicated for his successors.

Taaffe's agenda in the 1880s was replete with obvious political trade-offs, and while there were progressive, modern elements, there were also those that pandered to the Iron Ring's more reactionary members. Emulating Bismarck, and advised by Emil Steinbach, a Jewish convert, Taaffe passed a slew of social legislation for remedying the worst excesses of the new economy. Limits were placed on working hours and on the use of child and female labour; a system of accident and sickness insurance for industrial workers was implemented; and the liberal Industrial Code of 1859 was replaced in 1882 with a much stricter regulatory code for trades and crafts. Yet Taaffe also rammed through an Anti-Socialist Law to suppress the organization of working class protest. It was liberal pressure that eventually repealed this draconian measure in 1891.

Taaffe's progressive social legislation was almost all at the expense of liberal supporters in the industrial and commercial middle classes; worker protections and insurance were much scantier for agricultural and forestry workers owing to Taaffe's support from conservative landowners. Education policy also satisfied conservative supporters rather than responding to modernization's needs. The Education Act of 1883 rolled back liberal reforms, allowing peasants once more to take their children out of school after only six years of schooling to work on the farm. The Clericals were also rewarded with a requirement that all teachers have 'special competence' in the religion of the majority of pupils, in other words be Catholic. The law was not applied to Galicia, because too many schools there might have Jewish or Ruthenian majorities. Satisfying national interests, particularly those of the Czechs, was also a priority. In 1882 Prague's Charles University was split into linguistic halves, and the Taaffe administration was far more welcoming of the proliferation of Czech secondary schools in the Bohemian lands.

Czech support (and that of Croats and Slovenes) was also bought at liberal expense in political and administrative policy. The Bohemian diet's franchise reform of 1882 delivered a previously German-dominated body to the Czechs, just as the creation of a slew of peers in 1881 handed the formerly liberal Herrenhaus to the conservatives. Most contentious of all were the Stremayr Ordinances of 1880, which made Czech one of the 'external' languages of the political bureaucracy (the imperial bureaucracy directed from Vienna rather than the 'parallel' provincial administrative hierarchy run by the various provincial diets) in Bohemia and Moravia. On the face of it quite reasonable, these ordered officials to communicate with petitioners in the latter's language, whether Czech or German. The 'internal' administrative language, between officials, and the 'most internal' language, between the localities and Vienna, remained German. Because most Czech officials already spoke German, and most German officials refused to learn Czech as an inferior peasant language, however, these measures drastically reduced the number of official jobs for Germans. Germans feared, moreover, that this was only the beginning of a slippery slope to Czech domination of government in the Bohemian lands.

Even an apparently progressive measure such as expansion of the franchise led to a less progressive and less liberal political landscape. The electoral reform of 1882 reduced the tax qualification to 5 Gulden, bringing into Austrian politics the lower middle classes. Victims of economic modernization, the *Mittelstand* were anti-liberal and amenable to co-option by Taaffe's more socially minded, state-oriented regime.

Modernization and the expanded political terrain radically altered Austrian politics. Within the German middle classes there was a pronounced shift to the more socially oriented, nationalist end of the German liberal 'Left'. The Linz Programme of 1882 combined more emphasis on social welfare with a far more strident tone in defending Austrian Germans against Cisleithania's other nationalities. This programme became the basis of the German nationalist movement led by Georg von Schönerer. Under Schönerer the movement soon embraced racial antisemitism, even though the original programme had largely been written by Jews such as Heinrich Friedjung. Victor Adler, later Austrian socialism's leader, was also an original signatory.

Schönerer enjoyed great success during the Nordbahn Affair of 1884–5, when he assailed the generous terms on which Taaffe's government had renewed the contract to operate the railway held by a Rothschild-controlled company, but his career received a severe setback in 1888 when he was imprisoned and banned from political life for his attack on the offices of a liberal (and Jewish-run) newspaper, the *Neues Wiener Tagblatt*. His message, in more moderate but still racially antisemitic form, was nevertheless successfully adopted by other former liberals, such as Otto Steinwender and his 'German People's Party'.

There were similar developments in other nationalities' politics. The 'Old Czechs' were swept aside electorally in the early 1890s by the Young Czechs, who represented a combination of left-wing, socially oriented policy and strident nationalism similar to their German nationalist antagonists. It was the Young Czechs' success that foiled the Bohemian Compromise of 1890.

Parallel to this radicalization of the bourgeois Left, the Christian Social movement transformed the lower middle class, clerical and conservative German Right in Austria. This started as an artisanal protest movement in Vienna against both the harsh effects of the free market economy and also the supposedly 'Jewish' liberalism that such ideologues as Karl von Vogelsang blamed for fostering this system. In 1887 German nationalist antisemites joined to found the 'United Christians', but the decisive moment came when Karl Lueger, previously a politician of the democratic Left, became leader.

Lueger, the supreme opportunist in Austrian political history, recognized that antisemitism, the use of 'the Jew' as a scapegoat for the distresses of modernity, could bring together anti-liberal forces like nothing else. He was so successful in amalgamating a ragbag of dissident groups from the Right (lower clergy and cultural conservatives) and the Left (petit bourgeois radicals, democrats and German nationalist racial antisemites) that by 1891 liberal hegemony in Vienna started crumbling, and in the municipal elections of 1895 the Christian Socials achieved a majority in the city council. Francis Joseph's refusal to sanction Lueger's election as mayor was famously celebrated by Sigmund Freud, yet Lueger became mayor nonetheless in 1897. By then the Christian Socials dominated Viennese politics, and could not be budged until 1918. From Vienna they expanded into Lower Austria, and then, in alliance with clerical and conservative forces, into the Alpine Austrian provinces.

These new mass political movements were each other's fiercest rivals: German nationalists and Young Czechs were nationally at odds, while the Christian Socials were opposed to the anti-clericalism (inherited from liberalism) of the nationalists. All, however, shared hostility to Jews.

The rise of antisemitism in the 1880s was to be a fatal development for Austrian history. Its causes are complex, but among them was the identification between Jews and liberalism. The group that did best out of liberal hegemony was Austrian Jewry. Jews proved much better at adapting to the modern economy: from being a persecuted and relatively poor minority in the 1850s, they were now prominent in many fields, especially literature, the press, music and the liberal professions, adding to the established Jewish prominence in banking, commerce and industry. Many Jews had been victims of the 1873 Stock Market crash, but many others had been able to salvage their holdings, and the envious are only attentive to success, not failure.

Much of antisemitism's power arose from the envy of the largely Catholic populace, who would not accept that Jews, condemned in Christian theology to abasement, could legitimately deserve their new prosperity. Moreover, Jewish success when so many Christians were suffering was seen as breaching the unwritten contract that

Illustration 27. Antisemitism: 'Inexplicable what one experiences': Kikeriki: 'Thus and not otherwise did their fathers appear! And today the sons of such Polish Jews want to teach us Viennese about Germanness!' *Kikeriki,* 9 September 1883.

Jewish emancipation would lead to prosperity for all. The end of prosperity, and the end of liberal hegemony, severely compromised the Jewish position in society.

The replacement of liberalism's values by nationalism's far narrower world view also worked against Jewish integration. Had Jews been seen merely as a religious group, integration into the various nations should have been feasible. Yet the ethnic element was always present in Central Europe's nationalisms, and, with the large exception of the Magyars, these movements had early on designated the Jews as an alien ethnic group. In their mutual hatred, German and Czech nationalists nevertheless agreed on Jews as a pernicious, foreign element. Czechs, furthermore, saw Jews as a German fifth column in the German–Czech conflict. As the conflict between nationalisms sharpened, and divisions became more absolute, with pseudo-Darwinist biologism supplanting national by racial categories, the Jews' position became ever more insecure. Once a mere pariah group, with a lowly but tolerated status, they now became a foreign racial element that would have to be expelled or eliminated.

Christian Socials, more loyal to the concept of imperial Austria, did not quite fit the nationalist pattern. Their ideological roots in

Catholic social thinking, with its supra-national values, meant that their antisemitism was generally not as ethnically or racially modelled. One of Lueger's most famous sayings was 'I decide who is a Jew'. This shows opportunism, but also a certain elasticity in Christian Social antisemitism. Yet antisemitism was more important for Christian Socials than for nationalists, for the Christian Socials had no separate national identity to fall back onto, only what they were against – the Jews – as their uniting principle. Even clericalism was not a unifying theme, as many of their supporters, especially in Vienna, harboured anti-clerical attitudes. That is why the party named itself 'Christian' and not 'Catholic' – 'Christian' in this context meaning 'not Jewish'. Antisemitism was at the core of Christian Social identity.

Antisemitism's meteoric rise in Austria was not as inevitable as it appears in retrospect. Antisemitism was also strong in Hungary in the early 1880s, but the government quickly moved against it, and Hungary remained an island of relatively pro-Jewish sentiment. In Austria, by contrast, antisemitism's rise was left unopposed by a Taaffe administration more interested in using it to deter the Jewish leadership in Vienna from supporting the German liberals. The Viennese Jewish establishment, admittedly, was initially uncomprehending and paralysed in its response to this resurgence of Jew hatred. Nevertheless, the unfettered rise of antisemitism in Austrian political life was partly a product of Austrian-style *trasformismo*.

The one mass political movement in 1880s Austria that did not go down the antisemitic road was Marxist socialism. Although also a collectivist ideology, its retention of liberalism's humanist universalism allowed Jewish individuals to see themselves as among equals. Socialism had its own antisemitic heritage, and Austrian socialism in particular often lapsed into using antisemitic imagery and rhetoric when competing with their nationalist and Christian Social rivals. Marxism's atheism worked directly against the Jewish religion (and Christianity), and the socialist attack on 'capitalism' threatened the livelihoods of most Jews. Yet socialism accepted Jewish individuals as human beings and championed many of the Enlightenment values so dear to modern, emancipatory Jewry. It was no accident that many in the Austrian socialist leadership, from

Victor Adler down, and even more of its intellectual leadership, with Max Adler, Otto Bauer and Rudolf Hilferding, were of Jewish descent.

The 1880s were a period of crisis and rebuilding for Austrian socialists. Taaffe's crackdown succeeded in scattering the nascent workers' movement, but the dedicated work of new leaders, often disenchanted rebels from the ranks of the German nationalist Left, such as Victor Adler and Engelbert Pernerstorfer, both former Schönerer supporters, culminated in the movement's refounding at Hainfeld on 1 January 1889. The Austrian Social Democratic Party was henceforth to be the other party that, with the Christian Socials, was to dominate Austrian politics in the next century.

The rapid rise of the socialists allowed the originally radical and populist Christian Socials to become the defenders of the 'respectable' classes against the 'Reds'. The one sector of the middle class *Bürgertum* that found it hard to support the Christian Socials was the Jewish community. This constellation explains many of Austria's subsequent political travails, and its spectacular intellectual and cultural flourishing.

There was a much more fractured political scene in Austria by the end of the 1880s, and this partially worked in the Taaffe government's favour. As Steinbach remarked in 1893, the lack of a strong, stable majority in the Reichsrat virtually guaranteed the 'crown's full sovereignty'. Taaffe could rule above the political parties as the Kaiserminister, the emperor's minister, beholden to the monarch alone.

The monarch himself presided over a conservative 'muddling through' in foreign affairs similar to that in the domestic sphere. After the Bosnian crisis, the aim was to preserve the status quo, sticking with Germany but not antagonizing Russia (Three Emperors' Alliance, 1881), going along with Germany's alliance with Italy (Triple Alliance, 1882) and making alliances with the new Balkan monarchies, but also keeping in with Britain (Mediterranean Entente, 1887).

One critic of the drift in Austro-Hungarian policy was the heir, Crown Prince Rudolf. In 1888 he warned his father, anonymously but presciently, that the occupation of Bosnia-Herzegovina was 'one foot in the grave'. For his father, however, Rudolf was himself a problem. Rudolf's opposition to the German alliance, his surrounding himself with left-liberals such as the Jewish journalist Moritz Szeps, and his pro-Magyar stance, which he shared with his mother, Empress Elisabeth, might cause concern in imperial circles, but they were normal behaviour for an heir, usefully channelling opposition to the current monarch's policies in a dynastically loyal direction.

What was far less acceptable was the deterioration in Rudolf's personal behaviour, partly exacerbated by increasing frustration at his father's excluding him from any serious responsibilities. Whether as a result of disease or a psychological disorder, Rudolf's trials and tribulations culminated in his killing his lover, Marie Vetsera, and then himself at Mayerling, in the Vienna Woods, on 29 January 1889.

Rudolf's death was a body blow to the dynasty. He was Francis Joseph's only son, and, despite everything, a much loved one. The emperor was heartbroken, and did everything possible to ensure that the death did not appear a suicide, thus ensuring his son a decent burial. (His body resides in the Kapuzinergruft.) The elaborate cover-up, however, led to multiple rumours, so that Mayerling became a myth unto itself, the topic of everything from films to fancy cakes, but in the short term it meant a severe diminution of the dynasty's moral authority.

Meanwhile the nationality conflicts only worsened. The Bohemian conflict proved intractable. In 1890 the German and Czech political leaderships did reach a Bohemian Compromise that would have ceded political control of the province to the Czechs, but left German as the internal language of the political (imperial) bureaucracy, and given German Bohemians local autonomy. The agreement, however, was vitiated by the electoral defeat of the Old Czechs by the much more nationalistic Young Czechs, who had campaigned on rejection of the Compromise. By 1893 the diet was obstructed and Prague under martial law. 'Muddling through' had led to political chaos.

Taaffe responded with an electoral reform bill in 1893 designed to cripple the bourgeois national parties by giving the vote to all literate

Illustration 28. Mayerling as a business opportunity:
cakebox lid for a 'Kronprinz Rudolf Mayerling Torte'.

males over twenty-four. While not universal or equal suffrage, owing
to the franchise's curial structures, this was a dramatic expansion
of the electorate. It severely threatened the established parties, and
the result was a very odd political alliance between German liberals
and conservatives, along with the Poles and other vested interests,
which unseated Taaffe and imposed its own ministry, presided over
by the conservative Alfred Windischgrätz, but effectively led by the
liberal Ernst von Plener, on a reluctant emperor.

The Windischgrätz ministry was the last parliamentary government of Francis Joseph's reign and it was a disaster for the coalition

members. Liberal failure to deliver better pay and conditions for the bureaucracy led to many disgruntled officials voting for the Christian Socials, helping them to their epoch-changing victory in the municipal elections in Vienna on 1 April 1895. This election set Lueger on the path to the mayoralty, and Theodor Herzl on the road to Zionism. The liberals' attempt to regain control of Austrian politics ran aground and the coalition broke apart in June 1895 over another instance of the nationality conflict, the attempt to introduce a parallel Slovene class in the Gymnasium of the Styrian town of Cilli (Celje).

Francis Joseph now picked his own premier, a man with a reputation for decisive action, Count Casimir Badeni, governor of Galicia. Badeni initially showed promise, arranging negotiations for another Bohemian compromise, and getting a watered-down version of Taaffe's electoral reform bill passed in 1896 that created a new 'fifth curia' with universal male suffrage. This reduced German Reichsrat representation to a minority of seats (202 out of 425), and, as the elections of March 1897 showed, reduced the Left's power within that national bloc.

Having hoped to govern with a progressive coalition of Young Czechs and German liberals, Badeni ended up with a majority of the Right in the new parliament, and no German–Czech agreement over Bohemia. He decided to go ahead with his version of 'compromise' anyway. The concession to the Germans, administrative autonomy for German Bohemia, could only be managed through the Czech-dominated Bohemian diet, but the concession to the Czechs over administrative language rights could be achieved by administrative ordinance. So the decisive Badeni issued his language ordinances in April 1897, making Czech equal to German as an administrative language in Bohemia and Moravia, and requiring proficiency in both languages from all officials by 1901.

The Badeni Ordinances broke the political system of Cisleithania. The German Left went on political strike. The language ordinances, on the face of it reasonable, created such a furore because of the practical inequality between the two languages and because the Germans were convinced (correctly) that the Bohemian diet would not fulfil its side of the bargain. The fears raised in 1880 by the Stremayr Ordinances were now realized, for the ordinances promised a Czechification of the Bohemian administration with nothing in return.

Over the following months the German Left, liberals and progressives initially even more than the nationalists, launched a complete obstruction of parliament. When the majority Right tried to break this on 25 November by enacting new procedures in the 'Lex Falkenhayn', the crisis boiled over, with the government sending police to expel deputies, and German protesters taking to the streets. The threat to constitutionalism brought the socialists into the German camp, and even Karl Lueger, confirmed as mayor by the emperor in April in return for supporting Badeni's plan, now turned on his ally. Badeni resigned on 29 November, but the crisis had only begun.

For the next couple of years a series of Beamtenministerien (official-directed governments) ruled Austria, but none restored normality. German obstruction continued until the Badeni Ordinances were suspended (and eventually repealed in 1899), only to be replaced by Czech obstruction. The government managed to keep the state functioning by exploiting Article 14 in the constitution, which allowed emergency legislation to be decreed in the Reichsrat's absence. Obstruction would lead to the emperor proroguing parliament; the government then passed emergency decrees under Article 14; parliament was then recalled and confirmed the decrees passed *ex post facto*; after a brief lull obstruction would then resume . . .

With the ministry of Ernst Koerber of 1900–4, there was a certain stability, even efficacy, in this arrangement. Koerber concocted a new, improved version of Taaffe's interest politics, perfecting 'the politics of the bazaar'. An elaborate programme of public works and investment to boost the economy also provided, quite intentionally, large inducements for the political parties to be friendlier to the government. Cultural and educational policy, such as establishing Czech-language polytechnics, was also thus employed.

These pork barrel tactics were initially quite successful, but there were large drawbacks for policy and Austria's political health. The government could get by using Article 14, but the political consensus prohibited passing important legislation, such as tax reform or an increase in the army's size, by decree '*ex lex*' (outside statute); yet such legislation was increasingly needed. The new arrangement was also most detrimental to political health. The breakdown of parliamentary politics led to a new 'bureaucratic absolutism': political parties no longer dealt with each other or sought actual power; instead they competed with each other to make deals with the bureaucrat-led government. They therefore left government to the officials, and merely tried to obtain satisfaction of their interests. It was a recipe for interest politics at its worst, complete political irresponsibility, and extremism.

There were some state-sponsored compromises between the parties. The Moravian Compromise settled the German–Czech conflict there, but even it was based on national separation, not co-operation. In Bohemia there was no progress, and in 1904, with the economic trade-offs producing diminishing returns and the cultural trade-offs creating more antagonism, Koerber resigned and total obstruction resumed.

Cisleithanian politics had been totally 'transformed' by then. After the Badeni crisis the German bloc in parliament no longer acted on the lines of being the 'state nation' but as just another national interest group. This 'nationalization' of the Austrian Germans was even reflected in such cultural fields as architecture. After the devastating fire of 1892 in Leonfelden had destroyed its characteristically Habsburg and Baroque onion dome, the rebuilt parish church was given instead a neo-Gothic spire. This was partly a historicist identification of the spiritual with Gothic, but there was also, with Bohemia and the linguistic border so close, a nationalist aspect, for Gothic also represented *German* spirituality in a way that Habsburg Baroque did not.

The Christian Socials and the Social Democrats both counteracted this nationalizing tendency, to varying effect. The Christian Socials fancied themselves an 'imperial' party with an 'Austrian' identity, but they remained partial and regionally limited in their appeal. While their links to clericalism alienated many German middle class voters, they remained a German party, closely attuned to their constituents' interests. With their combination of irresponsible, anti-semitic rhetoric and pragmatic pursuit of political favours, they exemplified the transformation of Austrian politics.

Illustration 29. Leonfelden, a) before and b) after the 1892 fire.

The socialists by contrast extended across national boundaries. Ostensibly the most interest-oriented party of all – as champions of the working class – their defence of workers' rights and their ideological roots in the Enlightenment led them to become the liberals' successors in advocating the rule of law, responsible government and supra-national constitutionalism. It was from Austro-Marxist thinkers such as Karl Renner and Otto Bauer that some of the most innovative thinking about the 'nationality question' in Austria came. The one party dedicated in theory to the overthrow of the Habsburg Monarchy tried harder than any other to make the supra-national polity work. The Social Democratic Party, because of its own supra-nationality, became one of the Monarchy's best hopes for survival. Its splitting along national lines in 1910, when the Czechs seceded, was a blow not only to socialist internationalism but also to the Monarchy.

Hungarian politics had developed differently, but also were in crisis. In the 1880s Germans had formed 37 per cent of the Cisleithanian populace and Magyars 41 per cent of the Hungarian. While the Germans had been reduced to just one national interest group among many in Cisleithania, Hungary had become a Magyar state. King Francis Joseph never tried to upend liberal hegemony there as Emperor Francis Joseph had in Vienna. Instead he allowed Kálmán Tisza, prime minister since 1875, to pursue both liberal anti-clerical policies and a policy of largely permissive but also partially coercive Magyarization of the populace, resulting in growing Magyar dominance. Budapest asserted substantial control even in autonomous Croatia. The Hungarian parliament's deputies were almost exclusively Magyar. Instead of opposition to Tisza coming from a multi-national Right, it came from a nationalist Left wanting even more independence from Vienna.

After Tisza's resignation in 1890, Hungarian politics carried on in much the same way. The fight between the *labanc* moderates and the *kuruc* radicals (labels taken from the seventeenth-century rebellion) sharpened in 1898 over renewal of the Economic Compromise and then, in 1902, over the Joint Army. To achieve true nationhood, it was demanded, Hungarian regiments of the Joint Army should have Magyar as their language of command. As in the Badeni crisis, language was at the centre of the ensuing conflict and, although a Hungarian problem, it struck at the heart of the idea of 'Austria'.

The Joint Army crisis was not about military practicalities, but rather national symbolism: was Hungary going to have a Magyar-speaking (part of an) army, or was the emperor-king going to retain his united, German-speaking Habsburg army? There was also a vital *national* practicality involved: many national identities in nineteenth-century Europe benefited greatly from conscript armies being the 'school of the nation'. Francis Joseph, similarly, had reason to fear that the national division of the Joint Army would herald an end to the supra-national dynastic, 'Austrian' identity that held not only his army but also the Monarchy's peoples together.

This explains why Francis Joseph rejected any challenge to German as the language of command in the Chlopy Order of 1903, and why this outraged the Magyar political nation. In 1905 a massive electoral revolt against the moderate liberals led to the king's imposition of a 'loyal' government, provoking a tax strike, which in turn was answered by a royal plan for dramatic franchise expansion, increasing the enfranchised from 7 per cent to 16 per cent of the population, and including many non-Magyars. With the Magyar monopoly on power seriously threatened, the Magyar opposition caved in, and a deal was made: Francis Joseph retained his army and his royal powers, and in return he delegated franchise reform to the new coalition government, effectively ending it.

Electoral reform had been nothing more than a ruse to subdue the Magyars. Once broached in Hungary, however, it was adopted as a solution to *Cisleithania's* political travails. The Austrian Social Democrats had already launched a concerted campaign for universal male suffrage before the Hungarian crisis, and the 1905 revolution in Russia further highlighted the issue. The key moment came, however, when the emperor himself backed the measure. Quite why the old absolutist allied, bizarrely, with the forces of socialism is still not clear. He likely thought of electoral reform as a way to frighten the nationalist parties into being more co-operative, and keeping the Magyars compliant. Whatever the reasoning, imperial backing was crucial to the achievement of universal male suffrage in Cisleithania.

The law was passed on 20 January 1907, and elections for the new democratic Reichsrat were held in May. The old curial structures were no more (although they continued for all provincial and local assemblies). German representation in the new Reichsrat held up surprisingly well: with Germans being 36 per cent of the population but still contributing on one calculation more than 63 per cent of tax revenue, they were allotted 45 per cent of the seats in parliament. The composition of German representation changed markedly, however, with the Social Democrats and Christian Socials making large gains at the expense of nationalists and liberals. The nationalist Young Czechs also lost seats to new parties, such as the Agrarians.

Initially this was seen as encouraging, for the non-nationalist socialists and the 'imperially loyal' Christian Socials seemed to offer a way out of the national stand-off. Yet the socialists were the only party to have multi-national representation in the new parliament, whose membership had splintered into thirty different parties. The parliament thus required extremely deft handling to make it work. Max Vladimir Beck managed this for a while as prime minister, but by 1908 renewed crises in Bohemia and Galicia, and over the annexation of Bosnia, made Beck's task intractable, and he resigned in November 1908. His successor, Richard von Bienerth, tried to mitigate various national disputes, but then Czech deputies returned to obstruction, which led back to Article 14. By then the experiment in democracy as a cure for Cisleithania's political problems had been judged a failure.

While the political system appeared to be falling apart, the Austrian economy was doing remarkably well, Austrian society was modernizing rapidly, and the Monarchy as a whole, but Vienna in particular, was becoming a great centre of intellectual and cultural innovation. At first sight this might seem paradoxical, but there are many examples, such as the contemporaneous French Third Republic, of volatile political systems being paired with stable and even flourishing economies and societies. In Austria, the nationality conflict and economic, social and cultural progress might even have been mutually reinforcing.

The Austro-Hungarian economy was growing quite fast around 1900, faster than the British economy. Austria-Hungary had some catching up to do compared with Western Europe, but even so growth rates were impressive and the western, developed parts of the Monarchy, especially in the Bohemian lands and around Vienna, were approaching Western European levels.

Proximity to the German economic powerhouse helped. It was often German firms who provided the investment in Austria-Hungary in the new industries, such as electric machinery and automobiles. The Monarchy's economy also greatly benefited from the customs union of the 1867 Compromise. This, allied with the extensive railway network, allowed for a specialization and integration of the Danube basin's economy which boosted overall growth, even in the Monarchy's backwaters. The regional disparity in the Austro-Hungarian economy was considerably less than that in the United States at the time.

A key factor in this relative success might well have been the nationality conflict and the conflict between 'Vienna' and Hungary. Nationalistic efforts at Hungarian economic independence produced a relatively liberal industrial policy, as well as a remarkably tolerant policy to the entrepreneurial class, which was largely Jewish. In Cisleithania the horse-trading between the government and national blocs over infrastructure projects, the founding of educational institutions and other inducements, had a stimulating economic effect, even on peripheral regions such as Galicia. Koerber's 'politics of the bazaar' partly induced the boom of 1900. Obversely, many of the pressures involved with nationalism, whether from population migrations, the increased need for literacy and the concomitant increase in the salience of language and hence nationality, or the differentiation of the workforce on national lines, themselves arose from economic modernization and growth.

A similar dialectic developed in education. By 1900 Austria-Hungary had one of the most elaborate and extensive educational systems in Europe, and this partly explains its remarkable intellectual achievements and its good economic record. Here as well, nationalism played a large role. In Hungary heavy investment in schools was directly linked to Magyarization. In Cisleithania government policy and national considerations conspired to boost educational opportunities. Polish universities were established in

Cracow and Lemberg to placate Polish politicians, while a German-speaking university was set up in Czernowitz as a counterbalance. In Prague the Charles University became two universities and the prospect of Czech-speaking polytechnics or Italian-speaking law faculties was used as a bargaining counter by the government.

The government's fall in 1895 over a Slovene class in Cilli is not that odd considering that schools were one of the main national battlegrounds. Education was seen by nationalists as a power-ful weapon in the national struggle. Czechs in particular became adept at working the system of financing schools by national lan-guage, setting up private Czech-speaking secondary schools which, by law, became entitled to government financing on reaching a certain level of attendance. To counter this tactic the Germans, liberals and nationalists alike, invested heavily in the Deutscher Schulverein (German School Association), to increase German school enrolments in the Bohemian lands. The result was a race to the top, with many more well-educated individuals than otherwise expected, or even required. The oversupply of competent individu-als increased competition for state jobs, which in turn exacerbated the national conflict. A fight for jobs was behind the Badeni affair.

National struggles often had a positive effect on intellectual and cultural life. Nationalist energies were devoted to enhancing a nation's cultural prestige and were often bolstered by the Habsburg authorities' interest in placating national constituencies. Cracow flourished as the Poles' national cultural capital, as it was the one major Polish city where Polish culture and identity was not persecuted, unlike in Germany or Russia. At the same time, the Habsburg authorities were open to the argument that high culture, even modern high culture, could act as a binding counterforce to nationalist divisiveness. Thus the Viennese Secession initially gained state backing on the argument that theirs was an *Austrian* art that stood above and beyond national divisions.

The political crisis of the turn of the century has itself been seen as a spur to cultural creativity. Carl E. Schorske has claimed that the crisis in Vienna, which saw liberalism vanquished by Christian Social mass politics, induced a political alienation among the scions of Vienna's liberal bourgeoisie that led to a retreat into the temple of art and the psyche, and hence to the great cultural flowering that has made *fin de siècle Vienna* so famous.

On closer inspection, such explanations of cultural creativity from national conflict and liberalism's political crisis can only be partial at best, and often lead astray. National ambition in such cities as Prague, Budapest and Cracow does much to explain the cultural flourishing in those cities, but Vienna, as the capital of a supra-national empire, did not share in this, and the attempt at an 'Austrian' culture never carried much conviction. It is also not clear that the political alienation of the liberal middle classes in Vienna, as such, was that significant. Liberal parties continued to hold power in many provincial centres, and in Vienna Josephist liberals continued to be prominent in the bureaucracy. The political and legal structures of Austria remained those of the liberals (as they do, more or less, today). At the same time, it was not so much that Vienna's 'liberal' middle classes were alienated from power as that they ceased to be liberal, going over en masse to the anti-liberal, but still bourgeois, Christian Socials. The political crisis of liberalism is thus an unconvincing explanation for the flowering of Vienna 1900.

Then again, what is there to explain? Vienna was one of Europe's largest urban centres, with a population of more than two million by 1910, and had been a major centre of political power and cultural patronage for centuries. Hence it was one of Europe's leading cultural centres, especially in music, but also in theatre, opera and medicine. Viennese modern culture, moreover, was in many respects not that revolutionary compared with developments elsewhere. The art of Gustav Klimt and the Secession, and of Expressionists such as Oskar Kokoschka and Egon Schiele, is today highly prized, but it did not radically break with the past in the way of Picasso and Braque's Cubism, or Kandinsky's abstract art. The architecture of Otto Wagner was pioneering, but much of its innovation arose from Wagner's links with American architects. As striking as the functionalism of Wagner's signature buildings, such as the Postsparkasse or the Church am Steinhof, was his retention of classical architectural conventions.

Fin de siècle Vienna was not really *seen* as being at the cutting edge of modernity, unlike Paris, Germany or America. Most contemporaries, the Viennese included, regarded the city as a backwater.

Only in hindsight has Vienna 1900 come to be seen as 'the capital of the twentieth century'. Yet there are strong grounds for this claim.

What needs explanation is the emergence of a host of innovative cultural and intellectual movements and figures, who, unlike the artists and architects mentioned above, really did radically change Western culture and thought. Leading a very long list are two intellectual giants: Sigmund Freud, the founder of psychoanalysis, and Ludwig Wittgenstein, one of the most influential philosophers of the modern era. Then there are figures such as Arnold Schoenberg, whose explorations into atonal and then twelve-tone composition revolutionized modern classical music; or Adolf Loos, whose theories of functionalism in architecture were radical in a way that Wagner's were not.

Hans Kelsen revolutionized the theory of law; the Austrian School of Economics had a large influence on liberal economic thought; the Vienna Circle of philosophers developed logical positivism, and Karl Popper acted as that movement's leading critic; Alfred Adler developed individual psychology, the first of many rebels from Freudian orthodoxy who established their own movements; Austro-Marxism brought innovative reinterpretations of socialist theory. Vienna also became a powerhouse of literary innovation: Arthur Schnitzler, Hugo von Hofmannsthal, Karl Kraus, Hermann Broch, Robert Musil, Stefan Zweig and Franz Werfel, later Elias Canetti, were but the most prominent among a vast array of writers. It is the depth of intellectuality and talent that is perhaps the most impressive part of Vienna 1900. It is not only Freud and his disciples, but the many rebellious offshoots, not only Schoenberg but the others in and around his group, such as Alban Berg or Alexander von Zemlinsky, that are notable. The energy and fecundity of the intellectual and cultural milieu is almost more outstanding than the individual achievements.

Many figures in this multi-faceted explosion of creativity are eccentric to our own ways of thinking, and hence very difficult to comprehend under current categories, yet were central to the thought of the time. Otto Weininger, for instance, is vilified today as a Jewish self-hating misogynist, yet he was admired by Schoenberg, Kraus, Wittgenstein – and Stefan Zweig. There are no easy summaries of the Viennese contribution to modern culture. We can nevertheless discern three major trends.

As elsewhere in contemporary Europe, there was a fashion for aestheticism and impressionism, where the focus on individual will and rationality was replaced by emphasis on surface experience, aesthetic form and the irrational psyche. This 'modernism' of *fin de siècle Vienna* had its roots in French *décadence*, the positivism of the physicist Ernst Mach, with his idea of 'the irretrievable self', and the German cultural irrationalism of Richard Wagner and Friedrich Nietzsche. There was also a much more straight-forwardly progressive modernism, represented by such figures as Joseph Popper-Lynkeus and Ludwig Boltzmann (and indeed Mach). Freud as well, for all his 'Nietzschean' tendencies in emphasizing the irrational, sexual side of the psyche, was firmly situated in this pro-gressive, rationalist modernism, as was Schnitzler, for all his appar-ent aestheticism.

The most interesting variant of modern culture that emerged in Vienna in the first years of the twentieth century was what Allan Janik has termed 'critical modernism'. What marked critical mod-ernists such as Loos, Schoenberg, Kraus, Georg Trakl, Broch and, in his own way, Weininger, was their rejection of the convention-alities of both established historicist culture, and also of aestheti-cist modernism. They did not criticize modernity from outside, as traditionalists did, but rather from within the new art. Above all they sought to restore an *ethical* imperative to modern art, reject-ing the 'phrases' of convention, so that the work of art became an essay in realizing the artist's 'thought'. Schoenberg put it most suc-cinctly about music, that it 'should not be an ornament, it should be true'. Vienna's critical modernists were iconoclastic, but in the sense of rejecting the false idols of both tradition and an ahis-torical modernism, and all the accompanying ideologies, includ-ing the liberal ideology of infinite progress. They recognized that the modern world could only succeed with a realization of the limits to the modern, scientific and technological world view. It was through its critical modernism, through works such as Loos' Haus am Michaelerplatz, Wittgenstein's *Tractatus Logico-Philosophicus* and Schoenberg's music, culminating in the opera against opera, *Moses und Aron*, that Vienna 1900 made its most vital contribution.

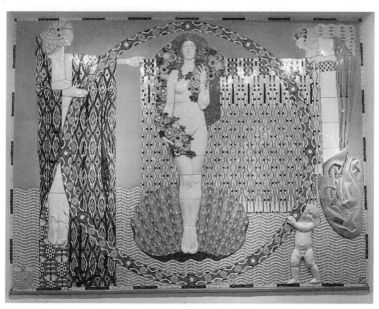

Illustration 30. Leopold Forstner, large mosaic in the dining
room of Grand Hotel Wiesler, Graz.

Vienna 1900 was indeed a vibrant centre of radical cultural
and intellectual innovation, with consequences that reverberated
through the twentieth century. Yet Vienna's eminence as a cultural
centre had rarely been associated with *radical* innovation of this kind
before. An explanation is still needed of why Vienna, why around
1900?

First, the remarkable phenomenon of Vienna 1900 was very much
an urban one, indeed almost exclusively Viennese. There was some
contribution from the 'Austrian' hinterland. Georg Trakl came from
Salzburg, Robert Musil from Klagenfurt, and Ludwig Ficker's *Der
Brenner* made an important contribution from Innsbruck. In the
graphic arts, there was even a Leonfeldener, Leopold Forstner, who
was a figure in the world of Viennese modernism, being a member
of the Secession and a major contributor to the Palais Stoclet and
the Church am Steinhof. Yet the provincial cities of the hereditary
lands tended to be culturally conservative.

The milieu of Vienna 1900 had much more in common with Prague and Budapest, albeit not the nationalist modern culture of Czechs or Magyars, but rather the culture of the remaining German-speaking (or bilingual) liberal bourgeoisies. An informal Central European network connected similar modern cultural milieux in these cities as well as in Berlin, Breslau and Frankfurt-am-Main in Germany, and such outposts as Lemberg, Czernowitz and Cracow, as well as Łódź in Russian Poland. The driving force behind this nexus of Central European modernity was the Jewish bourgeoisie.

In Vienna especially the Jewish role was predominant. Some of the major figures of Viennese modern culture mentioned above, such as Adolf Loos and Georg Trakl, Ernst Mach and Ludwig Boltzmann, were not Jewish, but the vast majority were. The Jewish presence among creative figures in the plastic arts was not that large, although Jews were prominent as patrons, art critics and propagandists, and eventually as art historians. In most other modern cultural fields, especially the movements and circles mentioned above, such as psychoanalysis, the Vienna Circle, Austro-Marxism and literary Young Vienna, the people involved were in a large majority Jewish or of Jewish descent. The liberal professions – lawyers, physicians and journalists – also had a majority Jewish presence, and it has often been claimed that the public for Viennese modern culture was also heavily Jewish. This Jewish predominance was based on solid socio-economic grounds, for the social reservoir of Viennese modern culture, the educated part of the liberal wing of the city's bourgeoisie, was largely Jewish.

Jews only comprised 10 per cent or so of Vienna's population, fewer than 5 per cent of Cisleithania's and even less, about 3 per cent, of the population of the lands of the later Austrian Republic. Yet Jews had a large presence in Vienna's 'liberal' socio-economic sectors, being 30 per cent of Vienna's commercial self-employed. Their emphasis on education was also much greater than normal. Roughly a third of all pupils in Vienna's Gymnasien (the elite secondary schools) were Jewish. Combining these factors, Jewish predominance in Viennese modern culture becomes not only explicable, but almost predictable: approximately two-thirds of all boys with a liberal bourgeois background who graduated from Vienna's central

Gymnasien between 1870 and 1910 were Jewish. (The equivalent proportion among girls was higher still.)

What this Jewish predominance represented was not merely the hypertrophic success of an enterprising minority, but rather a new, qualitatively different contribution to Austrian culture, thought and society. What made Vienna 1900 so exceptional was the integration of Central European Jewry into the mainstream of history.

Jews had lived in the Habsburg Monarchy for centuries, but it was only in the late eighteenth century that their integration into the larger, non-Jewish world began. Under the pressure of Joseph II's reforms and the influence of the Jewish Enlightenment (*Haskalah*), Habsburg Jewry slowly adopted a new, modern form of Jewish identity that came to identify Jewish values with the Enlightenment, liberalism and German culture. In the ideology of Jewish emancipation, traditional Jewish values, such as religious learning and emphasis on the ethical rather than the aesthetic side of life, were transformed and co-opted in a strategy of secular education and moral betterment – to allow Jews entry into the modern world of pure humanity, in which all would share the 'essence' of Jewish values. Jewish emancipation's sub-culture shared much with mainstream German liberalism but had different origins and different (Jewish) values, and hence produced different responses. The Jewish contributors to Viennese modern culture all grew up in some variant of this emancipatory culture.

This Central European Jewish emancipatory experience was particularly salient in Vienna. Identifying Jewish values with the German Enlightenment, Protestant emphasis on the Word and the Kantian categorical imperative might help integration in Protestant Berlin. The effect in Vienna, with its Catholic Baroque heritage of emphasis on the Image, aesthetic splendour and obedience to hierarchy, was different. The antisemitism that emerged in the 1880s fed off a real culture clash. A population brought up with a traditional Catholic mindset, disoriented by the modern economy, was all too willing to accept the mendacious accusation that the 'Jews' were to blame, for the one group who had completely identified their interests and values with the new, modern world was emancipated Viennese Jewry. Many former political, social and even ideological allies of the Jews also went over to the antisemitic side, whether out of conviction or self-interest. The contemporary prestige of 'scientific' biological and racial thought, as well as ideas of ethno-nationalism, encouraged even among many erstwhile liberal progressives the isolation of Jews as 'not-belonging'.

The fall of Vienna to political antisemitism in the 1890s left Jews threatened with social ostracization, politically alienated and faced with the atavistic return of Vienna's Catholic Baroque culture, albeit in modern disguise. Many of the more educated and articulate members of emancipated Viennese Jewry responded by further committing themselves to the emerging modern culture, as both beyond mere ethnicity and politics, but also as a means to liberation and eventual power. What emerged in Vienna 1900 as a result was a powerful re-examination of contemporary assumptions about progress and modernity, and a searing critique of the very foundations of modern thought and society.

One of the best descriptions of this 'ferment of humanity' in Vienna at the turn of the century was written in 1908. Schnitzler's *The Road to the Open* discusses the threatening situation that existed under the calm exterior of Viennese society, and all the possible 'ways to freedom' that his mainly Jewish protagonists try: psychology, socialism, liberalism, radical assimilation, emigration, literary satire, even Zionism. The one way to freedom that Schnitzler's spokesman in the novel, Heinrich Bermann, thinks has any chance of success is that of critical introspection, looking into one's soul, and being completely honest with oneself, which is ultimately an ethical stance: 'Yes, that must be the daily prayer of every decent person: never to let yourself be misled.'[2] It is that commitment which is the heart of the cultural achievement of Vienna 1900.

The first full year of the young Adolf Hitler's character-deforming sojourn in the city, 1908 was also the year of Francis Joseph's jubilee, which celebrated the Monarchy's remarkable national and ethnic pluralism, and the very fact of its continued existence. While Hitler's arrival augured a horrible future, confirming retrospectively Schnitzler's portrayal of a mainly Jewish cultural elite in existential crisis, it is also true that Hitler was then a non-entity, and Schnitzler

---

[2] Arthur Schnitzler, *Der Weg ins Freie* (Frankfurt, 1978), p. 205.

Illustration 31. Austrian modernism: Adolf Loos, Haus am
Michaelerplatz (1909–11), Vienna. The building 'without
eyebrows' was a pioneering and highly controversial
achievement in architectural modernism. It was built for the
tailoring firm, Goldman und Salatsch, run by the Jewish
businessman Leopold Goldman.

heavily criticized for exaggerating the problem. It was still possible in 1908 to be optimistic, to think the crisis for Jews, as with
the Cisleithanian and Hungarian political crises, desperate but not
serious: there was the imperial authority to prevent anything too
drastic, and somehow, some way, something would turn up. The
next decade proved this optimism false.

AN EMPIRE FALLS APART, 1908–1918

The Habsburg Monarchy's greatest advantage in nineteenth-century
European diplomacy was its status as a 'European necessity'. It provided a power bloc in the continent's middle that helped balance
the other powers and kept the region's patchwork of nationalities

contained. The Monarchy had hence survived events, such as the debacle of 1866, that might have led other polities to be dismembered. Yet what made the Monarchy a 'European necessity', the exceptional, inextricable relationship between its domestic and foreign affairs, also led to its falling apart.

The Monarchy in the 1900s was prostrated by its national conflicts. The long-running Czech and Magyar crises were particularly disabling, yet neither caused the Monarchy's destruction, for both were manageable within the Monarchy. What proved fatal to the Monarchy were nationality crises extending beyond the Monarchy's borders, for they led to an inextricable entangling of domestic and foreign policy. Irredentism, the wish for national populations and territory to be 'redeemed' for the national homeland, destroyed the Habsburg Monarchy.

On the face of it, this should not have been such a problem. Three irredenta, the German, Romanian and Italian, had nation-states that were Austria-Hungary's allies. Although domestic policies, such as Magyar persecution of Transylvania's Romanians, could compromise relations, these alliances insulated the Monarchy from nationalism's full consequences. The Ruthenian cause was muted by the alternative of Russian repression, while Galicia's Poles far preferred Austrian to repressive German or Russian rule and evinced little irredentist interest before 1914. (What would happen if there was a Polish nation-state was another question.)

The crucial problem of irredentism for the Monarchy was on its southern flank, with its assortment of Serbs, Croats and Slovenes. Relations between these groups within the Monarchy were thorny enough, and exacerbated by the Italian presence on the Adriatic coast. Dualism made the situation worse, for the South Slav populations in the Monarchy were split between Austrian and Hungarian jurisdictions. Carniola, Istria and Dalmatia (largely Slovene and Croat) were part of Cisleithania, and Croatia-Slavonia (mainly Croat but with a sizeable Serb minority) was part of the Hungarian kingdom. After 1878 the Serbs, Croats and Muslim Bosniaks of occupied Bosnia and Herzegovina further complicated the picture. What turned the hostilities within this variegated national and jurisdictional landscape into the Monarchy's fatal South Slav Problem was the presence to the south of Serbia, the 'Piedmont of the Balkans'.

Serbia, carved out of the Ottoman Empire in the nineteenth century, had not been perceived as a serious threat to the Habsburgs. For much of its existence, it had been an Austro-Hungarian satellite. Then, in 1900 the Serbian king, Alexander, turned away from Austria towards Russia; his assassination in 1903, and the replacement of the Obrenović by the more nationalist Karageorgević clan, only exacerbated this trend. Serbia was now a problem.

The Serbian problem for the Monarchy was both foreign and domestic. In foreign policy, Serbia was in the middle of Austria-Hungary's last sphere of interest, the Balkans, and as a Russian satellite might block Austrian influence and interests in the region. Bosnia-Herzegovina also had a large Serb population, and the Austro-Hungarian occupation fatally roiled relations with a Serbian government that eyed it as by right Serbian territory.

The domestic implications of a hostile South Slav power on the border were even more threatening. Serbia came to be viewed as an alternative power centre for the Monarchy's South Slavs, as Piedmont had been in Italy. There were actually far more South Slavs in the Monarchy (7 million, including 2.1 million Serbs) than there were in Serbia (2.6 million), and therefore the dynamic could have been reversed, with Serbia joining the South Slav provinces to form the third part of a trialist Habsburg Monarchy, anticipating the dynamic of European Union enlargement. The Monarchy's domestic politics prevented this. Instead many Serbs, Croats, and even Slovenes, looked to Serbia as the hope of the South Slav, Yugoslav, cause. The conflation of foreign and domestic aspects made Serbia appear, at least to Habsburg policy-makers, as a threat to the Monarchy's very existence.

The internal South Slav problem in the Monarchy revolved around the Hungarian government's abuse of the Nagodba, the Magyar–Croat Compromise of 1868. The imposition of Magyarophile governors (*bans*) by Budapest, pro-Magyar railway policies and the fostering of the Serb minority all riled Croat national opinion. The failure of Francis Joseph as Hungarian king to protect the traditionally Habsburg-loyal Croats against Magyar abuse was also deeply resented. Francis Joseph also refused as Austrian emperor to intervene on behalf of Hungarian Croatians, even when petitioned to do so by Austrian Croatians from Dalmatia and Istria in 1903, on the argument that it was no business of his to intervene in the Hungarian king's affairs.

The Habsburg authorities were hence blamed by the Croatians for Magyar policies. This led to a revolution in South Slav politics in 1905, when Serb and Croat leaders in both halves of the Monarchy allied to promote South Slav autonomy within the Monarchy. This Croato-Serb alliance even supported the Magyar nationalists in their power struggle with Francis Joseph. The Magyar nationalists soon reneged on their side of the deal, but the 'Yugoslav' alliance between Croats and Serbs remained, deeply unsettling the Habsburg regime. With Serbs in Bosnia, resentful of apparently preferential treatment for the Muslim landed class, looking to Serbia for support, the regime in Vienna started fearing Serbia as the core of an irredentist Yugoslavism.

In 1903, Count Agenor Goluchowski, the Austro-Hungarian foreign minister and a Pole, had warned of a 'Slav deluge' that threatened to turn the Balkans into a South Slav super-state detrimental to Austria-Hungary's foreign *and* domestic situation. When Serbia and Bulgaria announced a customs union in late 1905, Vienna therefore set out to put the Serbian upstarts in their place by launching a trade war. The 'Pig War' (1906–10), so named because of trade barriers imposed on Serbian export of live pigs, was a diplomatic catastrophe for Austria-Hungary. The Serbians found new markets, their resentment of Austria-Hungary increased and Vienna lost prestige for not even being an effective bully. It was only the prelude, however, to an even larger, and fateful, blunder: the annexation of Bosnia-Herzegovina.

Bosnian annexation was intended by Baron Lexa von Aehrenthal, foreign minister from 1906, as part of a strategy to use foreign policy to improve the Monarchy's dismal domestic situation. Russian preoccupation elsewhere had produced relative tranquillity in the Balkans. Even the First Moroccan Crisis of 1905–6 had seen the Austrians and Russians still maintaining a regional détente. Russia was now returning its attention to the Balkans, but Aehrenthal had a domestic rationale for his 'energetic' foreign policy and was determined to pursue it.

Aehrenthal had been one of the 'new men' grouped around the heir, Crown Prince Francis Ferdinand, in the Belvedere, and he shared that group's faith in a more muscular approach to policy. He thought a forward foreign policy would reinvigorate the Monarchy's status abroad, decreasing dependence on over-bearing Germany; at home, an assertion of Habsburg power would also be a rallying point for the Monarchy's peoples, strengthening Habsburg loyalty and identity. A key assumption in Aehrenthal's exercise in 'social imperialism' was his idea that annexation would enable a major restructuring of the Monarchy along trialist lines, including an autonomous Yugoslav kingdom. This was tragically unrealistic, given the inevitable Magyar opposition.

There were also more pragmatic reasons for normalizing Bosnia-Herzegovina's status. The success of the Young Turks in Istanbul, and their plan for an Ottoman constitution and parliament, produced the embarrassing prospect that there would be elections in Bosnia for neither the Cisleithanian nor the Hungarian, but a Turkish parliament. Yet for Bosnians to vote under Habsburg auspices constitutional structures were needed, requiring annexation. Aehrenthal also saw a Bosnian settlement as part of a larger deal solidifying the regional détente with Russia. While his outward policies promoted an assertive image, his actual goal was modest: to vacate the Sanjak of Novibazar, and formally annex territory that was already informally Austro-Hungarian: Bosnia-Herzegovina.

The Russians were also interested in co-operation, and negotiations in the summer of 1908 resulted in a deal at Buchlau between Aehrenthal and the Russian foreign minister, Alexander Izvolsky. Aehrenthal then announced the annexation on 5 October, without informing the other great powers, and without clearing it with Izvolsky, but letting Ferdinand of Bulgaria know. This was a disastrous mistake: the other powers were deeply offended; worse still, Izvolsky had not yet prepared the Russian government and public for the announcement, which an outraged Russian public saw as an attack on their Serbian 'little brothers'. Izvolsky denied agreeing to annexation. The attempt at shoring up the Austro-Russian détente ended up smashing it.

In the short term, largely owing to German support, Austria-Hungary did quite well out of the ensuing crisis. Aehrenthal even boasted that it could no longer be seen as a '*quantité négligeable*'. The long-term consequences were disastrous. The Monarchy was left even more dependent on Germany, the Russians were furious, and the Western powers severely alienated. Relations deteriorated further when the Zagreb treason trial of 1909 and the subsequent Friedjung libel trial revealed the Habsburg regime framing South Slav leaders with forged documents. This greatly damaged Austria-Hungary's image in Western liberal opinion. The trials became a *cause célèbre* for Austrian Slav leaders and led to a further breakdown of trust between the emperor-king and his South Slav subjects. Serbia meanwhile, having survived the Pig War and freed itself from economic dependency, was increasingly resentful of Austria, and eager to play the irredentist card against it.

By the Second Moroccan Crisis of 1911, Aehrenthal realized the damage that his 'forward' policy had done to Austria-Hungary's situation. His sarcastic explanation of Austrian unwillingness to support Germany was revealing: 'What more can I do? We can pursue no *Weltpolitik*.' For the foreign minister of the dynastic empire once ruled by Charles V, this was a stark admission of the reality of the Habsburgs' reduced position.

Even in the Balkans events were careening out of Austrian control. The events in Morocco and the annexation of Bosnia-Herzegovina led to a series of land grabs in and around the Balkans. Italy seized Tripoli in 1911, and the Balkan states now eyed the remaining territories of European Turkey. Aehrenthal died in February 1912. It was left to his successor, Count Leopold Berchtold, to experience the collapse of Austrian Balkan policy. First came the formation of the Balkan League, and then the First Balkan War, which saw European Turkey temporarily erased from the map over the winter of 1912–13 in favour of large gains for all the members of the Balkan League, but especially Serbia. The Second Balkan War of the summer of 1913 then saw Serbia joined by Greece, Romania and Turkey in a comprehensive defeat of Bulgaria, which resulted in an even larger Serbia, with even greater prestige among South Slavs, including Habsburg South Slavs.

Francis Joseph and his advisers watched their foreign policy being dismantled before their eyes. Conrad von Hötzendorf had called for a preventive war against Italy in 1911, but that went against the policy of both Aehrenthal and Francis Joseph, the 'peace emperor'. Allying with Turkey against all the Christian Balkan states was also out of the question. As it was, it took two large-scale mobilizations and some staring down of Russia and Serbia to gain Francis Joseph's minimum requirement, the creation of an independent Albania that prevented Serbian access to the sea. Francis Joseph's advisers, and the emperor himself, now concluded that only the threat of force, and if necessary its use, could halt further Serbian expansion.

The collapse of the Habsburg position in the Balkans was exacerbated by the continuing domestic crisis. In Croatia the constitution was suspended in 1912; in Bosnia the new diet had yet to find a working majority, and acts of terrorism by Serb radicals were mounting. In Hungary proper, the political conflict over parliamentary reform and relations with Vienna led to the instituting of what amounted to 'parliamentary absolutism' under István Tisza. In Cisleithania, the German–Czech conflict once more led to a complete obstruction of the Bohemian diet and then Reichsrat. Count Karl Stürgkh, prime minister since November 1911, responded by dissolving the Bohemian diet in 1913 and the Reichsrat in March 1914, so that Cisleithania reverted to 'bureaucratic absolutism'.

The domestic crises were, in themselves, manageable. There were even signs, in Galicia and Croatia, that progress towards compromise was being made. Yet the dysfunctional character of Habsburg political life, combined with a deteriorating economic and financial situation and perceived military weakness, made the threat of irredentist Serbia loom ever larger.

The Serbian threat was not only to material Habsburg interests, but also to perceptions of dynastic Habsburg prestige. If the Habsburg power could not keep even Serbia in its place, it would no longer deserve to be a great power. For centuries, however, this had been its whole *raison d'être*. Moreover, the concerns about the loss of prestige were not entirely irrational, for perceptions had consequences. The irredentist threat from Serbia was real. Flush with double victory, and with renewed backing from Russia, Serbia now targeted Serb areas of the Monarchy, especially Bosnia, for expansion. Romania, though an ally, eyed Hungarian Transylvania. Even the Italian allies were once again showing national interest in the irredenta of South Tyrol and the Adriatic coastline. The Monarchy's weak position after the Balkan Wars encouraged such irredentist thoughts.

Berchtold's initial response was a diplomatic offensive, for which German support was ever more important. The Matscheko Memorandum started out in June as a vehicle to persuade Germany to help Austria-Hungary regain its diplomatic status. Its function was radically altered only when another attempt to bolster Habsburg prestige in the Balkans, the visit of Francis Ferdinand and his wife to Sarajevo on 28 June 1914, ended in the assassination of the couple by Gavrilo Princip, a Bosnian Serb.

One month later, on 28 July, Francis Joseph signed the declaration of war against Serbia that started the First World War. There has been a heated debate ever since over who really began it. The prevailing view remains that the primary instigator was Germany, with its drive for a 'place in the sun' as a world power. The fact remains that the war was actually started by the Habsburg Monarchy as a response to events in the Balkans, for far less ambitious reasons.

Those 'reasons' included the need to defend the honour and prestige of the dynasty against such an assault on its core values. Even if no direct responsibility of the Serbian government for the Habsburg heir's assassination was proved, the Serbian upstart had to be punished. Its crushing would act as a deterrent to the other irredentist nationalists with designs on Habsburg territory. Previous experience of the unreliable German ally also gave the Monarchy a strong motivation to use the German 'blank cheque' offered by William II after Sarajevo, before it was withdrawn again. Yet declaring war against Serbia, in the full knowledge that this would cause at least a European conflagration, was a quite irrational act.

Given the internal (and external) fragilities of Austria-Hungary, large-scale war in 1914 was an act of self-destruction as an independent great power. Many in the Habsburg circles of power had seen this, including Francis Ferdinand. While arch-conservative, the crown prince also recognized the Monarchy's internal weakness and the need to ameliorate the nationality problem, largely by tackling the Magyars' privileged position. He also wanted an accommodation with Russia, whose tsarist regime was an ideological ally. Sarajevo not only radicalized Habsburg hostility against the Serbs, but also removed one of the main champions of peace from the Habsburg regime. Habsburg policy was hence reduced to the equivalent of a street slogan: 'Serbien muss sterbien' (Serbia must die). Germany, having decided the time was right to launch a long-intended war, might well have enticed and cajoled the Austrians to war; but if Vienna was Berlin's stooge, it was a willing stooge.

War should have been avoided by Austria-Hungary at all costs, because it desperately needed to solve its internal problems. Francis Joseph had long been convinced of the Monarchy's need for peace and stated explicitly to Conrad in 1911 that *his* foreign policy was a 'policy of peace'. Yet even Francis Joseph became persuaded that the Austro-Hungarian Dual Monarchy had to act against Serbia, for only then could it fulfil its purpose of maintaining the status of the House of Habsburg as one of the world's great powers. As Berchtold later put it, the emperor's main reason for war was 'the concern for the continuation of the patrimonial legacy which he had inherited'. The reasons given at the time in the imperial-royal War Manifesto of 29 July, addressed 'to my peoples', were similar: the honour of 'my monarchy' had to be protected; so had its good name and position among the powers; and its possessions had to be secured. Austria-Hungary went to war in 1914 for reasons of dynastic power politics, because, as Berchtold wrote, 'our role in world history would be over if we feebly allowed fate to do what it willed'.[3]

This was false logic. The only way to keep the Monarchy's fate in its own hands was *not* to go to war. Then again, ultimately Francis Joseph went to war because he felt he was fated to: that, as stated in the Manifesto, providence was behind the events of Sarajevo. He had initially seen the assassination as providential punishment of Francis Ferdinand for his morganatic marriage, and there is in his attitude in late July a fatalistic air. On signing the declaration of war, he told Alexander von Krobatin: 'Go, I can do nothing else.' A few days before he told Conrad: 'If the Monarchy must perish it should at least perish with decency.' Left unsaid in 1914 was how many of the emperor's subjects were supposed to perish along with the Monarchy – to ensure *its* decency.

From the beginning the war was a catastrophe. The declaration on 28 July led to the war by timetables that by early August had

[3] Leopold Berchtold, 'Der Herrscher wie ich ihn bekannt', in E. von Steinitz (ed.), *Erinnerungen an Franz Joseph I* (Berlin, 1931), pp. 313–14.

Illustration 32. Albin Egger-Lienz, 'To the Nameless 1914'.

much of Europe engulfed in armed conflict, but this was not a surprise to the Austrians and Germans. The Germans claimed to be
disappointed by Britain's siding with the Entente, but should not
have been, and the fact that Italy, the third member of the Triple
Alliance, did not immediately join in was predictable, as its alliance
was only defensive and Austria-Hungary was the aggressor against
Serbia.

The initial popular reaction in the Monarchy to war seemed to
belie the previous experience of unending national conflict. The
same outpouring of martial enthusiasm from the public seen in
other combatant nation-states was also evident in the multi-national
Monarchy, even in many Slav regions. The Habsburg army, the subject of so many national disputes, also held together remarkably
well, considering. There were some mutinies, by Czech units especially, but they were far fewer than expected. The discipline and
coherence of the army was to remain surprisingly high until war's
end.

The initial, disastrous flaws in the Austro-Hungarian war effort
came from the army being badly prepared and provisioned, and,
above all, badly led. Nationalism had done large indirect damage.
The pre-war national conflicts had led to severe underfunding of
the armed forces for many years, with the Monarchy having the

worst-funded military of all the major powers, Italy included. The Military Bill of 1912 had partially corrected this situation, but by 1914 the net effect of such a long period of neglect was still considerable. Habsburg troops went into the war poorly trained and equipped, with predictable results. Egregious errors by the High Command, and especially its chief, Conrad, compounded this material weakness. Faced with a two-front war, against Serbia and Russia, Conrad dithered fatally about which to tackle first, leading to a chaotic mobilization, immortalized in Jaroslav Hašek's *The Good Soldier Švejk*.

Habsburg forces failed to conquer Serbia in August, and then, with the Germans reneging on promised support, the Habsburg army was thrown back by the Russians, losing Lemberg in September, and retreating across the Carpathians. It was only in December, at the battle of Limanowa-Łapanow, that the Russians were stopped, and then only with German help. By the end of 1914 the front had stabilized, but the cost to the Habsburg forces of the opening months of the war was devastating: four-fifths of the trained infantry and half of the army's original officer corps had been lost. The traditional Habsburg army was effectively destroyed on the battlefields of Galicia, and Austria-Hungary never fully recovered.

The following year was one of mixed fortunes for the Monarchy. On the diplomatic front the refusal of Francis Joseph (again) to give up territory to Italy resulted in the former ally declaring war on Austria-Hungary in May. On the actual battlefield, however, 1915 was a year of military success both in Galicia and in the Balkans. On the Eastern Front, the joint Austro-German Gorlice-Tarnow offensive made huge gains, retaking Lemberg in June. In the Balkans, another joint Austro-German force, with Bulgarian assistance, conquered Serbia in November. Yet these successes were only achieved with German help. When Conrad launched an independent operation, the 'black-yellow' Rovno offensive of August and September, it was a failure. By the end of 1915, the Austrians might be winning, but at the cost of increasing subordination to Germany.

On the home front, internal political relations were fraying over such issues as the supply of Hungarian grain to Vienna. The

188 A Concise History of Austria

Austro-Hungarian infrastructure proved inadequate to the demands of modern warfare, especially for supplying food and fuel to the major population centres. The strict censorship imposed by the authorities at the beginning of the conflict also proved detrimental to the war effort, for it led to great distrust of officially sanctioned information, and allowed rumours to run riot. The co-option of the media by the authorities, chronicled by Kraus in *Die Fackel* and later in his magnificent diatribe against war, *The Last Days of Mankind*, only exacerbated the loss of credibility of the Habsburg regime among the populace. The clampdown on nationalist leaders, such as the Czech Karel Kramář, similarly increased national resentments. Even Austrians who continued to support the war effort often displayed an almost diffident attitude from quite early in the conflict, retreating Biedermeier-like into the private world of the family. The bombast of the newspaper editorials very soon gained little resonance in an increasingly worried, and sullen, populace.

In 1916, Conrad's May offensive in Italy ended in failure. In June the Russians launched the Brusilov offensive, initially sweeping through the Austrian forces. The situation grew even graver when Romania, another former ally, joined the Russians in early August and overran Transylvania. German forces again intervened: in September the Russian advance was halted and by December German troops had entered Bucharest. By then, Austria-Hungary was hardly an independent power. The setting up of an Austro-German Joint High Command, led by Germans, had formalized Austrian military subordination to Germany. The Salzburg Agreement between German and Austrian parliamentary deputies – with only German deputies involved – was a further indication of a creeping transformation of the Monarchy into a German satellite.

With Austro-Hungarian independence eroding, and increasingly bleak and chaotic economic conditions, the pressure for peace in the Monarchy mounted. Francis Joseph himself, shut away in Schönbrunn, demanded peace by next spring, and by October even the foreign minister, Count Stefan Burian, was advocating a quick settlement. When the Austrian premier, Stürgkh, was assassinated by Friedrich Adler (the son of Victor Adler) on 21 October, the increasingly frail Francis Joseph signalled his wish to return to constitutional government and to seek peace by reinstating his most successful premier, Koerber. The emperor, however, died a few weeks later, on 21 November 1916.

Francis Joseph's funeral on 30 November was a great demonstration of Habsburg pomp, but it could not distract from the traumatic effect of this loss. For all his mistakes, Francis Joseph had gained through his longevity and the omnipresence of his image throughout his Monarchy an authority that was based on familiarity and custom. Yet this authority was largely affixed to his person alone. His successor, Charles, did not have the same authority. He also did not have his predecessor's experience of the Monarchy's complexities, at a time when that Monarchy was in a severe, life-threatening crisis. Had he been wilier or stronger, this might not have mattered, but subsequent events showed that it did.

Initially Charles's continuation of liberalization could be seen as a rejuvenation of the Habsburg cause. Charles, influenced by his wife, Zita (of the Bourbon-Parma dynasty), and with the advice of his foreign minister, Count Ottakar Czernin, set upon a course of seeking peace abroad and returning to constitutional rule at home. Good policy on paper, it was disastrous in practice. In March 1917 the Habsburg regime secretly sent out feelers to the French through Zita's brother, Sixtus, but without any positive result. On the home front, with increasing unrest in Vienna and the provinces and news of revolution in Russia, Charles released prominent political prisoners such as Kramář and recalled the Reichsrat in May, only for the assembly to become a forum for calls by the various nationalist deputies for virtually independent national states. In June Charles sacked an obdurate Tisza, but Tisza's successors proved no more open to serious reform or concessions to Hungary's other nationalities.

There was military success for the Central Powers in 1917, but also an ever greater domination of Austria-Hungary by Germany and an increasingly threatening diplomatic situation. On the Eastern Front, the February revolution destroyed the tsarist regime in Russia. When the new, constitutional government launched the July offensive at the behest of its Western Allies, the Austro-German forces repelled the attack, and the end result was the revolution of October and the virtual capitulation of the new Bolshevik regime to the Central Powers at Brest-Litovsk, provisionally in December 1917, and formally in March 1918. Germany and Austria-Hungary won the First World War – in the east.

In the south, the Italian offensive on the Isonzo that summer stalled, ending with a major Austro-German victory at Caporetto in October and Italian retreat all the way to the Piave (as described in Ernest Hemingway's *A Farewell to Arms*). By now, however, the Austro-Hungarian forces were almost never without German support and direction, and the peace arrangements in the east were made by the Germans with little heed paid to the Austrians. Meanwhile the domineering German ally, in starting unrestricted submarine warfare in the Atlantic in February 1917, had sealed the fate of itself and Austria-Hungary by provoking the United States' entry into the war in April.

Faced with looming disaster and German overlordship, Charles and Czernin continued secretly to negotiate peace with the British and the French into 1918. With talks stalled, however, and with all German resources deployed for the March offensive on the Western Front, Czernin decided to change tack and throw in the Habsburg lot with Germany. In a speech on 2 April 1918, he averred that Austria-Hungary would back the Germans to the hilt, even over Alsace-Lorraine. In response, the infuriated French leader, Georges Clemenceau, revealed Charles's peace offer of March 1917.

The ensuing Sixtus Affair obliterated the Habsburg Monarchy's credibility as a great power. Austrian relations with Germany were utterly compromised. The Germans insisted on, and received at Spa on 12 May, the 'Austrian Canossa', surrender of any remaining Austro-Hungarian independence. This capitulation of Habsburg to Hohenzollern then led the Western Allies to give up on the Habsburg Monarchy as a 'European necessity', for it could not be such if it was just a puppet-state of Germany. It was only after Spa that they started taking seriously the idea of breaking up the Monarchy along national lines.

By May, the fortunes of war were also turning. The Austrian offensive on the Piave in June was an abject failure. In the Balkans, Bulgaria's collapse led to broad retreat by the Central Powers. On the Western Front, the failure of the spring offensive proved to be Germany's last gasp, and Allied troops, now with fresh American reinforcements and new tactics, made advances not seen since the beginning of the war.

Domestically, the Monarchy was falling apart. Problems of food and fuel deliveries caused by the dislocation of war had resulted in severe labour unrest, with a wave of strikes over the winter of 1917/18, and growing popular unrest in the streets and bread queues. Demands for autonomy for the various nationalities were only radicalized by the events of the summer. The focus of many of these demands was President Woodrow Wilson's 'Fourteen Points', enunciated in January 1918 and demanding widespread autonomy for the Monarchy's nations. Charles responded to this nationalist pressure by proposing in the autumn a far-reaching federalization of the Monarchy. Yet when Charles's Manifesto of October 16 was published, it was very quickly overtaken by events.

On 18 October, Wilson rejected an Austrian call for peace. On 26 October, Charles withdrew from the alliance with Germany; but on 28 October the founding of Czechoslovakia was declared in Prague; on 29 October the Croatian parliament in Zagreb declared Croatia's union with Serbia. One effect of the Manifesto was to elicit a protest by the Magyar leadership at its reworking of the Compromise of 1867, which they now declared null and void, withdrawing from the Dual Monarchy as part of the revolution of November 1: the empire on notice had come to an end.

On 3 November the Habsburg authorities signed an armistice, but by then the Monarchy had to all intents and purposes ceased to exist. The Habsburg dynasty was not even welcome in Vienna. The 'provisional national assembly of German Austria', formed on 21 October from German deputies from the Reichsrat, passed a provisional, republican constitution on 30 October and declared German Austria a constituent part of the German Republic, with the Babenberg colours of red-white-red adopted as the new Austrian state flag. On 1 November, in an atmosphere of revolution, the Social Democrats demanded a republic. There was no room in any of this for the Habsburgs: on 11 November, Charles renounced his imperial powers. On 23 March 1919, Charles and his family left Austria for exile in Switzerland. After a restoration attempt in Hungary, he moved for health reasons to Madeira, where he died on 1 April 1922.

With Charles's departure ended more than six centuries of Austria as the seat of the Habsburgs – and half a century of the Habsburg Monarchy's attempting to come to terms with the modern age.

The Habsburg Monarchy was not alone among monarchies in failing to survive the First World War. The Hohenzollerns fell in Germany; the Romanovs in Russia; the Ottoman Empire was dismembered. In Italy the constitutional monarchy was soon to be usurped by fascism. Yet none of the states involved suffered quite the Monarchy's fate of virtual disappearance. There was still a considerable Turkish state in Asia Minor; Germany was still a large nation-state; the Bolshevik Soviet Union was still a huge territorial state. In contrast, there seemed nothing left of the Habsburg Monarchy.

Two successor states, Czechoslovakia and Hungary, were only interested in claiming what pertained to their national heritage. The Hungarian regime was eventually a regency, but determined to be without its Habsburg monarch. Most of the rest of the Monarchy's territory was integrated into the surrounding 'nation-states': newly restored Poland, Romania, Italy and newly created Yugoslavia. The part of the former Monarchy that was seen as its main successor was the collection of German-speaking provinces that had pronounced themselves 'German Austria' in late October 1918. Yet even this entity initially saw itself as just another national group whose goal was to join the new German Republic. Even what we now think of as 'the Austrians' wanted nothing to do with the Habsburg Monarchy's heritage in 1918.

How an empire can collapse so completely has been an often debated question: did the Monarchy fall apart on its own, or was it ripped apart by external forces? It was clearly a combination of the two, for the lobbying of the national liberation movements might have influenced Allied policy somewhat, but it was the Monarchy's ceding of effective sovereignty to Germany, thus surrendering its right to be regarded as a 'European necessity', that led to them countenancing the Monarchy's dismantlement. The Monarchy *self-destructed.*

On 6 July 1914 Berthold Molden, a journalist with links to Francis Ferdinand's Belvedere circle, addressed the question of how to improve relations with the Monarchy's Serbs. Referring to earlier

Habsburg experience, he wrote: 'the Venetians, in their time, used to say that they did not wish for Austria to govern them well – it should not govern them at all'.[4] The central problem for the Habsburg Monarchy was that it could not adapt its imperial heritage to the demands for self-government brought on by modernization. In the past, the role of empire as umpire had proved advantageous for the Habsburgs, who, as Holy Roman Emperors and then as Austrian emperors, could act as mediators and arbitrators between the elements in their multi-faceted empires.

Modernization, however, had brought forth the notion of popular sovereignty, the right of the people to govern themselves, and henceforth the Monarchy's days as an empire, whether mediatory or not, were numbered, unless it adapted to the logic of constitutional, representative government, along federalized lines. It never did. It made major adjustments, but some of these, such as the Compromise of 1867, probably made matters worse. The Monarchy's leadership, especially the 'old emperor', could never give up the idea of the Monarchy as the Habsburgs' patrimony, its main goal the preservation of dynastic power and status. This was irreconcilable with modernization's principle of self-determination.

The Monarchy was therefore never able to establish in modern form the authority and legitimacy that it had possessed in the premodern past, and so could not finesse national loyalties by developing an effective supra-ethnic and supra-national 'Austrian' loyalty and identity. There was some such identity, and there was, for Francis Joseph at least, a strong residue of dynastic and even personal loyalty among much of the Monarchy's populace; yet the attachment to the larger Austrian state, let alone to Austria-Hungary, was poorly developed.

The Monarchy had sufficed for its populace when there was no better alternative, and as long as it continued to deliver relative prosperity, relative good order and security, and relative toleration. Over the course of the First World War, and especially in the summer and autumn of 1918, this equation changed radically. In the chaos caused by the war's exigencies, the Monarchy proved incapable of

---

[4] Solomon Wank, 'Desperate Counsel in Vienna in July 1914', *Central European History*, 26 (3), p. 308; Beller, *Francis Joseph*, p. 158.

Illustration 33. Executioner Lang and Cesare Battisti. This picture, originally published as a postcard, was called by Karl Kraus 'The Face of Austria'.

providing the economic, social and above all political benefits that it once had, even in such basic terms as food and fuel; at the same time, in the ideologically radical atmosphere after the Russian Revolution, opportunities erupted for self-determining political development, whether on nationalist or socialist lines, that fitted much better with the 'modern' spirit of the times than the fusty relic of the Monarchy. The Monarchy ultimately failed to fulfil its functions, and was cast aside for something better.

Many of those hopes for a future Central Europe of national democracies, or socialist republics, proved tragically mistaken. Many came to regret the passing of the Monarchy, especially in its roles as a unified economic area and as protector of the region's small nations from Germany and Russia. By then it was too late.

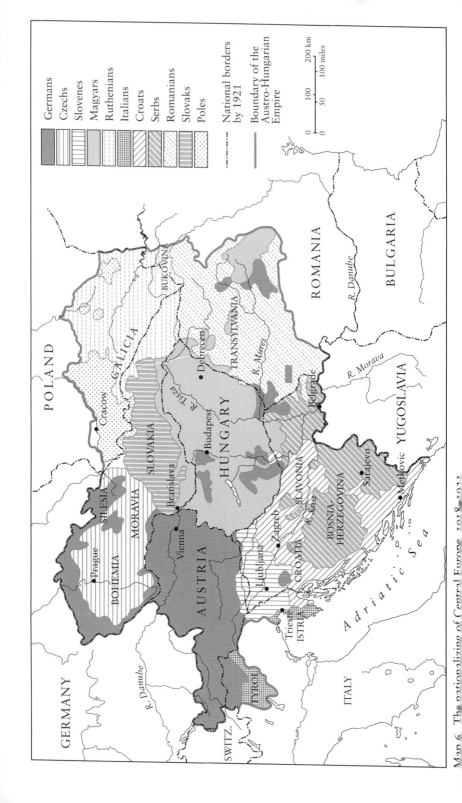

Map 6 The nationalizing of Central Europe, 1918–1921

Legend:

Germans
Czechs
Slovenes
Magyars
Ruthenians
Italians
Croats
Serbs
Romanians
Slovaks
Poles

National borders
by 1921

Boundary of the
Austro-Hungarian
Empire

0   50   100   200 km
0   50   100 miles

GERMANY
POLAND
SWITZ.
AUSTRIA
TYROL
Vienna
BOHEMIA
Prague
SILESIA
MORAVIA
SLOVAKIA
Bratislava
Cracow
GALICIA
BUKOVINA
HUNGARY
Budapest
Debrecen
R. Tisza
TRANSYLVANIA
R. Mureş
ROMANIA
R. Danube
BULGARIA
Belgrade
R. Morava
YUGOSLAVIA
Sarajevo
BOSNIA-
HERZEGOVINA
SLAVONIA
R. Sava
CROATIA
Zagreb
Ljubljana
ISTR.
Trieste
ITALY
Adriatic Sea
Metkovic
R. Danube

5

The land without qualities, 1918–1945

In 1930 Robert Musil published the first volume of *The Man without Qualities*. The setting of this novel was Vienna in 1913. Its hero, Ulrich, is a man without qualities, or characteristics, because he refuses to be typecast by dysfunctional Habsburg society. Instead he is determined to be his own man, and it can be seen as typically 'Viennese' that this turns into an investigation of his sexual and psychological identity. *The Man without Qualities* is not simply a historical novel about pre-war Vienna; it is also a discussion of Austria (and Germany) during the period in which it was written, the interwar years. It is not only about a man without qualities, but also about the land without qualities, a country in a severe identity crisis – as well as a spiritual, economic and political crisis – that never recovered from the trauma of having had its imperial character stripped from it in 1918.

Austria in 1918 had become a land without qualities against its will. Austrian history from 1918 to 1945 is a history of people struggling, and failing, to resolve the profound issues raised by the Habsburg Monarchy's collapse. This is a story not only of the Republic of Austria failing to create a new 'Austrian' identity, but also of the destructive consequences of the political logic that insisted on the 'nation' as the primary political unit. 'Austrians' so easily became 'Germans' in 1938 because they already saw themselves as part of the German nation. It was only the experience of a second catastrophic defeat as part of the Third Reich that persuaded the inhabitants of Austria that they were, after all, nationally 'Austrians'.

The crucial period of modern *Austrian* history, when Austrian national identity was first formed, was when Austria was part of Nazi Germany. Yet after 1945 part of that new Austrian identity was an unspoken agreement to exclude precisely this Nazi period from Austrian history. The traumas of the interwar years and the 'Hitler Time' profoundly shaped modern Austrian identity; that this identity was formed at a time of such a severe identity crisis for Austrians and Austria is what lies behind the surprisingly acute problems of recent Austrian politics.

THE ORPHAN REPUBLIC, 1918–1927

Central Europe, along with much of the rest of the continent, was in a state of turmoil after 1918. The crisis that had started in 1914 did not end with the armistice of November 1918, but extended well into the 1920s. The defeat of the Russian, Ottoman and German empires led to collapse and revolution in all three. Even in some of the 'victor' countries, the crisis led to radical change, in Italy's case to fascism. Yet nowhere was the change as radical as in formerly Habsburg Central Europe. The Weimar Republic remained Germany, and the Soviet Union by the early 1920s had regained most of Russian imperial territory. Even the Ottoman Empire was succeeded by a substantial Turkish nation-state. Only the Habsburg Monarchy disappeared into thin air.

It was replaced by what were supposed to be 'nation-states'. Some territories were hived off to neighbouring nation-states: Italy, Romania and Poland. Much of the Monarchy's southern lands went to the new kingdom of Yugoslavia. Three states were created out of the whole cloth of the Monarchy: Hungary, Czechoslovakia and 'German Austria'.

The Republic of 'German Austria' was founded on 12 November 1918, by an assembly of the Reichsrat's German members. From its beginning it was regarded as that part of the Monarchy that was left over, orphaned, the state that no one wanted.

In the Peace of Versailles that ended the war, the victorious Allies, Britain, France and the United States, rewarded the national leaderships and the states that had sided with them against Austria-Hungary. Just as the Treaty of Versailles with Germany punished the German Empire's successor, the Treaty of St Germain, imposed on German Austria on 10 September 1919, and the Treaty of Trianon, imposed on Hungary on 4 June 1920, punished the apparent dual heirs of the Habsburg Empire. The two treaties crassly favoured the Allies' friends at German Austrian and Hungarian expense, in many cases contravening the Wilsonian principles of national self-determination on which the peace settlement was ostensibly based. Hungary was reduced to a third of its previous territorial area, with many Magyars outside its borders. St Germain, while not quite as disastrous, imposed conditions on German Austria that were nevertheless very harsh, and in national terms very unfair.

The northern border with Czechoslovakia retained the historic borders of Bohemia and Moravia, except where the Czechs asked for and received 'strategic' and 'national' realignments. This meant that many German-speaking 'Austrians' in southern Bohemia, the 'language islands' of Moravia and the 'Sudetenland' of northern Bohemia and Moravia, found themselves the wrong side of the national border.

In the south, heavily Slovene Carniola became part of Yugoslavia, as did, more controversially, a large block of southern Styria. Much of Carinthia was also occupied and claimed by Yugoslavia, but this move was met by resistance from local *ad hoc* militia units, the Heimwehr, and the issue was eventually resolved by plebiscite in October 1920. The voting by largely Slovene-populated Zone A for Austria kept territorial losses in Carinthia relatively small.

For Austrians the worst 'crime' of St Germain was the rewarding of Italy with not only the Italian-speaking areas of the former Monarchy, but also the Carinthian Canaltal and, notoriously, the solidly German-speaking area of Tyrol south of the Brenner Pass. The 'rape of South Tyrol' made a mockery of national self-determination, had little strategic basis and was simply a sop to wounded Italian national pride. Italy went fascist anyway – but South Tyrol was to roil Austro-Italian relations from then on.

On the eastern border, German Austria and Hungary were both regarded as enemies by the Allies, so neither was particularly favoured. Once a Czech proposal for a north–south Slav corridor between them had been dismissed as too arrogating, the national principle was more or less followed. German Austria thus gained territory in western Hungary. Even here, though, the accession of what became the province of Burgenland was only agreed in 1921, and without Ödenburg (Sopron), where a plebiscite under Hungarian auspices, probably rigged, resulted in an unlikely vote for Hungary.

Of the almost ten and a half million 'German Austrians' claimed by the government in Vienna, only slightly more than six and a half million were in German Austria; the other almost four million ended up in non-German states.

Some 'German Austrians' appear to have wished to leave the state of their own free will. Roughly 80 per cent of Vorarlberg voters in an unofficial plebiscite in May 1919 opted for accession to Switzerland. The Swiss were not interested, and neither Vienna nor the Allies recognized the decision, so it became moot. It indicated, however, the low degree of 'Austrian' identification remaining after the Habsburg Monarchy's collapse.

Most 'Austrians' in 1918–19 did not want an independent Austrian Republic. They regarded 'German Austria' as a stepping stone to integration into the larger German Republic. The inclusion of the more than two million Germans in northern Bohemia in 'German Austria' in 1918–19 only made sense if 'German Austria' joined Germany, and the newly elected constituent national assembly openly declared on 12 March 1919 that 'German Austria is a part of the German Republic'. The Allies, particularly France, would have none of it.

The grounds for the Allied veto on the *Anschluss* (union) of German Austria to Germany in 1919 were obvious: it would be absurd, given German war guilt and defeat, for Germany to become even larger and stronger than it had been in 1914. Nevertheless, forbidding the union of Austrian Germans with Germany contravened the principle of national self-determination, and it had a disastrous effect on Central European politics. The goal of *Anschluss* was a running sore in Austrian politics throughout the interwar period, until its realization in 1938.

More immediately, the *Anschluss* veto upended the basis on which the state had been founded; even its name had to be changed, at the Allies' behest, from 'German Austria' to 'Republic Austria'. The law of 21 October 1919 instituting this change also explicitly denied that the new Austrian Republic was the legal heir of 'Austria' (Cisleithania), despite St Germain. Yet now that the *national*, German basis for the new state had been denied, the only other identity available was as 'what remained' of Habsburg Austria. Whether it acknowledged it or not, the Austrian Republic was treated, and perforce acted, as the heir to old Austria.

This led, especially on the conservative Catholic Right, to a revival of the idea of a Catholic Baroque Austrian identity different from 'Protestant' Germany. Instilling this new identity was the rationale of the Salzburg Festival, which held its first season in August 1920. Even this most 'Austrian' of cultural projects, however, explicitly situated Austrian culture within the larger *German* national culture. The reluctance of many conservatives to take on the mantle of supranational Habsburg Austria led them back to the Babenberg Middle Ages for a new Austrian identity. This was facilitated by the fact that the new republic's eventual borders approximated those of Babenberg Austria, or at least the very early Habsburg period. Yet the irony of this medieval 'Austrian' identity was that the Babenbergs were even more clearly a *German* dynasty. Moreover, many of the new republic's territories had never been part of Babenberg Austria, including those most 'Austrian' provinces: Tyrol and Salzburg.

The other main political groupings did not even have an interest in creating an independent Austrian identity. The German nationalist camp by definition was uninterested, and the more internationalist socialists saw no objective reason for an Austria independent of more progressive Germany. At base, no part of Austrian society had great faith that the new republic could, or indeed should, survive.

Meanwhile, much of the rest of Europe, including on Austria's borders, was in a state of crisis bordering on chaos. Revolution in Hungary led to a Bolshevik regime under Béla Kun, and then a vindictive counter-revolution led by Admiral Miklós Horthy. Bavaria was under a radical left-wing government in 1919, before this too was brutally put down by right-wing forces. In Berlin the Spartakist revolution was crushed, but Germany was beset by various right-wing coup attempts, culminating in Hitler's failed Beer Hall putsch in Munich in 1923. There were times in 1919 when it looked as though the 'permanent revolution' espoused by Leon Trotsky would actually come about, and Austria was not immune to this apparent

Illustration 34. Aryanization 1: Gustav Klimt, 'Amalie
Zuckerkandl', 1917–18. Amalie Zuckerkandl and her
daughter were murdered by the Nazis, probably at Belzec.
The portrait was 'Aryanized' in 1938. Its ownership has been
the subject of long-running dispute.

communist tidal wave. Working-class unrest reached threatening
levels, especially when stoked by prisoners of war returning from
Russian camps, and there were frequent strikes and even riots in the
winter of 1918–19, often led by workers' and soldiers' councils that
paralleled the 'soviets' of Russia.

   Underlying this general political crisis, a severe, in places devastating, economic, social and medical crisis engulfed all of Europe, and
was especially severe in Austria. The Spanish influenza epidemic of
1918–19 took a severe toll, claiming figures such as Gustav Klimt,

Otto Wagner and Egon Schiele. The epidemic was made worse by the weakened condition of a population near starvation in some areas. The confusions of the war effort had already strained the economic and transportation infrastructure of the Monarchy, and the break-up of the Empire only added to dislocation.

Vienna was especially hard hit by the disintegration of the Monarchy on national lines. As the imperial capital, and hub of the Monarchy's free trade area, Vienna had come to depend for its food supplies on Hungary and for much of its industrial materials, especially coal, on the Bohemian lands. Its economic relations to the lands now in the Austrian Republic had been secondary in comparison. The new national borders cut off Vienna from its economic lifelines. The situation was made worse by the former supplying countries using their hold over Vienna to exact revenge for the past, and better terms for the future. Hungary's refusal to supply food to Vienna had already caused a wartime crisis, but Czechoslovakia's embargo on coal supplies in the harsh winter of 1918–19 was an especially hard blow. Many Austrians were only kept alive in this period by Allied food aid, under the direction of Herbert Hoover. Another programme sent children to countries such as the Netherlands to escape the hell of deprivation called Austria. The worthlessness of wartime savings bonds and runaway inflation also left many middle-class Austrians in unprecedented economic straits. The inflation had been started during the war by the printing of ever larger quantities of paper money, but worsened in the post-war crisis. It never reached the absurdity of Weimar hyperinflation, but it still caused profound social upheaval, for it virtually eradicated the capital savings that had provided the Austrian middle classes with much of their income. Radical working-class unrest was thus matched by the resentments of a déclassé bourgeoisie.

The emergency in which the republic was founded was met initially by remarkable co-operation between the political parties, with the socialist Karl Renner as the premier in an all-party coalition government formed on 31 October, before the republic's declaration on 12 November. One of the major achievements of this first coalition government, largely attributable to the skill of its foreign minister and the leader of the Social Democrats, Otto Bauer, was avoidance of the kind of radical revolution that occurred in both Budapest and

Illustration 35. The interwar legacy on the Left: Bruno
Kreisky celebrates Otto Bauer's centenary, 1981.

Munich. By maintaining party discipline with the help of such heroes
of the radical Left as Friedrich Adler, and, crucially, adopting a radical left-wing ideological position, Bauer was able to outmanoeuvre
the communists and ensure working-class loyalty to the democratic
republic. In saving the republic from Bolshevism, however, Bauer
gave many hostages to fortune, for he created a large gap between
his radical ideological rhetoric and his pragmatic, constitutional and
democratic practice.

   Initially democratic politics seemed to be heading in a radical
socialist direction anyway. In the crisis of 1918–20, many progressive measures were contemplated, including extensive workers' control of businesses, and quite a few implemented. The eight-hour
working day became law, the right of workers to a paid holiday
instituted. The election of the Constituent National Assembly on
16 February 1919 was the first in Austrian history in which women
had the right to vote. From this election the Social Democrats
emerged as the largest party, and remained as senior partner in the
coalition government.

The constitution enacted on 1 October 1920 was a progressive document, although Christian Social influence, and Social Democratic compromise, was evident in the retention of considerable legal privileges by the Catholic Church, effectively maintaining it as the established church of Austria. Written largely by Hans Kelsen, the constitution framed the Austrian Republic as a federal state, with the provinces represented in the Bundesrat (Federal Chamber) to partner the Nationalrat (National Chamber), where deputies were elected in national elections in a reasonably sophisticated system of proportional representation. This was a fairly centralized federal system, with the Bundesrat only having a delaying veto on the Nationalrat's legislative decisions. The constitution also instituted as head of state a president, who, however, had only largely representative and formal duties.[1] Real power in Austria in the 1920s lay with whomever controlled the Nationalrat.

In those terms the election of 1919, despite leaving the Social Democrats as the largest party, already heralded the end of their more revolutionary hopes, for it left the Left in a minority against the 'bourgeois' parties. The Christian Socials, owing to their Catholic–conservative–corporatist approach, initially went along with the Social Democrats in passing some progressive social and economic legislation. Their own workers' wing, led by Leopold Kunschak, promoted progressive labour legislation to compete with the socialists. In most matters, however, they remained adamantly opposed to the 'Marxism' of the Social Democrats. Once the worst of the crisis surrounding the republic's founding receded, the Christian Socials began demanding retrenchment in the more progressive policies of the Social Democrats, for instance in the field of education.

Even before passage of the 1920 constitution, the two parties had stopped working together in the government. When the elections of 17 October 1920 returned the Christian Socials as the largest party, the Social Democrats withdrew into opposition. They thought that inevitable social change would soon provide them with a majority,

---

[1] The 'reform' of the constitution in 1929 moderately increased the president's powers, and made the presidency a nationally elected office. Thus amended, the constitution of 1920 was readopted after 1945 and remains Austria's constitution.

when they could institute by democratic means their 'revolution' and the radical reforms in Austrian society that had been frustrated in 1919–20. As with the progressive German Liberals of 1879, the Social Democrats thought history was on their side, incorrectly; the Social Democrats were not to regain power until 1945.

Excluded from national power, the Social Democrats pushed forward with their plans for a progressive, socialist future in their new bastion, Vienna. The constitution of 1920 had made Vienna its own federal province, independent of Lower Austria. Universal suffrage meant that political power in Vienna changed from being a Christian Social to a Social Democratic monopoly. 'Red Vienna', led by its mayor, Karl Seitz, hence became a showcase for the policy prescriptions of interwar socialism. Julius Tandler instituted a very progressive system of public hygiene and health care; Otto Glöckel, after having to give up his plans for federal educational reform, continued his campaign for a more open, egalitarian school system in Vienna. The socialist leadership, influenced by Austro-Marxist intellectuals such as Max Adler and by the progressive heritage of German (and Jewish) liberalism, also put a great deal of effort into workers' education programmes. Activists such as Joseph Luitpold Stern and David Josef Bach attempted to create a new, humanist proletarian counter-culture, a new, socialist man to match the new, socialist world being developed *in nuce* in Vienna.

The greatest expression of this new world was the municipal building programme. Under the Christian Socials there had been a dire housing shortage. This was partly a result of pre-war Vienna's rapid rise in population, but also because of landlords' quasi-monopolistic preference for raising rents rather than investing in building new housing units. The Christian Socials, who counted landlords as a key constituent group, did little to encourage new housing, despite the obvious need. The exigencies of war, including the influx of thousands of Galician refugees, had then made a poor situation critical.

The market having failed, the Social Democrats instituted their own, government-run building programme to solve the housing shortage. Hugo Breitner, the city's financial chief, instituted a progressive housing tax and luxury taxes to fund a large portion of this programme. Over 60,000 units were built between 1919 and

1934, including such temples to socialist living as the Karl-Marx Hof in Heiligenstadt, where lecture rooms, laundry rooms and nurseries nestled in the large courtyards of the barrack-like apartment buildings.

For the planners and for many residents of these housing projects, their fortress-like design was seen as protective, and the housing programme was a source of socialist pride. Critics saw the projects as bastions of socialist dominance, Breitner's taxes as an undue burden, and the housing programme as distorting the housing market. Admittedly, by 1934 the number of homeless had actually risen to 80,000; and the amenities in the new housing were fairly basic. The rise in homelessness was mostly a result, however, of the ongoing economic crisis of interwar Austria, and the amenities were much improved on previous conditions. Overall, the housing programme was a great achievement, as was the municipal socialism of Red Vienna.

It was, however, a very vulnerable achievement. Red Vienna, for all its heroic self-image, was a socialist island in a sea that was 'bourgeois', or worse. The new jurisdictional borders of the federal province could not keep the storms of national Austrian politics out of the Viennese socialist idyll.

From 1920 Austria was governed at the national level by a series of conservative 'bourgeois' coalitions, whose main initial aim was to restore 'normalcy'. After such traumatic change, this proved difficult. In Austria, as in Germany, even the basic restoration of a solid currency required financial resources that were lacking. Austrian politics in the early 1920s were dominated by the struggle to defeat inflation and restore the state's credit. Austria had a twin credit problem. Financially, it lacked the resources or credit to create a hard enough currency to stop inflation; politically few within Austria or outside really believed that the state or economy was viable. The pressure for *Anschluss* remained high, with unofficial plebiscites in Tyrol and Salzburg both returning almost unanimous votes for union with Germany in the spring of 1921.

Independent Austria was saved financially because of its role in preventing the French nightmare of a larger Germany. When the Allies provided the Austrian government with a large loan to finance currency reform, in the Geneva Protocol of October 1922, one of the main conditions was that all signatories, Austria included, guarantee that Austria remain independent, and not join Germany.

Even with the Geneva Protocol, Austrian financial problems were not over. Inflation only reached its high point in the autumn of 1924. The Protocol put Austrian state finances under the supervision of a League representative, Alfred Zimmermann, making Austria virtually a 'League of Nations colony'. Austrian financial and fiscal policy was very deflationary, resulting in a strong currency, the schilling, which replaced the crown in 1925, at a rate of 1:10,000. By the 1930s Austrians were bragging about the schilling as the 'Alpendollar'. Yet the conservative policies pursued by Austria under League tutelage meant that the unemployment crisis was never overcome, with a concomitant, deflationary impact on demand, even in the relatively good years of the mid-1920s. Unlike in Weimar Germany, there really were no 'good years' for the interwar Austrian economy.

The attempt to restore 'normalcy' in other fields was only partially successful, and brought with it more problems. One of the most obvious failures was in security. St Germain had put severe constraints on the size and character of the Austrian army. In the war's aftermath a Social Democrat, Julius Deutsch, was able to form a small, professional army, loyal to the republic and the constitution. His successor, however, Carl Vaugoin, politicized the army, so that, from being left-leaning in 1920, it became a right-wing institution, loyal more to a party, the Christian Socials, than to the republic.

The state, moreover, was never able to achieve a monopoly of force. Private armies continued to exist even after the state and its borders had been secured. On the left, the Social Democrats had their own military force, the Republikanische Schutzbund (Republican Defence League), led by the former army minister, Julius Deutsch. On the right, there were initially groups of 'Frontkämpfer' (battle-front veterans), but these were eventually superseded by the Heimwehr (Home Defence).

This militia claimed roots in the self-defence forces of the immediate post-war period, but was in reality a new organization, based on right-wing local groups, whose aim was not to protect the republic from foreign armies, but rather to protect 'Austria' from the forces of Marxist revolution. The Heimwehr was sometimes a direct political actor, while at other times it acted as a military back-up for the 'anti-Marxist' political right. It also came to have strong, if unofficial, links with the state's army, but remained an independent and often unpredictable political factor.

In comparison with the Heimwehr, the National Socialists were initially insignificant. Yet many of the various Heimwehr units, rife with political infighting and sectarianism, were often sympathetic to Nazi thinking. Even if opposed to the Nazis, most in the Heimwehr were also hostile to parliamentary democracy: the Heimwehr's Korneuburg Oath of 1930 was explicitly fascist in its ideology. For many Heimwehr members, the republic was more the enemy than the cause to be protected.

Private armies were the sharp end of the central fact of interwar Austria: the division of the country into two political camps, the Social Democrats and the Christian Socials, with the German Nationals constituting their own, somewhat smaller outpost. The Social Democrats developed an extensive support network for their proletarian counter-culture, extending to such areas as sports, the arts and leisure. Socialist workers could live their lives fully within this world. On the Right, the large presence within the Christian Social world of the Catholic Church, and all its attendant social and cultural involvements, also enabled a self-contained life for a bourgeois, conservative Catholic.

Between these two groups there was not much ground for normal 'civil society', and what remained was fractured. There was still a liberal bourgeoisie, especially in Vienna, but it was heavily Jewish and facing a massive growth of antisemitic sentiment since the end phase of the war. Jews, or 'the Jew', were blamed for everything from Bolshevism, to the 'stab in the back', to economic corruption, to modernity itself. The presence of many Galician Jewish refugees in wartime Vienna had exacerbated this, but even when most refugees had left after 1918 almost everybody, even at times the Social Democrats, continued to blame Austria's ills on 'the Jews'.

The much larger German National camp also claimed Austrian liberalism's mantle, and was the successor to most of liberalism's middle-class constituency, but by the interwar period its otherwise liberal precepts, such as anti-clericalism and free-trade economics, were subsumed in a (German) nationalist ideology informed with antisemitism, and German nationalist ideologues were in the vanguard of antisemitic accusation.

What would have been the 'liberal' camp in Austrian politics was thus split by antisemitism, with Viennese Jewry voting heavily for the largely non-discriminatory Social Democrats, and the German National camp siding for the most part with those who shared their opposition to 'Jewish' modernity and 'Jewish' Marxism, the Christian Socials. There was little or no middle ground in Austrian interwar politics.

The resulting confrontation between the 'anti-Marxist' Right and the socialist Austrian Left effectively prevented the formation of any new *national* political consensus in Austria, because of the extremist positions taken by both sides, but particularly the Right. Bauer might be criticized for retaining a radical Marxist ideology – evident in the Linz Programme of 1926 – long after his pragmatic actions had belied his revolutionary words, but he explicitly endorsed the procedures of republican democracy. His rival, the Christian Social leader and Catholic priest, Ignaz Seipel, was just as radical in his 'anti-Marxism', but, as a speech at Tübingen in 1929 made plain, he regarded 'parliamentarism' and democracy as expendable, if a version of Catholic corporatism could replace it. The only political camp that truly supported the First Republic's 'bourgeois' democracy was the 'anti-bourgeois' Social Democratic party of revolution.

The background to these political divisions was a still disastrous economic situation. Some pre-war economic links were re-established, but national animosities kept the region's economy severely fractured. Czechoslovakia, which had both an advanced industrial base and the requisite resources, prospered in this new, nationalized environment, but for Austria, separated from its former economic hinterland, the necessary restructuring was both painful and incomplete. Hydroelectric power compensated somewhat for reduced coal supplies from Czechoslovakia, but its development was hobbled by a lack of capital investment. Despite the currency stabilization of 1925, the economy continued to suffer a severe credit shortage.

The class war between workers and business made matters worse, but it is unclear on which side fault lies. Friedrich von Hayek blamed Austria's economic woes on socialism and excessive regulation, pointing to Vienna's housing crisis as stemming from property taxes and rent control. Yet these measures were part of the socialists' response, as noted above, to a pre-existing crisis caused by a market failure. The lack of capital investment was owing not so much to the disincentives of socialism and union power, as to the absence of entrepreneurial will, which in turn was a result of lack of confidence in Austria's future.

The outcome was economic stagnation. In the very brief period of relative 'prosperity' from 1925 to 1929, the Austrian economy did grow, by 1929 reaching the pre-war level of 1913. Yet the recovery was fragile and weaker than in Germany. The banking system never fully recovered, and Austria remained dependent for its international credit on the League of Nations. This left both Austria's foreign policy and its domestic politics beholden to the dictates of its creditors in the League, most notably France.

Against this backdrop a succession of 'bourgeois bloc' coalition governments ruled Austria in a fairly conservative manner. A major source of contention was the Catholic Church's continuing political influence, personified in Seipel. Seipel, a Catholic priest, was chancellor several times, and even when he was not he was the leading figure in government throughout the period. Conversely, Red Vienna was resented by conservatives for defying their hegemony in national politics. Breitner and Tandler were decried as class enemies, and several figures of the Left, such as the writer Hugo Bettauer, were assassinated by right-wing fanatics, whom middle-class juries then often left unpunished. Federally appointed officials in Vienna, most notably the chief of police, Johannes Schober, increasingly asserted their power against the socialist municipal government. Even when the economy recovered to some extent after 1922, labour–business relations were still bad, the ideological tensions palpable, and private armies on left and right still faced off. It was one such confrontation that marked the beginning of the end for the republic.

A fire fight between Schutzbund and Frontkämpfer units in Schattendorf, Burgenland in January 1927 led to the deaths of a man and a child. At the subsequent murder trial of the accused Frontkämpfer, the jury acquitted them in a travesty of justice that infuriated the Viennese working classes. This led to a mass demonstration on 15 July that got out of Social Democratic control, and the Justice Ministry was set alight. When the police failed to restore order, Schober called in army units. There were scenes on the usually urbane Ringstrasse resembling civil war, and by day's end 89 demonstrators were dead, 600 severely wounded. In protest the Social Democrats called a national general strike for 16 July, but the response was patchy, and the government, aided by Heimwehr units, rode the strike out. The Social Democrats were defeated at home; the government was strengthened, as was the Heimwehr. The republic had suffered a body blow from which it never fully recovered.

CULTURE WARS, 1927–1938

That same year, 1927, also saw the publication of Ludwig Hirschfeld's *Was nicht im Baedeker steht: Wien und Budapest*. In this humorous travel guide is a chapter on 'Peculiarities that one must get used to' about Vienna. One of these peculiarities is the question: 'Ist er ein Jud?' (Is he a Jew?) According to Hirschfeld, the first thing asked in Vienna about a prominent individual is whether he is Jewish or not. Only then do people decide what they think of him. Hirschfeld explicitly cites as proof of this question's power the fact that Sigmund Freud, 'our greatest scholar', is still not a full professor at the university. He also goes on to warn the prospective traveller to Vienna not to be too 'interesting or original, otherwise you will suddenly, behind your back, become a Jew'.[2]

The culture clash between the 'Jewish' modern culture of Vienna 1900 and the conservative culture of the rest of Austrian society had only been exacerbated by war and the ensuing crisis. The Jewish element of Austrian culture was still regarded by most Austrians pejoratively, as something foreign to what was 'Austrian'. Yet not only high 'modern' culture but also the popular culture so integral to 'Austrian' identity was created and fostered largely by Jews.

Much of what has made Vienna 1900 famous was actually the product of the interwar period, and Jews had an even larger

[2] Ludwig Hirschfeld, *Was nicht im Baedeker steht: Wien und Budapest* (Munich, 1927), p. 57.

presence in high cultural life then than before the war. Many major developments in Freudian psychoanalysis took place after 1918, and this was also the heyday of Alfred Adler's Individual Psychology. Vienna's interwar literary world was a powerhouse of German literature. Older writers continued producing major works, such as Schnitzler's brilliant interior monologue, *Fräulein Else*, or Hofmannsthal's *Der Schwierige*, while Karl Kraus continued to berate society in *Die Fackel*, and published his anti-war masterpiece, *The Last Days of Mankind*. A younger generation also emerged, including Musil, but also Joseph Roth, Hermann Broch, Stefan Zweig, Elias Canetti, Alfred Polgar and a whole host of others, such as Anton Kuh, Egon Friedell, Friedrich Torberg and Hilde Spiel. Musil was the only one named here who was not Jewish, or of Jewish descent.

In the musical world, Arnold Schoenberg, together with his (non-Jewish) students Alban Berg and Anton von Webern, perfected his system of twelve-tone composition in this period. The war years, and those following, saw the greatest achievements of Viennese philosophy, in Wittgenstein's *Tractatus Logico-Philosophicus* and the logical positivism of the Vienna Circle. The Circle had prominent non-Jewish members, such as the Germans Moritz Schlick and Rudolf Carnap, but a majority, including Otto Neurath, Philipp Frank, Hans Hahn and Friedrich Waismann, were of Jewish descent, as was the Circle's most prominent critic, Karl Popper. Ludwig von Mises' seminar was a forum for the economic liberalism later represented by his (non-Jewish) pupil, Friedrich von Hayek. A majority of the seminar's members were Jewish by descent. The pedagogic achievements of Eugenia Schwarzwald reached their apogee in the interwar years. Hans Kelsen was the main author of the Austrian constitution.

Owing to the plight of interwar Austria many prominent thinkers left for richer pastures abroad. Schoenberg became a member of the Prussian Academy in Berlin, Josef Schumpeter went to America, Hayek to Britain. The gravitational pull of Weimar Berlin for Viennese cultural and intellectual figures is obvious. Yet interwar Vienna remained a remarkable centre of cultural and intellectual innovation, partly because of the continued existence of Viennese modern culture's social reservoir in the Jewish bourgeoisie.

Austro-Marxism's theorists were also mostly of Jewish descent, including Bauer, Max Adler, Rudolf Hilferding and Gustav Ehrlich. They propounded an individualistic, neo-Kantian interpretation of Marxian theory that offered a more attractive theoretical alternative to the era's totalitarian trends. There were non-Jews such as Otto Glöckel, Adolf Loos and Karl Bühler in the cultural and intellectual landscape of Red Vienna, but Jews such as Käthe and Otto Leichter, Paul Lazarsfeld, Hans Tietze, David Josef Bach, Otto Neurath, Josef Frank and Charlotte Bühler predominated.

Even in the cultural politics of the conservative Austrian Right, individuals of Jewish descent were prominent. A coping stone of the interwar Habsburg myth, albeit a subtly critical one, was Joseph Roth's *The Radetzky March* of 1932. The most significant 'Jewish' contribution to conservative Austrian politics was to the Salzburg Festival. Hugo von Hofmannsthal and Leopold von Andrian, two key figures in its founding, were both the descendants of prominent Jewish families, Andrian being the grandson of Giacomo Meyerbeer, Richard Wagner's archetypal 'Jew in music'. While the non-Jewish Richard Strauss was the festival's main musical figure, its theatrical maestro was Max Reinhardt. Many other festival collaborators, such as the artistic director, Oskar Strnad, were Jewish.

Jews also played an extensive part in Austrian popular mass culture; indeed they predominated in Austrian showbusiness. In the film world Jews were very prominent as directors, producers and cinema owners; both Erich von Stroheim and Billy Wilder had their start there. Jews, Hermann Leopoldi foremost, wrote some of the most famous *Wiener Lieder*, Viennese popular songs, including that most 'Viennese' of songs, the *Fiakerlied*, by Adolf Pick.

Jews were particularly prominent in the world of Viennese operetta, as impresarios, agents, producers, financiers, but also as performers, composers and above all as librettists. Even the Strauss dynasty, composers of the Radetzky March, the Blue Danube Waltz and *Die Fledermaus*, were partly of Jewish descent (a fact that the Nazis tried to cover up in 1938). In the 'silver era' of operetta, starting before the war and extending into the interwar period, Jews were especially prominent. There were many non-Jewish composers as well, most famously Franz Lehár, but many of the period's great operettas were written by Jews such as Imre Kálmán, Oscar Straus and Leo Fall. Moreover, most of the best-known librettists were

Illustration 36. Interwar Austrian identity: Josef Danilowatz, 'The Poet Princes'. This interwar cartoon shows the Jewish operetta librettists Julius Brammer and Alfred Grünwald on a pedestal; underneath there is an adapted version of Grillparzer's salutation to Radetzky: 'In your camp is Austria'.

Jewish, including the team of Julius Brammer and Alfred Grünwald, whose popularity elicited an interesting pictoral interpretation of interwar Austrian identity.

The Jewish presence in operetta, as in Hollywood, was usually left unarticulated. Occasionally, however, an explicitly Jewish figure would appear, and in a positive light. *Frühling am Rhein* (1914) even had a Jewish hero, Moritz Frühling, whose (Jewish) cleverness helps him overcome the amorality of a German baron and enables his Christian, but Jewish-raised step-daughter to marry the man she loves in a reworking of Lessing's *Nathan the Wise*.

Several operettas showed their authors' origins by having a strongly emancipatory message. Two of Brammer and Grünwald's wartime operettas, *The Rose of Stamboul* (1916) and *Bruder Leichtsinn* (Brother Frivolity) (1917/18) tackled social issues of the time, women's rights and race relations, and in both they took a liberal, progressive view. *Bruder Leichtsinn* is especially striking, as it is an ideological defence of the 'frivolity' of operetta, and has as its hero a half-black American, Jimmy Wells. The libretto makes plain that the 'frivolous' decision of the Belgian heroine, Musotte, to marry Wells is the right decision. The lesson could not be plainer: the underlying human reality, and not the colour of one's skin (or the shape of one's nose), was what mattered. In such matters the frivolity of operetta (and carnivalesque modernity) could see more clearly than divisive social conformism.

Jews were also heavily involved in the interwar attempts to develop a new, tourist-friendly Alpine identity for Austria in the genre of the *Heimatoperette*. The most famous of these was *Im weissen Rössl* (The White Horse Inn) of 1930, which combined shameless advertisement of the beauties of the Austrian Alpine landscape with Habsburg nostalgia and a critique of the economic hard times: Francis Joseph himself makes an appearance in an operetta set in the 1920s. Ralph Benatzky, the main composer, was not Jewish, nor was Robert Stolz, composer of the operetta's big hit. The other composers involved, Bruno Granichstaedten and Robert Gilbert, were Jewish, as were the librettist, Hans Müller, and the director, Karl Farkas. There was also a Jewish presence in the cast of characters: 'Sigi Sulzheimer', the lisping son of a Berlin underwear manufacturer, played by Farkas himself, one of the era's most famous Jewish comedians, in the Viennese premiere. It is Sulzheimer, who, newly acquainted with the wonders of love, resolves the plot with an innovation: 'a wedding dress with a zip'. Even within the Alpine fairyland of the *Heimatoperette*, Viennese 'Jewish' modernity was able to inject a combination of technological progress and Freudian psychology in the form of a joke.

Jews were central not only to Austrian high modern culture, but also to the type of mass popular culture on which much of inter-war Austrian identity, and even current Austrian identity, is based. For all that, Jews were still not recognized by other Austrians as *bodenständig*, belonging to the land. There was a tragic conflation between the way Austrians understood their national identity and their attitudes to the political and ideological splits in the country. To the extent that there was an Austrian national identity in the inter-war period, it was dominated by the Christian Socials' conservative and Catholic definition. Beyond the Austrian popular culture of the operetta was another, more engrained, traditional popular culture, the actual culture of the *Heimat*. This was a world where beauty was defined by girls in dirndls set against a backdrop of Alpine scenery, a world in which Jews were seen as foreign and hence as intrud-ers. In this world, under this definition, one could not possibly be 'Austrian' *and* Jewish.

Jews might have helped promote the touristic image of an Alpine and Baroque Austria, but they were not of that world. The Jewish figure in *The White Horse Inn* was an industrialist from Berlin; the Salzburg Festival might be a 'cosmopolitan' project, but this was consciously not the 'Western internationalism' associated with Jews, but rather a cosmopolitanism tied to both *German* culture and *Catholic* religion. The festival was reactionary and anti-modern, trying to recreate the totalizing effect of both medieval and Baroque Catholic culture, a totality that excluded Jews or kept them in total subjection.

Encouraging tourism was itself a conservative strategy. Even before 1914, local leaders in the 'Alpine' Austrian provinces had latched on to tourism as a means of achieving economic develop-ment without the need for industrialization, avoiding the full effects of modernization such as an independent working class. Tourism in turn reinforced Alpine society's conservatism, retaining very patri-archal social and familial patterns. Hotels and resorts continued to run on hierarchical lines at a time when union power in facto-ries and offices was transforming the modern workplace. Provincial Austria invited foreigners from the modern world in order to keep that world out. The resentment of 'rich' Viennese tourists in the provinces was partly owing to the usual envy, but it was also a result of fear of the new, modern ideas and habits they might be bringing with them. That 'touristic' Austria relied for its livelihood on such guests from Vienna and the foreign modern world only made matters worse.

Beyond the polar divide between modern, progressive, 'Jewish' Red Vienna and the conservative, provincial Austrian *Heimat* lay a related and even more destructive division: the three-way battle between socialist, Christian Social and German nationalist *political* cultures.

The Social Democratic camp came to represent not only socialism and the interests of the working class, but also the progressive, emancipatory, modernist and anti-clerical agenda of Austria's erstwhile liberal forces. This led Austria's Jews to vote almost entirely for the Social Democrats in interwar Austrian and Viennese politics. The Social Democrats might occasionally use antisemitic rhetoric, and they might be antagonistic to the Jewish religion, but they accepted Jewish individuals as equals. For Viennese Jews, despite being mostly 'bourgeois' in status, with material interests threatened by socialist policy, that was enough.

Jews, admittedly, had no reasonable alternative. Both of the other camps were explicitly, and quite strongly, antisemitic – in ideology and policy. The Christian Socials represented the conservative 'bourgeois', capitalist part of Austrian society, and as a result some Jews, more interested in preserving social order and property than in full social equality, supported them. The party of Seipel operated, however, from a very socially conservative position, heavily influenced by the Church. Its attitude to capitalism, at least in its rhetoric, was heavily qualified by religious considerations and concern for the 'little man'. It defended the interests of the propertied, but often while preaching *against* 'Jewish' market forces. Its economic and social ideal was corporatist, not capitalist.

The 'national' (German) camp included remnants of the old German liberals, and in its support for 'liberal' free market economics and its anti-clericalism retained elements of the old progressive agenda. The German nationalist element, however, was dominant in the interwar era, and the 'national' camp was strongly antisemitic, often on racial criteria. While the 'national' camp was the weakest and also most diverse of the three, it was also very influential in the non-Jewish part of Austria's intelligentsia. Its exclusivist nationalist ideology was to make its supporters highly susceptible to the rationale of National Socialism.

The two *bourgeois* political camps, the Christian Socials and the German nationalists, both ranged themselves after 1920 against the *city*, Red Vienna. Thus the political struggles of the interwar period mirrored the dual cultural divide between modern 'Jewish' Vienna and the 'reactionary' Alpine provinces. On one side were the supporters of 'Progress', including the Social Democrats, the 'cosmopolitan' (largely Jewish) liberal bourgeoisie centred on Vienna, with a few progressive stragglers from the national (German) camp; on the other were the traditionalists, with a conservative vision of Austrian society. This was Christian Social at heart, but most German Nationals adopted it. German Nationals might be anti-clerical in principle, but the threat they saw to German national 'culture' in the Western 'civilization' represented by 'Jewish' modernism and 'Judeo-Bolshevik' Marxism meant they sided for much of the interwar period with the clerical Christian Socials.

Right-wing thinkers attempted to bind the two sides of the Austrian Right more closely together. Richard von Kralik proposed a German form of Catholicism; Othmar Spann advocated a quasi-fascist brand of neo-medieval corporatism. The Salzburg Festival's organizers wanted the festival to be a vehicle for a conservative ideology uniting anti-revolutionary, Catholic social thought (as in Jedermann and the Salzburger grosse Welttheater) with its own, albeit cosmopolitan, Baroque, and Catholic–South-German–Austrian brand of organicist German nationalism. Such thought blurred the boundaries between Catholic traditionalism and German nationalism in order to facilitate a new coherence of Austria's anti-Marxist Right. Antisemitism plastered over any remaining seams.

Despite the 'anti-Marxist' political coalition of the 1920s, such efforts at a conservative synthesis were never entirely successful, for the clerical and the national world views were not so easily spliced. Hence it was the *triple* division of political cultures – stemming from the division *within* Austrian 'bourgeois' politics – that in the 1930s fatally complicated any strategy for the republic's survival.

After the crisis of the Justice Palace fire and ensuing massacre of 1927, the political situation was already fraught, with battles between Schutzbund and Heimwehr units becoming ever more frequent. The world economic downturn a few months later had a particularly harsh effect on the fragile Austrian economy and financial system, and several banks collapsed. The takeover of the Bodenkreditanstalt forced on the Credit-Anstalt by the government in October 1929 provided momentary stability, but the economy continued to deteriorate, with unemployment up to 15 per cent by 1930.

Along with the economic crisis was the threat now posed to constitutional government by the Heimwehr as a potentially independent political force, along fascist lines. The agenda of Austria's 'bourgeois' governments of the early 1930s was thus dominated by the need to achieve economic recovery, keep the Social Democrats at bay, but also 'tame' the Heimwehr, especially the leading figure, Ernst Rüdiger Starhemberg.

In 1930 Johannes Schober's government attempted to regain control of events by solidifying relations with both fascist Italy and democratic Germany, a trade treaty being signed with Germany in April 1930. Meanwhile, the Christian Socials answered the Heimwehr threat first by bringing Starhemberg into government, in September, and, when that failed, setting up their own paramilitary organizations in December. In November 1930 the opposition Social Democrats gained 41 per cent of the votes in national elections, once more becoming the largest party in parliament. Clearly, something more was needed to secure the situation for the forces of bourgeois order.

In March 1931, Schober, now foreign minister, tried again to improve the government's situation by secretly negotiating a customs union between Germany and Austria. This would have had economic benefits and also achieved part of the *Anschluss* that Schober, his German nationalist supporters and so many other Austrians desired. It was a fatal mistake: the French government vetoed this covert union-by-other-means, and exerted financial pressure to get its way. As an indirect result there was a run on the Credit-Anstalt in May 1931, which brought the effective ruin of that bank, but also that of much of the financial order in Austria, and also Germany, whose major banks had large investments in their Austrian counterpart. The Credit-Anstalt was taken over by the Austrian government with the help of emergency foreign loans, but its initial collapse destroyed any remaining confidence in the Austrian economy, and tragically brought crashing down economic recovery in Germany. Thus did the question of *Anschluss* return to haunt post-Versailles Europe.

The Credit-Anstalt disaster made a severe crisis even worse. The battles of the private armies continued. In September there was an attempted coup by the Heimwehr leader Walter Pfrimer. Unemployment skyrocketed: by 1931 it surpassed 20 per cent, and only levelled off in 1934 at just under 40 per cent, with many unemployed now without benefits. Seipel, still *de facto* Christian Social leader, made a half-hearted effort at another emergency all-party coalition government, but the Social Democrats refused to join, still looking to a democratic electoral majority. So the Buresch government of June 1931 saw all 'bourgeois' parties, including the Heimwehr's Heimatblock, united against the 'socialist threat', echoing the fascist regimes in Italy and Hungary.

The crisis only deepened. In January 1932 the German Nationalists left the government, but they were in any case a diminishing asset. In April 1932, the National Socialists began to make inroads in provincial elections, largely at German Nationalist expense. In May, the Christian-Social-led government of Engelbert Dollfuss was formed, dependent on the Heimatblock and the agrarian Landbund. Desperate for further financing, Dollfuss obtained in the Lausanne Treaty of July 1932 a large League of Nations loan, at the price of renouncing all ideas of union, even customs union, with Germany. Although this helped financially, politically it further enflamed divisions in the country, with Social Democrats, German Nationalists and National Socialists protesting this 'surrender' to the Western powers.

The treaty was narrowly ratified by parliament, but it brought the government neither economic recovery nor political strength. The Social Democrats looked towards the next election, and the National Socialists increased their propaganda and their public outrages; meanwhile the Christian Socials feared for their electoral future. Nazis, Schutzbündler, Heimwehr units and the Christian Socials' own paramilitary groups took to the streets to practise the extra-parliamentary politics of bombings, shootings and general mayhem.

The National Socialists were not yet electorally that successful in Austria, partly because of competition from the Heimwehr, but rampaging Nazi success in Germany overshadowed Austrian politics. Austria's economic misery reinforced doubt in the country's sustainability, which in turn increased capital flight. It also made *Anschluss* ever more attractive, and hence Hitler's rise an ever greater threat to Christian Social hegemony in Austria.

Dollfuss decided a radicalization of Christian Social policies was needed. Although sceptical, Seipel had gone along with parliamentary government; with Seipel's death in August 1932, Dollfuss began shaking off parliamentary bonds. He did so, ostensibly, to meet the Nazi threat, which was real. Hitler became German chancellor on 30 January 1933, and the Nazis and their allies gained a majority in the German Reichstag in the elections of 5 March. Dollfuss's response was to exploit a constitutional accident in the Austrian parliament on 4 March, when all three presidents of the assembly resigned, to declare the parliament defunct. The Christian Social response to the Nazi takeover in Germany, far from defending the republic's principles, was to abandon parliamentary politics and institute a form of authoritarian, quasi-fascist government of their own: 'Austro-fascism'.

Dollfuss imposed the complete Christian Social conservative agenda on the country. Austria was to be transformed in the image of the papally backed corporatist state. A Vaterlandsfront was instituted on 20 May, a supposedly supra-partisan organization, which individuals from all walks of life were urged to join, as long as they were 'loyal to the government'. All local elections were postponed after the National Socialists gained 40 per cent of the vote in Innsbruck's municipal elections in April. Hitler responded in late May to Dollfuss's anti-Nazi measures by imposing a 1,000 mark tourist tax on all Germans entering Austria.

Dollfuss did not give in to this bullying. Called affectionately 'Millimetternich', Dollfuss possessed a short leader's pugnacity, and in standing up to Hitler he earned the respect of many in Austria, including Karl Kraus. Tragically for Austria, however, Dollfuss's courage was not matched by political wisdom or perspective. He remained trapped in the narrow ideology of his Christian Social roots. Despite Hitler and the Nazis now being obviously the greatest threat to Austrian independence, he chose to respond by fighting the 'threat' of the Social Democrats instead.

Days after the coup against parliament in March, Dollfuss's government decided on a radicalization of the 'anti-Marxist' course and declared the Schutzbund illegal. This was partly to please Mussolini, Dollfuss's purported 'protector' against German threats; but the main reason for Dollfuss's crusade against socialism was his own conviction of the need to rid Austria of this scourge.

The strange stand-off between the still democratic socialists and the obviously anti-democratic Christian Social government continued for almost a year, in which time Austria was remade in a conservative and Catholic image. In June 1933 a Concordat was signed with the pope, greatly increasing the Church's domestic influence. In September, Dollfuss announced the establishing of a new 'Ständestaat' and the *Kruckenkreuz* was introduced as the regime's new symbol, an Austrian clerico-fascist answer to the swastika. In the same month a concentration camp for political prisoners was instituted at Wöllersdorf. By the end of 1933, long before February 1934, Austria had already become an authoritarian, corporatist state that brooked neither National Socialist nor Social Democratic opposition.

The showdown with the Social Democrats eventually came on 12 February 1934, when government forces and the Heimwehr, now enthusiastic supporters of the authoritarian regime, provoked a socialist uprising in Linz, and in response the socialist leadership in Vienna called a general strike. The government and Heimwehr were waiting for this opportunity finally to put down the 'Austro-Bolshevik' threat, which they did ruthlessly over the next few days. At one point the Karl-Marx Hof, emblem of Red Vienna's housing achievement, was subjected to heavy artillery fire. Until a few years ago, shrapnel damage could still be seen on its walls. By 15 February the fighting was over, and the socialist leaders had fled to Czechoslovakia; on 16 February the Social Democratic Party was abolished and its funds confiscated. More than a hundred government troops had been killed; but socialist losses were, for the times, horrendous, with more than a thousand Schutzbündler killed in Vienna alone. Austria's civil war was over in a matter of days, and with it the culture war between provincial and urban Austria. The

Heimat had conquered Red Vienna. The Austrian Republic was to be remade into something new, the Ständestaat, the state of estates.

Dollfuss's Ständestaat was an attempt to return post-1918 Austria to somewhere between interwar conservative provincialism and traditionalist Habsburg legitimacy. The constitution of 1 May 1934 set out an Austrian state in which central power was articulated through a corporatist hierarchy. Instead of the troublesome *demos*, functionally based councils together elected a central parliament. The president was elected by Austria's mayors. The state's foundations were explicitly 'Christian and corporate', confirming the Church's regained prominence. The state's new heraldic symbol was, once more, a Habsburg double-headed eagle, though with a Babenberg red-white-red shield. This symbolism paralleled a more positive attitude to the Habsburg family, with its rights and property in large part restored from 1935. This was an Austria as it ought to be – from the provincial perspective.

Officially, the state was quite accommodating of those who did not belong: the May constitution promised religious equality, Jewish religious institutions were not touched, and some Jews were allowed to join the Vaterlandsfront. The Austrian Ständestaat was undeniably better for Jews than Nazi Germany. Yet official tolerance masked a large degree of informal antisemitism. Jewish prominence in the socialist intelligentsia explains why many Jews either lost their jobs or were not promoted after February 1934. Yet this does not explain why pro-socialist Jewish doctors were denied promotion at a much higher rate than pro-socialist non-Jewish doctors. Jews were again 'unerwünscht', unwelcome, the new-old state ultimately only for the *bodenständig* Austrians of the Heimat. The new political culture was one of cultural exclusion, of what Freud had called the 'compact majority' against the outsiders: socialists – and Jews.

The Ständestaat was also a defence against the other hostile political culture: National Socialism. While Dollfuss and the Heimwehr were snuffing out the Austrian Left, Nazi thugs were committing most of the terrorist outrages destabilizing Austria. The Austro-fascist government took measures against the obvious Nazi threat, but its anti-Nazi strategy was tragically compromised by a deep ambivalence. Dollfuss, and even more Kurt Schuschnigg, were never quite sure whether to oppose Nazism outright, or compete with

Hitler for the loyalty of Austria's fascist and German nationalist elements, while reaching some *modus vivendi* with the Third Reich.

The problem was that the two 'bourgeois' cultures, now both anti-democratic, were not as distinguishable from each other as they were from socialist political culture or 'Jewish' modern culture. The fascist culture of the Heimwehr was quite close to that of the Sturmabteilung (SA), with only ultimate loyalties differentiating them. Then again, that was not as much of a difference as one might assume. Even the Austro-fascists, Schuschnigg among them, conceived of Austria as a *German* state, albeit as the better one. The Salzburg Festival, although more truly international after the 1933 tourist tax took away its mainly German audience, still remained a symbol of a better, more cosmopolitan *German* culture. School textbooks still featured oaks as the German, and hence Austrian, national trees. The Austro-fascist–National Socialist argument remained one *within* the German family.

It should have been obvious that the Nazis were the mortal threat to Austria, but the attempted coup and successful assassination of Dollfuss at his Ballhausplatz office by Austrian Nazis on 25 July made this insight unavoidable. The international outrage caused by Dollfuss's death allowed his successor, Schuschnigg, some breathing space in the struggle to maintain Austrian independence. He also had the promise of help from Mussolini's Italy, which played a part in deterring Hitler from intervention. Austria's situation in relation to Nazism, however, steadily worsened.

Austrian national ambivalence allowed the phenomenal economic success of Hitler's Germany to have a powerful effect on the thinking, and loyalties, of ordinary Austrians. Psychologically, spiritually almost, Hitler's Third Reich was a far more impressive and 'uplifting' spectacle than Schuschnigg's homespun Ständestaat. The Austrian government could brag about the strong schilling, but the austere fiscal and financial policies involved provided little in the way of economic growth or new jobs. Unemployment remained near 20 per cent in Austria while it fell precipitously in Germany.

Austria's position internationally also deteriorated. In April 1935 the 'Stresa Front' of France, Britain and Italy had guaranteed Austrian independence as part of its stand against Hitler's treaty revisionism. Yet neither of the two democracies, Britain and France, was prepared to do much to protect the Austro-fascist Ständestaat. Fascist Italy, a neighbour and far more ideologically sympathetic, was thus Austria's main protector against German designs.

Since the Rome Protocols of March 1934, Austria had effectively been an Italian client state. When Italy invaded Abyssinia in October 1935, Austria refused to condemn its ally. Obedience counted for little in international politics, however: rebuffed by the Western powers, Italy began its rapprochement of Germany. The collapse of the Stresa Front left Hitler free to continue his rollback of Versailles, and Mussolini was now moving towards the alliance with Germany of 25 October 1936 that would establish the Rome–Berlin Axis. Austria was well and truly boxed in. While Italy, Austria and Hungary tightened their alliance with additional Rome Protocols in March 1936, Mussolini also pressured Schuschnigg to reach an accommodation with Nazi Germany. Schuschnigg had little choice but to comply.

On paper the agreement of 11 July 1936 was a reasonable compromise whereby Germany recognized Austria's sovereignty and Austrian internal political developments as Austria's concern. The 1,000 mark tourist tax was lifted. Yet the German government never meant to honour the implied promise of non-intervention, and Austria's concessions spelled the beginning of the end of Austrian independence. Austria promised to act as a German state, to cease its anti-Nazi propaganda, and to amnesty its approximately 17,000 Nazi political prisoners. Schuschnigg also allowed two representatives of the 'national' camp into the cabinet, ostensibly to protect 'German' interests: Edmund Glaise-Horstenau and Guido Schmidt. The radical Austrian Nazi 'illegals' might have disliked this compromise, but it gave Hitler what he wanted: now Germany had two stalking horses in the Austrian government, and plenty of opportunity to intervene to 'protect' 'national' interests.

One result of the July Agreement was the diminishing of Heimwehr influence in favour of the 'German way', co-opting German nationalists and moderate Nazis into Austro-fascist circles. The Heimwehr had proved very useful to the Ständestaat in its early days, but the fractiousness among its units and erratic behaviour of its leaders, especially Starhemberg and Fey, meant it was now more trouble than it was worth.

Starhemberg was deputy chancellor, in charge of national security, and leader of the Vaterlandsfront, but he was an ideological misfit in the regime. Schuschnigg was an authoritarian, rather than a fascist. He was a conservative Catholic, and at heart a legitimist and monarchist. Starhemberg saw political Catholicism as an enemy, and wanted to turn Austria into a real fascist state. With Italy's shift towards Germany, Starhemberg's position in Austria was severely compromised. When he congratulated Italy on its conquest of Abyssinia in May 1936 with the words 'Long live the fascist idea', Schuschnigg sacked him. Ostensibly in response to the protests of France and Britain, this was really to be rid of an ideological adversary and to start bringing at least the *patriotic* private armies under control.

The turn to the 'German way' accelerated the taming of the Heimwehr. The two 'national' members of the cabinet replaced Heimwehr members. In October all militias, including the Heimwehr, were dissolved. In a November cabinet reshuffle Schuschnigg jettisoned the remaining Heimwehr elements, and strengthened the 'national' presence, Glaise-Horstenau becoming interior minister and Schmidt *de facto* foreign minister.

By the end of 1936 Schuschnigg had switched from allying with Italy and Austrian fascists to placating Germany. He really had very little alternative. Austria could still expect very little from France or Britain, because of Abyssinia, distaste for the Ständestaat – and British appeasement of Hitler. Italy, after the Axis agreement in October, was no longer as concerned about preserving Austrian independence. Mussolini's warning to the Austrians in August of German intentions, saying that Austria 'had twenty months left', did not augur well. Italian acquiescence in Austria's takeover was sealed as early as April 1937, when Germany promised to leave South Tyrol to Italy.

Bereft of any credible foreign support, Schuschnigg tried to finesse increasing German pressure by co-opting the 'national' and Nazi groups. A Committee of Seven was instituted in February 1937 to include the hard-core Nazi 'illegals'. A Volkspolitisches Referat (national-political department) for 'national' interests was set up in June. Arthur Seyss-Inquart, supposedly a 'national' moderate, became a member of the Staatsrat. Yet it was unclear who was co-opting whom. While Schuschnigg tried to entice the 'national' camp by inclusion in the Ständestaat, the 'national' camp retained its German loyalties, and the German government was preparing to 'co-opt' Austria entirely. In April Glaise-Horstenau was in Berlin for 'informal talks' to receive instructions. In June, as Schuschnigg was embracing the 'national' camp, the German general staff developed 'Special Scenario Otto', the first draft of the plan for *Anschluss*.

Economically and financially, conditions in Austria by the end of 1937 were markedly improved, with unemployment down to 233,000. Public works projects such as the Grossglockner-Hohenalpenstrasse, Reichsbrücke in Vienna and the Wiener Höhenstrasse had been effective; foreign currency reserves were at an all-time high. Economic improvement, however, could not undo the politically disastrous chain of events – and choices – since 1927 that left the Schuschnigg regime in a desperate position.

The crushing of the Left in 1934 had led the alienated and excluded into either backing more extreme elements of the Left, including the communists, or lending their support to the one remaining, *other* focus of Austrian non-conformism, the 'national' camp and the Nazis. Relative economic success in 1937 did little to assuage the mass resentment felt by probably a majority of Austrians at the monopolization of power by the authoritarian Catholic Right. Having large gold reserves simply made Austria an even more tempting target for the Third Reich.

Abandoned abroad, divided and adrift at home, the Austrian Ständestaat by the beginning of 1938 was at Nazi Germany's mercy. In September 1937 Mussolini had given Hitler free rein over Austria. In early November Hitler had laid out his plans to invade both Austria and Czechoslovakia to his generals, and the German ambassador to Vienna, Franz von Papen, was helping to plot a Nazi takeover. The details of the 'Tavs Plan' were uncovered in late January 1938, but by now there was no thought of Nazi retreat as in 1934. Instead Hitler adopted the tactic of the bum's rush: on 5 February Hitler had Papen invite Schuschnigg to the Eagle's Nest above Berchtesgaden, just over the border at Salzburg, for talks to 'clear the air'. Schuschnigg accepted and, accompanied by Guido Schmidt, he arrived on 12 February.

In a one-to-one conversation in the morning, Hitler terrorized Schuschnigg, and in a more public afternoon meeting presented a non-negotiable ultimatum effectively making Austria a quasi-Nazi satellite of Germany. Seyss-Inquart was to be interior minister; all imprisoned Austrian Nazis were to be released, National Socialism in Austria to be legalized, and all Nazis to regain their state jobs. Hitler's one concession was to allow Schuschnigg three days' delay, for the Austrian president, Wilhelm Miklas, to approve these changes.

Schuschnigg left Berchtesgaden broken and cowed. On 14 February he persuaded Miklas to approve the changes demanded by Hitler, and on 16 February they were fulfilled: Schmidt became official foreign minister, Seyss-Inquart became interior and security minister, with Glaise-Horstenau also in the cabinet. An amnesty was proclaimed for political crimes, and Austrian Nazis now operated virtually undisturbed.

The supporters of independence tried to rally. On 17 February Otto Habsburg, son of former Emperor Charles, offered to take over the government (Schuschnigg declined on 2 March). On 24 February Schuschnigg responded to Hitler's demand of 20 February for Austro-German union by declaring that he would never abandon Austrian independence, finishing with: 'Red-white-red, until I'm dead.' This provoked more Nazi unrest in the provinces, but was not credible. There were last-minute attempts to reach out to the remnants of the socialist movement, who were willing to help oppose Hitler. Yet the memory of 1934 still cast a pall, with Otto Bauer proclaiming in exile that the Left would collaborate *against* Hitler, but not *for* Schuschnigg. Efforts to organize a united socialist–conservative front against the Nazis proved ineffectual.

On 6 March Schuschnigg decided to defy the Nazi tide once more by holding a national referendum on independence, announcing on 9 March that it would be held on the 13th. It never took place. On 10 March there were mass Nazi demonstrations in many of the provincial centres, and though there were also anti-Nazi demonstrations, the Nazis gained the upper hand in most cases. The German border was closed on 10 March, and on 11 March Hitler ordered Operation Otto, the invasion of Austria, to go ahead.

On the morning of 11 March Seyss-Inquart and Glaise-Horstenau delivered to Schuschnigg an ultimatum from Hitler to abandon the referendum or resign. Schuschnigg ended up both abandoning the referendum and resigning, at 4 p.m. Miklas at first refused to appoint Seyss-Inquart chancellor, but Austria was effectively finished as an independent state. At 7.50 p.m. Schuschnigg made his resignation public in a radio speech and urged that there be no resistance to the looming German invasion, so that no 'German blood' (either German or Austrian) would be spilled. The fatal ambivalence of interwar Austrian identity over its German national character remained to its very last words. Schuschnigg ended his speech with 'a German word and a heartfelt wish: God protect Austria!'

With Miklas still resisting, Göring ordered the invasion of Austria to go ahead, and Seyss-Inquart to take power. At 11.14 p.m. the radio announced that Miklas had appointed Seyss-Inquart chancellor and at midnight Miklas approved the new, Nazi-dominated cabinet. Before even one German soldier had crossed the border, Austria was in Nazi hands.

When the German invasion began at 5.30 a.m. on 12 March, there was virtually no opposition and it became a victory parade. Having been hastily organized, the invasion's only serious problems were logistical, with petrol tanks running dry; but eager Austrians soon filled up the German tanks as a patriotic act. By the evening of 12 March, Hitler was already on the balcony of Linz town hall, orating to the adoring multitude. Next day, encouraged by the rapturous reception, Hitler had drafted a law for the full union of Germany and Austria, which was then sent to Vienna for enactment. Miklas refused to sign this bill, resigning instead, and the cabinet made the bill law. Austria 'legally' had ceased to exist.

In the events of 11–13 March remarkably little 'German blood' was spilled. The Nazis immediately arrested many political opponents, and some of these 'committed suicide'. Yet overall there was little physical violence – except for Austria's Jews. The *Anschluss* was accompanied in Vienna and elsewhere by hideous scenes of cruel persecution that have become seared into both the Jewish and Austrian historical imagination. Jews were forced by Nazi thugs to scrub the pavement, while happy onlookers crowded around.

Jewish businesses and homes were looted and Jews beaten up. In the euphoric *Judenhatz* of the *Anschluss*-pogrom some Jews were murdered.

While the Austrians on the streets in March 1938 jubilantly greeted *Anschluss*, Jews had seen their world collapse. In 1927 the question 'Ist er ein Jud?' had been an annoying sign of the incomplete acceptance of Jews as truly Austrian. After 13 March it became a question of life or death.

THE HITLER TIME, 1938–1945

On 13 March 1938 Austria as such ceased. In May Hitler ordered that the renamed Ostmark be divided into seven Gaue (Nazi provinces), fully integrated into the German Reich. In 1942 the Ostmark became the 'Donau- und Alpengaue' to eradicate any remaining separate identity. The history of 'Austria' was thus officially suspended under Nazi rule, and this has been reflected in post-1945 Austrian historiography, which until very recently skirted around the period 1938–45 as not really part of *Austrian* history. Austrian histories published after the travails of the mid-1980s treat the period more fully, but there is still a remarkable, if understandable, reticence about seeing the 'Hitler Time' as part of the *Austrian* experience.

There are more continuities between Austrian and Ostmark history than many post-1945 Austrians would care to admit. In most respects life went on after March 1938 much as it had beforehand, and many Austrian state institutions were simply adapted by the new rulers to their own ends. At the Austrian Gallery in the Belvedere the director, Franz Martin Haberditzl, was replaced by his Nazi deputy, Bruno Grimschitz (while his other, Jewish deputy, Heinrich Schwarz, fled), but otherwise the gallery's administration was largely untouched, and it used the same notepaper, headed with 'Austrian Gallery', well into the war. In many informal, cultural and structural ways 'Austria' continued.

Even if Austria was wiped off the Nazi map, the territory was still there, and its inhabitants, the once and future Austrians, mostly remained in it. Indeed the once and future Austrian economy and

Illustration 37. Hitler in Leonfelden, 20 October 1938, coming from Krumau.

society experienced under Nazi rule one of the greatest transformations in 'Austrian' history.

Most Austrians were euphoric when the German troops invaded
and Hitler ordered the *Anschluss*. There were scenes of mass adu-
lation at Hitler's speech at the Heldenplatz in Vienna on 15 March,
where he announced 'the entry of my homeland into the German
Reich'. Such scenes do not necessarily mean that all Austrians supported *Anschluss* – the Viennese feted Napoleon's army too – but
it remains unclear what they did represent. Relief at the end of
a fraught political crisis? Joy at liberation from the authoritarian Catholicism of the Ständestaat? Acceptance of the historical
inevitability of the 'return' of German Austria to the German father-
land, even by *force majeure*?

All of these considerations, and more, contributed to the
acceptance of the *Anschluss*. The Nazis expertly created the sense

of the invasion-cum-coup being an unstoppable *fait accompli*, so that fatalistic Austrians saw themselves as surrendering to the inevitable. The endorsement by Austria's Catholic bishops of the Nazi takeover smacks very much of this time-honoured Austrian bowing to the powers that be. There were also few good alternatives: the Ständestaat's poor record had alienated large swathes of the Austrian populace, especially in the working class, who could not discern much difference between clerico-fascism and National Socialism.

One could also approve of the long-sought union of Austria with Germany without approving of Nazism. There had been a strong pan-German tradition among not only Austrian German national-ists, but also progressive liberals and socialists, many of whom felt torn between despising Hitler and welcoming the fact of *Anschluss*. Renner approved of *Anschluss*, and even a liberal Jewish exile such as Heinrich Gomperz could express satisfaction at the fact of Austria's 'reunion' with Germany.

The response to the *Anschluss* was complex, but it is probable that a majority of Austrians supported it. The plebiscite of 10 April passed with an outlandish 99.75 per cent voting for 'reunification', which says much about the urge to conformism on such occasions, but with the Catholic Church and the remaining socialist leaders all urging 'Yes' it was probably a fairly accurate representation of the *acceptance* of the Nazi takeover. Given Austrian popular sen-timent in the 1930s, a period of large Nazi gains in (covert) sup-port, many Austrians, possibly a majority, actively wanted *Anschluss* in 1938, and most of the rest were content to go along with the inevitable.

There were losers in the *Anschluss*. Political opponents were rounded up: many were packed off to the Dachau concentration camp, and many died there. Some of the more outspoken adver-saries, such as Emil Fey, were forced into committing suicide. Of the roughly 20,000 arrested in the immediate aftermath of 13 March, though, about three-quarters were released after a few weeks, and for most Austrians not much changed after March 1938, certainly not for the worse. The Nazi leadership immediately started a large programme of economic investment in the land: as early as 13 May the ground was broken for the Hermann Göring steelworks in Linz.

The main losers of March 1938 were Austria's Jews. The 'wild Aryanization', where gangs of Nazis and their opportunistic followers took the 'law' into their own hands and expropriated Jewish homes and businesses by force, began on 12 March, even before the *Anschluss* was complete. After a few weeks, the Nazi authorities clamped down to stabilize the situation, and the 'wild Aryanization' was transformed into a system of organized, state-sanctioned robbery. The takeover of many Jewish firms by Nazi 'commissars' after 12 March was legally recognized after the fact; remaining Jewish firms were transferred to Nazi members as a form of middle-class welfare, or were turned into Nazi-run co-operatives of the non-Jewish employees.

Thousands of Jews lost their jobs, were forced to 'sell' their property at absurdly low prices, or had their property confiscated on various trumped-up charges. Jewish children were expelled from 'Aryan' schools and Jewish attendance in institutions of higher learning severely limited. Jews were quite clearly no longer welcome in Vienna, and many made the hard but life-saving decision to leave their Austrian homeland. The Nazi authorities were also intent on having Jews leave, albeit at as steep a price as possible. From August 1938, Adolf Eichmann, who had grown up in Linz, headed the Central Office for Jewish Emigration in Vienna, where he perfected a process for fleecing the prospective refugees of most of their cash and belongings, before letting them emigrate. The Nazis thus got rid of a large number of Jews for a large amount of money: by November 1939 more than 125,000 Austrian Jews had escaped the 'Ostmark'.

Among those who left were some of Austria's greatest artists and thinkers, including Sigmund Freud, as well as many up-and-coming individuals, who were to make the Central European (Viennese) intellectual a fixture of *Western* culture. Yet not all who left found success in their adopted Western homelands. Restrictions on refugees in Britain, America and British-controlled Palestine remained strict, so that many Viennese Jews were forced into a desperate search for any country that would provide them with a visa, and a way out. One group ended up on the island of Mauritius in the Indian Ocean. Another sizeable group found refuge in Shanghai, even under Japanese occupation. Many of those who escaped Vienna fled to other continental countries, Czechoslovakia, Holland or France, and so were caught up in the Nazi web again during the war. Even for those who reached safe havens, the trauma of exile sometimes proved too much. The suicide rate among Jews in Vienna after March 1938 was extremely high, but that among refugees was also elevated; more banal forms of despair and hardship also took their toll. Perhaps a third of all refugees did not survive the war.

For those who remained in Vienna, the situation grew ever more dire. To Austrians' discredit, it appears to have been popular pressure in Vienna and the initiative of responsive local Nazis that inspired many of the policies of the Third Reich's Final Solution. *Reichskristallnacht*, the Night of Broken Glass, of 9 November 1938 was a cataclysmic event for Jews all over the Third Reich, but it was particularly horrific in Vienna, where the radio commentator narrated the burning of the Leopoldstadt Synagogue as though it were a jolly, Nazi version of Guy Fawkes Night. Forty-two synagogues and prayer-rooms were destroyed that night, at least twenty-seven Jews were murdered and eighty-eight severely injured. Despite apparent ideological inconsistency, Jewish women were raped.

Vienna's remaining Jews became the guinea pigs and the local Nazi leadership the pioneers for the plan to remove and then murder European Jewry. In order to meet the perennial housing shortage in Vienna, Jews were expelled from their apartments and forced to live in quasi-ghettoes, mainly in Leopoldstadt. As early as July 1939, with local Nazis pointing to the resentment of the populace at having to live near Jews, plans were drawn up to deport Jews to concentration camps near Vienna. Only when victory in Poland opened up the prospect of sending Jews there were these plans dropped, but this Viennese initiative may have contributed to the policy of mass deportation of Jews 'to the East', and their eventual annihilation.

In October 1939, about 66,000 Jews by religion and another 39,000 'race-Jews' were still in Vienna. Their dehumanization, marginalization and immiseration accelerated when war began in September 1939 and foreign aid was cut off. Nazi intentions for Viennese Jewry, however, went beyond mere wretchedness. As early as June 1940 Hitler informed the Viennese authorities that all remaining Jews in Vienna would be deported to Poland; when deportations began in early 1941, the authorities ordered the Jewish

Community's administration to provide deportee lists and appoint 'marshals' to deliver those on the list to be transported. When the Community was dissolved in November 1942, its functional replacement, the Council of Elders, became responsible for determining who should be shipped off. The Nazis thus had Vienna's Jews decide who among them should live and die.

The preparations for war against the Soviet Union, and policy indecision concerning Jewish deportees once in Poland, led to a pause in deportation in the spring of 1941. By the beginning of 1942, however, the huge gains made on the Russian front in the previous summer, and the decision at the Wannsee Conference in January 1942 on a coherent plan for the 'final solution' of the Jewish problem, meant Viennese Jewry's deportation could resume with more deadly efficiency. The transportations, many now directly to extermination camps, reduced Vienna's Jewish population by up to 5,000 a month: by April 1943 there were fewer than 8,000 Jews in Vienna, and the rest of that year and 1944 saw yet more Jews sent to their deaths. Before the *Anschluss* Vienna had been home to 170,000 Jews by religion, and in excess of 200,000 if defined by 'race'. By the end of the war in 1945 there were 5,700 Jews in Vienna and 2,142 Viennese Jews still alive in the death camps. More than 65,000 Viennese Jews died in the Holocaust. About 1,500 Jews in Vienna were saved by non-Jews hiding them. Based on his study of Austrians among the SS and concentration camp personnel, Simon Wiesenthal estimated that Austrians in the service of the Third Reich were responsible for the death of approximately three million Jews.[3]

Historians have recently questioned this estimate. Yet the over-representation of Austrians in the Holocaust's death machine remains remarkable. Austrian individuals also played a very active role in pushing for anti-Jewish measures and formulating them; policies in Vienna often were a model for policies of the Third Reich. The Austrian state no longer existed, so the question of *state* responsibility remains moot. Yet the question of *national* responsibility is not so easily dismissed.

[3] Cited in Gerhard Botz, 'The Jews of Vienna from the *Anschluss* to the Holocaust', in I. Oxaal, M. Pollak and G. Botz (eds.), *Jews, Antisemitism and Culture in Vienna* (London, 1987), p. 202.

Austrians during the Nazi era were not even 10 per cent of the Third Reich's population, and yet Austrian individuals filled many key positions in the Holocaust's command structure, and Nazi anti-Jewish policy was apparently shaped by Austrian initiatives. 'Germany' and 'Germans' have traditionally been held solely responsible for the Holocaust, often guilty of it. Yet Austrians had a proportionately far larger share in responsibility for the Holocaust than Germans, given relative numbers. The 'Austrian' Hitler had become a German citizen long before 1938; yet many of the other perpetrators in the extermination of the Jews had been Austrian until 1938. Austrians then – and Austrians now – share a responsibility for the worst genocide in human history.

The central, painful problem for Austrian history during the Hitler Time is that for much of the period Austrians and the Austrian economy received huge benefits from Nazi rule, and most Austrians supported, actively or passively, the regime, especially the Führer. Austrians, generally speaking, did not act like an occupied nation and were not treated as one.

The Nazis gave a massive modernizing boost to the Austrian economy and society. Individuals might have made large 'windfall' gains from the 'Aryanization' of Jewish property, but there was a much greater economic boost from capital investments for Germany's war needs. Much of Germany's military infrastructure was set up in Austrian territory because it, unlike most of Germany, was out of range of Allied bombers (until 1943). Linz, Hitler's home town, was the site of some of the largest investments, with both the state-of-the-art Hermann Göring steelworks and a large chemical works for nitrogen production. Wiener Neustadt became home to the largest aircraft factory of the Third Reich. Many of the hydro-electric projects planned before 1938 but never realized for lack of funds were now started, including Kaprun. Large sections of the railway network were electrified; an 'Autobahn', the trademark of the Nazi economic miracle, was started from Salzburg to Vienna. Within months of the *Anschluss* Austria's unemployment problem had virtually vanished, and the Austrian economy had been put on a much more modern footing.

The economic changes brought in their wake major social change. The labour demand generated by Nazi investments enabled many farm labourers and house servants to escape to the towns and industrial centres. The Nazi era was hence for many a period of emancipation from the quasi-feudal world of the Austrian countryside. Nazi social policy itself was far more 'modern' than the interwar Austrian norm, especially the Ständestaat.

The power of the Catholic Church was reduced: divorced Catholics could now remarry, albeit in a civil ceremony. While the instituting in April 1939 of a church tax might appear to strengthen the Church's power over the faithful, its intent was to create a financial incentive to leave the Church and declare oneself only 'gottesgläubig' (believing in God). Such measures show the Nazi regime pursuing the goals of Austrian liberal/German nationalist anti-clericalism. The hostility shown by the Nazi regime to Cardinal Innitzer and Church hierarchy was felt by many Austrians to be part and parcel of a liberation from clerical, 'pfäffisch' control that was overdue, for some by about four centuries.

The Nazi period also saw the beginning of some of modern Austria's most cherished cultural institutions. The famed New Year's concerts of the Vienna Philharmonic trace their origins back to a concert that took place in the winter of 1939–40 (admittedly on New Year's Eve).

Not all this modernization was positively received by the Austrian populace (although the new, well-paying jobs, the improved public infrastructure and the fruits of Aryanization were). The attacks on the Church were resented by most Austrians, and were ameliorated in response to the public's obvious disapproval. The economic and social changes were resented in the conservative social establishment. Now that the Jews were no longer available, the target of discontent became the 'Piefkes' – North Germans, but eventually any Reich German.

There was some basis for resentment. The German regime had always seen the *Anschluss* in terms of political and material gain. A major goal of annexation had been acquisition of Austria's gold and foreign currency reserves. In the 'integration' after March 1938 the homegrown Austrian Nazis felt themselves short-changed. Some leading Austrian 'nationals' were rewarded for their (dis)loyalty in engineering the takeover with plum jobs elsewhere. Seyss-Inquart became Reich Commissioner for the Netherlands in 1940;

Glaise-Horstenau was put in charge of Croatia. The new man in charge of Austria after March 1938 was, however, a Reich German, Josef Bürckel. In early 1939 he replaced the local man, Odilo Globocnik, as Gauleiter in Vienna (Globocnik going off to a career in mass murder in Lublin), and in April 1940 became Reichsstatthalter in Vienna, before he in turn was replaced in August 1940 by Baldur von Schirach, another Reich German. Under Bürckel and Schirach, Reich Germans filled most key jobs, including academic positions at the university. Part of the reason for the large concentration of Austrian Nazis in the command structure of the Holocaust was displacement by Reich Germans on their Austrian home turf.

This Nazi carpet-bagging led to unrest among Austrian Nazis, and Austrians in general. The Nazi regime came up against the law of rising expectations, with large material gains creating only further demands, and envy of the more successful. This syndrome was described succinctly by Helmut Qualtinger as 'Herr Karl' in 1962. Relating how in March 1938 he had only forced one Jew to clean the pavement, while others had made huge fortunes from helping persecute many Jews, Herr Karl comments: 'I hab nur an Juden g'führt. I war ein Opfer' (I only collared one Jew; I was a victim).[4]

Many of the newly arrived Reich German Nazis were astounded at the vehemence of Austrian antisemitism and tried to restrain the fervour of their local Austrian counterparts. This emphasis on order over brigandage was resented by the Austrian Nazis, who then saw the fruits of their hatred plucked by Reich German functionaries. Austrian Nazis therefore came to be especially frustrated by the new regime.

The discontent of the local population was one of the factors in the replacement of Bürckel by Baldur von Schirach. Envisaging Vienna as his own powerbase within the Third Reich's hierarchy, Schirach tried to co-opt Viennese local patriotism by reviving 'Viennese' traditions and encouraging Heimat authors such as Josef Weinheber. Schirach played the role of the great art patron; at his behest the Künstlerhaus put on the most comprehensive exhibition ever staged of that great 'German' artist, Gustav Klimt, with Adele Bloch-Bauer's first, golden portrait shown under the 'ethnically cleansed'

---

[4] Helmut Qualtinger and Carl Merz, *Der Herr Karl* (Reinbek, 1964), p. 16.

title of 'Portrait of a Lady in Gold', as it was known for many years *after* 1945. Under Schirach, Vienna reasserted its own identity, different from the rest of the Third Reich.

This has made authors such as Weinheber appear as covert 'Austrians', proclaiming a local identity against Reich German imperialism, even as they remained feted by the Nazi regime. This internal resistance through local loyalties has been cited as a sign of crypto-Austrian patriotism among Austrians generally. Yet appearances can be deceptive. The experience of frustrated rising expectations, carpet-bagging 'Piefkes' and insolent, demanding 'Piefke' tourists did stoke resentment against Reich Germans, but most Austrians still had enormous faith in the Führer, Hitler and his Third Reich being seen as greater than just Germany. The Heimat literature of writers such as Weinheber actually fitted well into Nazi ideology, with its marrying of Nature and local tradition with the larger nation of 'blood and soil'. Weinheber celebrated Vienna as a German author praising a great German city: the local reinforced the national, and the National Socialist. The Salzburg Festival was still performed, now as a celebration of a *united* Germany.

Overall the Austrian populace received large economic benefits from Nazi war-driven investment. Unemployment disappeared, replaced by an employment deficit. Many of the crucial infrastructure projects that contributed so greatly to Austrian modernization during the Second World War, and after, were built with foreign forced labour. The expansion of the Third Reich into Czechoslovakia, coupled with its hegemonic economic role in south-eastern Europe, also greatly aided the Austrian economy. The links with Austria's economic hinterland, frayed and broken after 1918, were now restored in full.

On the local level, Leonfelden's links with such towns as Hohenfurth (Vyšší Brod) and Krumau (Český Krumlov) were even better than before 1918, being now without Czech interference. Hitler had actually passed through Leonfelden in October 1938, on the way back from Krumau. Given the new prosperity, the reuniting with 'German' southern Bohemia and the great optimism in the Third Reich in the early war years, it is understandable that the Nazi Party members of Leonfelden (most of the village dignitaries) would be proud to have themselves photographed at a party meeting in 1940 under a large banner that read 'We thank Adolf Hitler'.

Illustration 38. NSDAP meeting, Leonfelden, 1940. The sign reads: 'We thank Adolf Hitler'.

The dominant cause for celebration in 1940 was the stunning German success in the war, which had appeared to prove all of Hitler's claims about the racial and cultural superiority of the German people. The Wehrmacht had swept all before it in its conquest of Poland and then continental Western Europe, awing its enemies with its innovative 'Blitzkrieg' tactics. By 1941 the Third Reich dominated Western and Central Europe, and the Axis armies had swept through south-eastern Europe as well. If Britain had proved a harder nut to crack than anticipated, it was an isolated and puny power compared with the proven might of Hitler's armies, which even secured victories in North Africa.

In the summer of 1941, with German armies racing towards Moscow after shattering the Soviet forward defences in the surprise invasion of 22 June, it seemed nothing could stop German triumph. At that point in the war Hitler was immensely popular, for nothing succeeds like military success; most Germans basked in the reflected glory of the feats of 'their boys' and looked forward to lording it over Europe, and perhaps the world. Austrians could fully share in this German triumphalism, for those 'German' forces included many Austrians, as often as not in units composed of other Austrians.

When the young Kurt Waldheim 'fulfilled his duty' by serving in the Wehrmacht, he did so in a unit commanded by General Alexander Löhr, formerly a high-ranking officer in the *Austrian* army. Austrians were regarded by the Nazi regime as fully German, and entirely trustworthy, and were completely integrated into the German armed forces. Those Austrians called to serve did so as willingly as other 'Germans', for they were 'simply fulfilling their duty'. If Austrians in the Wehrmacht did consider what they were doing as fulfilling a duty to a legitimate authority, then they accepted the *Anschluss* and regarded themselves as full members of the Third Reich. In doing so, they were implicitly accepting responsibility for what the Third Reich perpetrated.

There were those Austrians who remained faithful to their Austrian identity, and many thousands of them, with communists as elsewhere being heavily over-represented, engaged in various forms of resistance throughout the Nazi period, although the bulk of such resistance occurred very near war's end. Two thousand seven hundred Austrians were executed for resistance-related activities; roughly 32,000 non-Jewish Austrians died in prison or concentration camp (compared with 65,000 Jewish Austrians); approximately 100,000 Austrians were arrested on political grounds. If one adds the more than 20,000 killed in the Nazi euthanasia programme, then the number of Austrian opponents or victims of the Nazis was significant, given the Austrian population was only around seven million. Yet these resistance numbers are dwarfed by the number of Austrians who served in the Third Reich's war machine and laid down their lives for the Führer.

Austrian mountain units played a key role in Norway in April 1940. Austrians were heavily involved in the sweeping Balkans campaign of the spring of 1941 and subsequent campaigns against Yugoslav resistance movements. Many Austrian troops were also involved in the Russian campaign from June 1941. The direct successors to Austrian regiments of the First World War, such as the Fourth Hoch- und Deutschmeister Infantry Regiment, found themselves, now in German uniforms, once again fighting in the Balkans and on the Eastern Front. For many Austrians the Second World War was the continuation of the First, just with greater integration into the German war machine. When that war machine began to go wrong, Austrian troops were among the first to suffer. At

Stalingrad in the winter of 1943, roughly 50,000 Austrian troops in the German Sixth Army were encircled by Soviet forces. Only about 1,200 of them returned home. This national tragedy was long taboo in Austria, for it is a clear indication of the dimensions of Austrian participation in the German war effort.

Overall, 247,000 Austrians died as soldiers in the Wehrmacht, a figure commensurate with their proportion of the overall German population. Austrians played a disproportionate role in the Final Solution. The German military campaigns of the Second World War are a part not only of German history, but also of Austrian history: Stalingrad was not only a German national catastrophe, but an Austrian one as well.

It was Stalingrad that proved the turning of the tide not only in the Third Reich's military fortunes, but also in the Austrian populace's sense of identity. What had seemed so glorious in 1941 had turned hideously sour by 1943, and it was really only at that point that Austrians began to regret their Germanness and rediscover their Austrian persona. Yet, despite disillusion with the Third Reich, and despite anti-Piefke resentment, many Austrians stayed loyal to their leader, Adolf Hitler, to the bitter end. He was, after all, one of them, and many convinced themselves that the Führer was not to blame for the catastrophe, but rather his corrupt advisers, and the Jews.

There was a resistance movement, and the bravery of its members was exceptional and most praiseworthy. Yet only a tiny minority of Austrians actively resisted the Nazi regime; the vast majority went along, some grudgingly but very many enthusiastically, with Hitler's policies. This was so even as the Allies closed in. In August 1943 the Allied advance into Italy enabled American bombing raids on Austria for the first time. Wiener Neustadt was bombed on 13 August 1943. In the east, the Russians kept rolling back the German forces; in the west, on 6 June 1944, the D-Day invasion began. On the home front, the war's deprivations became increasingly severe. Hitler survived the assassination attempt of 20 July 1944, and so the war went on, but with an ever decreasing likelihood of German success.

In September 1944 the first serious American bombings of Vienna began and defeatism spread. Pleas that Vienna be made a demilitarized 'open city' were made to Schirach, who took this request to

Hitler, but Hitler summarily rejected it in late October, ordering Vienna to be defended 'to the last stone'. With total defeat staring Germans and Austrians in the face, a more effective Austrian resistance arose, taking formal shape in December under the codename 'O5'. The Russians came ever closer (Budapest fell to them in February 1945) and the bombing intensified, reaching a highpoint in the raid on Vienna of 12 March 1945, with many landmarks severely damaged. Defeatism and resentment at the Nazis – for having failed – mounted.

Yet the degree of loyalty to the Nazi regime remained remarkably high, especially in the east, where the enemy was the Red Army. Paranoia induced by Nazi propaganda, guilt at known German excesses on the Eastern Front and the harsh realities of Soviet military practice combined to stiffen Nazi resistance. As late as 2 February, when about 500 Soviet officers imprisoned at the concentration camp at Mauthausen in the Mühlviertel, roughly 30 miles from Leonfelden, attempted to escape, about 150 successfully, the Nazi authorities could count on the local population to help. In the 'Mühlviertler Hasenjagd' (Mühlviertel Hare Hunt), the Russians were hunted down like vermin; only 11 survived.

In the east, the Austrian resistance was ineffective. A plot within the German military command in Vienna to surrender the city to the Soviets was uncovered and the plotters summarily executed. The German forces obeyed their orders, and so the week-long Battle of Vienna, from 6 to 13 April, was bloody and destructive. Even after this, German forces (including many Austrians) made a last stand at the Marchfeld. By 8 May, when American and Russian troops met on the Enns, most hostilities in eastern Austria were over, but firefights persisted. Hitler had committed suicide in his Berlin bunker on 30 April; Admiral Dönitz had signed Germany's unconditional surrender on 7 May.

It was only in the war's very last stages that the Austrian resistance became at all effective. It was on 13 April, after the fall of Vienna, that the resistance in western Austria, led by Karl Gruber, finalized their plans for rebellion, and it was only on 1 May that they decided to launch it. This duly took place the next day, and the German forces in western Austria capitulated. By the time American troops entered Innsbruck on 5 May, Gruber had taken over the city and the liberators were greeted by a crowd of red-white-red-flag-waving

Austrian patriots. The Nazi plans to make western Austria into an impregnable 'Alpine fortress' fizzled out for lack of materiel, manpower and local support. They did mean, however, that many prominent Nazis were captured in Austria, not Germany. Ernst Kaltenbrunner was caught in a cottage in Alt Aussee, an Alpine resort renowned for its associations with the (Jewish) literary stars of Vienna 1900.

The relative success of the resistance in western Austria was a sign of not so much the strength of Austrian patriotism as the sensible preference for American over Russian occupation. Thus it was that the Russians had to fight for every inch of Austrian soil, but the Americans met very little resistance, if any, with all 'Austrians' now willing the Americans to get to them before the Russians did.

Now that the pan-German identity of the Hitler Time was bankrupt, what could be the new identity of this group of formerly Austrian Germans? Would they remain German, or would they try something new, such as becoming, somehow, non-German Austrians? Conveniently, the Allied occupiers had a ready-made solution.

The exigencies of wartime propaganda and diplomacy, as well as the influence of some Austrian émigrés, had led the Allies to reassess the Austrian problem. Winston Churchill was particularly keen to reassert the idea of an independent Austria, partly on principles of self-determination, but largely because he thought the prospect of separate treatment might help undermine Austrians' new German loyalty. Churchill's promise to fight for Austria's 'liberation' in the Mansion House speech of November 1940 was thus not only a sop to émigrés' pleas, but also an exercise in *Realpolitik*.

The restoration of Austria became an agreed war aim in December 1941, after the entry of the Soviet Union and the United States. Although asserting, as Churchill did in February 1942, that Austria was the 'first victim of Nazi aggression' might be wishful thinking, it provided a carrot-and-stick approach to undermine Austrians' support for Hitler. The best-known formulation of this, key to Austria's subsequent future, was the Moscow Conference's declaration of 30 October. The declaration promised Austria's liberation from 'German domination' but had a quite stringent caveat: 'Austria is reminded, however, that she has a responsibility, which she cannot evade, for participation in the war at the side of Hitlerite Germany,

Illustration 39. Gerhart Frankl, 'The Watchtower', 1964. In the *In Memoriam* series.

and that in the final settlement account will inevitably be taken of her own contribution to her liberation.'

Initially the British draft of this had talked, more accurately, of the 'Austrian people' and not 'Austria', but the Soviets had insisted on 'Austria' to facilitate legal claims against a future Austrian state.

The British and Americans enabled Austrian émigrés to volunteer in the armed forces to fight for Austria's freedom (and beneficial treatment), and in late 1944 Austrian POWs and deserters were being organized to fight alongside the Slovenian resistance. The Allies clearly did not trust Austrian loyalty: in March 1945 Austrians were warned not to allow the Nazis to make the Alps their last redoubt, and the Yalta Conference of February 1945 saw Austria treated as a smaller version of Germany in terms of being divided into occupation zones. Yet the Allies' position officially remained that they were coming to liberate Austria from the German yoke. As General Tolbuchin, commander of the Soviet forces at Vienna, declared in late March 1945: 'the peaceful populace of Austria has nothing to fear'.

By the end of the war, much of what remained of Austria's inter-war political class was only too happy to accept the Allies' bargain. The German National camp had been totally compromised, and so were no longer a factor in *Austrian* politics. Catholic conservatives, by contrast, had always been for some sort of Austrian indepen-dence from the 'Protestant' German Republic, so their embrace of a truly independent Austria was relatively easy. The key group was Austria's socialists. In the interwar period *Anschluss* had remained socialist policy to 1933, and many remained in favour of it thereafter. The experience of Nazi rule changed this. The prominent post-war Austrian politician Adolf Schärf claimed to have stated in early 1943 to a German Social Democrat that 'Anschluss is dead.' Many of his comrades might still have disagreed with him then; a couple of years later, with a ruined Third Reich facing severe retribution from the Allies, Schärf's view had become virtually universal among Austrian socialists. In the wish for separation from the fate of Germany, and the return of an independent Austrian state, the two viable camps of Austrian politics, the Catholic conservatives and the socialists, now found themselves in novel agreement.

Thus it was that Renner, pre-1914 Austro-Marxist, first chancellor of the Austrian Republic, endorser of the *Anschluss* in 1938, but long since retired from public life, roused himself on 2 April 1945 to plead with the Russian invading forces at Hochwolkersdorf, and soon found himself agreeing to set up a provisional national government for an independent Austria, which was recognized by the Soviet occupying authorities on 27 April 1945.

Austria, as an independent nation-state, was going to have a sec-ond chance, not only at becoming a functioning polity, but also at creating a cogent identity. The Hitler Time had destroyed for Aus-trians the option of becoming once again German. Could Austrians now, with a little historiographical legerdemain and some help from the Allies, become – Austrian?

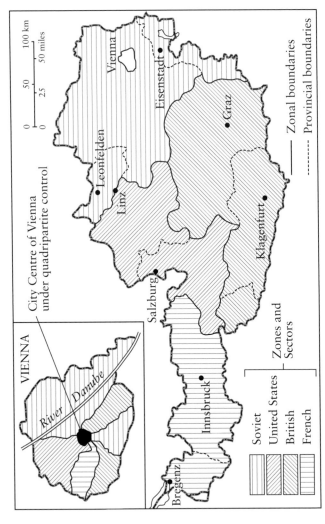

Map 7. The Allied occupation zones and the sectors of Vienna, 1945–1955

6

Austria Inc., from 1945

When the Republic of Austria was proclaimed restored on 27 April 1945 its land and people were in a state of utter disaster and moral degradation. Austrian participation in the Third Reich had had as its reward only physical, economic, moral and political ruin. Sixty years later, Austria is one of the world's most prosperous and secure countries. In 2006 it (again) held the presidency of the European Union. The phoenix-like rise of the Austrian Second Republic from the ashes of 1945 has been one of the most remarkable success stories of post-war Europe.

This transformation has not been without its setbacks, and some potentially tragic flaws. The economic prosperity and political cohesion of the Second Republic, so sorely missing in the First, were made possible partly by a socio-political pact that led to political stagnation, and partly by a conspiratorial manipulation of the Austrian past. This abuse of history helped cement Austrian national identity, at the expense of Austrian self-understanding. Austrians today are still living with the unsettling consequences.

In the chaotic days of May 1945, as American troops were invading Upper Austria, a teenage girl in Leonfelden heard a rap at the front door. She went to open the door, but on seeing an African-American GI, she was so shocked at his black face that she slammed the door shut and ran back upstairs. Nazi indoctrination and cultural prejudice made this reaction virtually inevitable. Yet people change, and there was no running away from the new reality of occupation.

According to the Allies, however, Austria was officially a *liberated* country that was being freed from *Nazi* occupation. While the Allied forces acted as occupiers, theoretically they were liberators. This ambivalence was of immense benefit to Austrians after 1945, for a liberated Austria was obviously far less responsible for *German* actions before 1945 than would be a conquered German province. A very convenient Austrian dual consciousness thus developed whereby the period from 1945 to the State Treaty of 1955 was called the 'occupation time', and 1955 the year in which Austria became free, whereas the founding myth of the Second Austrian Republic was that 1945 had been a liberation of Austria as 'the first victim of Nazi aggression'.

The Western Allies could be persuaded of this myth's truth, because they had created it, to coax Austrians away from Germany and enlist them in the developing Cold War. From this marriage of convenience between Austrian interest in avoiding the consequences of Austrians' misdeeds and Western Allied interest in reshaping the map of Europe was born the *Lebenslüge* (vital lie) that is central to post-war Austrian history.

By the First Control Agreement of 4 July 1945, the Allies put Austria under the control of an Allied Council, composed of four military commissioners. Distinct occupation zones were set by the agreement of 9 July. This resulted in some troop repositioning, with the Americans evacuating the Mühlviertel to make way for the Soviets, much to the dismay of Leonfeldeners. The French were handed Vorarlberg and the Tyrol; the Americans controlled Salzburg and Upper Austria south of the Danube; the British Carinthia, Styria and east Tyrol (pushing out Tito's Yugoslavs in the process); and the Soviets Upper Austria north of the Danube, Burgenland and Lower Austria. Vienna was divided between the four occupying powers in blocks of districts, with the inner city being jointly administered. This led to the four-man patrols made famous by their depiction in the film *The Third Man*. Although 'liberated', Austria looked on a map like a smaller version of occupied, 'guilty' Germany.

One of the Allies, the Soviet Union, also treated Austria as a conquered country. The Soviet military leadership did little to curb their

Illustration 40. Aryanization 2: The Riesenrad in the Prater. Originally built in 1897 for the amusement park 'Venice in Vienna', run by the Jewish entrepreneur Gabor Steiner; in 1938 the Riesenrad was 'Aryanized', stolen from its Jewish owner, who died at Auschwitz in 1944. Famous as the site for the scene in *The Third Man* (1949), when Harry Lime (Orson Welles) tells Holly Martin (Joseph Cotten) about the Borgias and the cuckoo clock.

troops' rape and pillage of the Austrian populace, with an estimated near 100,000 women raped in Vienna alone. The savagery
moderated in July, but the 'Russian zone' became notorious for
the brutality of its administration, and its ruthless, destructive economic policies. General Kurasov's 'Order No. 17' of 27 June 1946,
exploiting a loophole in the Potsdam Conference accords, effectively
confiscated large swathes of eastern Austria's economy, including
Lower Austria's oilfields, as 'formerly German assets'. It was the
exacting of reparations from Austria by other means, amounting to
$2–2.5 billion by 1955. Large amounts of machinery were shipped
to Russia, and the USIA (Administrative Authority of Soviet Assets
in Eastern Austria) became a hated and boycotted symbol of Russian
occupation.

The experience in the other occupation zones was quite different.
The French occupation in the far western provinces was very benev-
olent, and accordingly well received. The British, in the south, were
also appreciated, if only as protection against Yugoslav territorial
ambitions. The British zone was the scene of a disgraceful episode,
when the British handed over Cossack refugees to certain death at
Soviet hands, but that was not an Austrian concern. Otherwise, the
British did what they could to help in humanitarian relief and in the
resuscitation of the Austrian economy.

The most positive boost was provided by the Americans. Though
initially suspicious of the 'liberated' Austrians, they soon adopted
the positive approach of Britain and France, and the Truman administration became Austria's foremost benefactor. From August 1945
the Americans had advocated emergency humanitarian relief to 'liberated' Austria, and Herbert Hoover was (once more) in Vienna in
April 1946 to organize relief efforts. The UNRRA food relief was
vital in tiding over the Austrian populace in 1946 and the cruel winter of 1946–7, when the Austrian economy was brought to a virtual
halt.

The Marshall Plan, first articulated in June 1947, was central to
Austria's future prosperity. Over the next few years Austria received
from the European Recovery Program roughly $1 billion (at a rate
of $137 per capita, compared with West Germany at $19 per capita).
Over half of these funds were invested in industrial and infrastruc-
tural projects such as the Kaprun dam. This was the financial basis

Illustration 41. Occupation powers, September 1955. The
'four-men-in-a-jeep' became a symbol of post-war occupation.

for Austria's spectacular economic take-off. In the same summer of
1947 the Americans also forewent the payment for occupation costs
and reimbursed the Austrian government more than $300 million
charged to that point.

Western benevolence towards Austria was heavily influenced by
the onset of the Cold War, and Austria's pivotal position between
'East' and 'West'. In the critical period 1947–8 there were fears of
the Soviet Union instituting a permanent division of eastern Austria
from the western part. Fortunately, it remained content with bleed-
ing its sector dry, while the Americans pumped capital into theirs.
American solicitude for the communist-threatened Italian government may have contributed to Austria's failure to regain South
Tyrol in 1946, but containment of communism was also the main
reason for the economic support that set in train Austria's post-war
success.

Austrian leaders made the most of the propitious circumstances
created by the Cold War. As early as September 1945, the new

provincial leaders in the Western zones agreed to unite with the 'national' government set up in Vienna by Renner, thus presenting a united Austrian front to the occupying powers. The success of national elections on 25 November cemented the new government's legitimacy and helped persuade the Allies early on to grant Austrians a large degree of autonomy. The Second Control Agreement of 28 June 1946 left the Allied Council in a largely supervisory role. It retained a veto over Austrian legislation, but only if all four powers agreed, greatly reducing the threat of Russian obstruction. Hence, when in July 1946 the Austrian parliament responded to the Soviet grab for the 'formerly German assets' by nationalizing the main banks and most heavy industry, the Russians could only protest – and ignore the law in their zone.

The united Austrian front was not only across zones, but also between the socialists and the conservatives. Both reconstituted themselves, with some changes. The socialists changed their name, from the Social Democratic Party to the Socialist Party of Austria (SPÖ), a gesture towards the Revolutionary Socialists who had persevered 'illegally' after 1934. For the Christian Socials, the changes in 1945 were much more radical. Relinquishing their formerly close Church ties to facilitate a rallying of conservative and capitalist forces, the Christian Socials' successors reconstructed themselves as something new for Austria, the Austrian People's Party (ÖVP), a secular conservative party on Western lines.

From Renner's provisional government in April 1945 these two parties provided the core Austrian leadership. At first, circumstances (Russian forces) dictated that they share power with the communists (KPÖ), but in the autumn of 1945 the Western provincial leaders joined the government, and the November election, where the KPÖ received only 5 per cent of the votes, left the communists only a vestigial governmental presence. With National Socialists banned from the elections, this left the ÖVP with 50 per cent and the SPÖ with 45 per cent. As after the First World War, the two parties formed a government of national unity on 20 December, with Leopold Figl of the ÖVP as chancellor, and Adolf Schärf as vice chancellor; this time, however, the Grand Coalition proved to be much more successful and substantial.

As a matter of course, both parties completely rejected any German identity for Austria. The enthusiastic support of many Austrians, including Renner, for *Anschluss* was elided from the collective memory in a wave of political amnesia. The two camps also rejected divisive interwar politics. Whether or not it was the legendary 'spirit of the camp street', the shared experience of being inmates of Nazi concentration camps, that taught the party leaders the virtues of co-operation, a new, co-operative practice did indeed typify Austrian politics after 1945.

Both parties remained powerful. Party membership grew rapidly, with more than 500,000 in each party by 1955, with both parties again having complex organizational structure and wielding substantial power. Neither party much trusted the other, but this was addressed brilliantly by the complex (and secret) agreement between the two parties to exclude the communists from any real power after the November 1945 elections. It split up power at the centre, in the provinces and the municipalities, in great detail, on the principle of *Proporz*, proportionality reflecting party strength. There was a system of checks and balances, whereby, for instance, each minister was balanced by an under-secretary of the other party, and any disputes were referred to a coalition committee, as were upcoming bills, before they reached parliament. Once the hard-headed realists on both sides saw the need for collaboration, the system of *Proporz* provided a form of mutually assured power. Thus was born the 'Austrian way'.

Proporz became the basis of not only politics but also Austria's economy. A complex neo-corporatist system developed around the two parties. Agriculture and business were organized into associations in the ÖVP camp, while labour was organized into unions largely in the SPÖ camp. Most major economic policies were decided behind closed doors by the respective interests and then rubber-stamped by parliament. Initially there were some hiccoughs, such as the attempted general strike of September 1950, but generally this co-operative corporatist approach ensured a remarkable level of industrial peace, and was a major boost to prosperity. The 'social partnership' of capital and labour formed a parallel economic complement to the political Grand Coalition that made parliamentary politics at most secondary. The Second Republic resembled more a corporation, Austria Inc., than a parliamentary democracy.

The corollary of this political neo-corporatism was a narrowing and ethnicization of Austrian identity. The rejection of German identity did not result in a return to the supra-national, cosmopolitan and pluralist, 'old' Austrian identity of the Monarchy. That identity was occasionally employed to burnish Austria's image with the Western Allies, and Austria gratefully accepted membership in the United Nations. Yet supra-nationality was not something that the new, *national* Austria much wanted.

There was a closing of ranks after 1945. Austrians wanted to be left to work out their differences 'among ourselves', and national neo-corporatism necessitated, apparently, the sort of integral national coherence that only a narrow and exclusive, quasi-ethnic form of identity provided.

Identity was admittedly a complex subject in a post-war Austria where thousands were in transit. Not only were there the occupying forces; there were also the many non-Austrian Germans who had come after 1938, and were now forced to return to 'Germany' (though many were allowed to stay); there were also the captured German soldiers, and a remarkable assortment of displaced persons (DPs), running the gamut from Nazis to former concentration camp inmates, including many Jews such as Leon Zelman, who had barely survived the mass murder of the Shoah. The Allied forces, in the confusion of the time, sometimes put war criminals and Holocaust survivors in the same camp.

Then there were Austrians who had also been uprooted or captured. Austrian POWs generally benefited from being regarded as not German, and were released earlier than their German comrades-in-arms. The Western Allies had repatriated all their Austrian POWs by mid-1947. The Russians were slower, and conditions in the POW camps there were often awful, but even so Russian-held Austrian POWs were released earlier than Germans, with half back by 1948, and the rest by late 1956.

The new Austrian nation also accommodated many Germans who had been uprooted from east-central and south-eastern Europe. *Donauschwaben* (Danube Swabians), who had lived in the lower Danube valley for centuries, were forced out and some were accepted in Austria; similarly, the Germans in Czechoslovakia were expelled en masse and many were allowed to settle in Austria. One family from Krumlov settled in Leonfelden and found employment with a sympathetic family. These 'German Bohemians', as 'old' Austrians, became new Austrians. There were some exceptions, but the criterion for who belonged in the new Austria had a distinctly ethnic German – and antisemitic – tinge, as the differing approaches to Jewish émigrés and former Nazis make plain.

The new Austria presented a united front *against* Austria's Jewish exiles. It is true that many Jewish émigrés had no intention of returning to an Austria with which they could only associate persecution, hatred and terror; it is also true that there were exceptions, where Jews did return and were accepted, though usually only if they were prepared to accept the new Austrian dispensation, with its myths of innocence and victimhood. Yet the number who returned was very small, a few thousand, and it is clear now that this absence of return was actively encouraged by the Austrian government.

In a cabinet meeting of November 1948, in a discussion about an American request to facilitate the funding of the return of Jewish émigrés, Oskar Helmer, the socialist interior minister, averred: 'Ich bin dafür die Sache in die Länge zu ziehen' (I am for dragging the issue out).[1] This became official (if covert) government policy towards Austria's Jews. Gestures were made, the Austrian government went through the motions of compensation and restitution, but usually Jewish victims were referred to the German government for compensation, for impecunious Austria could not compensate people for acts for which it, as victim of German aggression, was not responsible. 'Austria', as a state, had not even existed between 1938 and 1945, so how could it be held responsible for another state's actions? And so Austrian Jews were given the runaround.

Many 'normal' Austrians resented Jewish émigrés for having sat out the war abroad and then expecting special treatment on their return, when Austrians had had to suffer the war. The same 'normal' Austrians outwardly distanced themselves from the Third Reich (though polls from 1948 show more than a third still supported

---

[1] Hella Pick, *Guilty Victim: Austria from the Holocaust to Haider* (London, 2000), pp. 206–7.

National Socialism in Vienna, and more than 40 per cent in Salzburg).[2] Yet they happily accepted the many material benefits that the Third Reich had brought to Austria, and one of these was the absence of Jews, and the transfer of so much Jewish property to 'Aryans' ('normal' Austrians). The government's resistance to Jewish claims thus rested on broad popular support.

The Austrian state had been quick after 1945 to nationalize 'formerly German assets', which were largely wartime Nazi investments. It had also benefited directly from the looting of Jewish property. The Austrian Gallery in the Belvedere happily regarded as legal the many 'acquisitions' of the Nazi period, even if many had been stolen from Jewish owners. The Austrian state rejected the Nazi heritage and at the same time accepted its material inheritance.

Austrian treatment of former Nazis stood in stark contrast to that of Jewish émigrés. Initial attempts at de-Nazification and punishment of war criminals were quite harsh, but disorganized and ineffective. In November 1945 more uniform procedures were instituted according to the two laws passed by the Provisional Government, the Prohibition of National Socialism Law (May 1945) and the War Criminals Law (June 1945), and the Austrian government was put in charge of de-Nazification, under Allied supervision. Over the course of 1946, 537,000 Nazi Party members were registered, including about 100,000 'illegals', party members from before March 1938, who were seen as real traitors as opposed to the mere conformists and opportunists who joined afterwards. People's courts were set up, and more than 136,000 investigations were started, resulting in the indictments of 28,148 and the conviction of 13,607. Of these, 43 were sentenced to death.

Allied military courts in Austria sentenced many more war criminals to death, and Austrian de-Nazification efforts soon slowed. The sheer numbers of registered ex-Nazis clogged up the system, especially as almost 90 per cent appealed for exceptional status. In February 1947 a new National Socialists Law was passed that provided for punishment according to party rank, with two major categories: 'incriminated' and 'lesser incriminated', with only 42,000

---

[2] Ernst Hanisch, *Der lange Schatten des Staates: Österreichische Geschichte, 1890–1990* (Vienna, 1994), p. 422.

in the former group. Any stringency in this law was only there as a result of Allied insistence. In 1948 an amnesty for the 'lesser incriminated' effectively ended mass de-Nazification. Trials of war criminals continued, and the 'incriminated' group had to wait until the 1957 National Socialist Amnesty Law for full relief, but after 1948 there had been a steep decline in cases brought. The people's courts were terminated in 1955, and thereafter war criminals were tried by jury, with a paltry eighteen convictions out of only thirty-nine cases.

The precipitous decline in cases was a result of Austria's changing circumstances. The Cold War distracted the occupying powers from the old enemy, and discouraged them from prosecuting potential allies against the new one. The amnesty of 1948 similarly gave the two main Austrian parties more incentive to gain the allegiance of the 480,000 amnestied Nazis than to preserve any ideological purity. The emergence of the Union of Independents (VdU) in early 1949, largely composed of ex-Nazis and nationalist 'liberals', added to the pressure to compete for this influential voting bloc.

Most Austrians came to see the former Nazis as having been victimized. According to the public perception, most Nazis had become party members in a banal conformist and careerist way, or had simply been following the party's 'invitation' (a *de facto* command) to join. They had been *coerced* into enjoying the advantages of party membership, just as Austria itself had been *forced* to enjoy the material benefits of the Third Reich. If Austria was a victim of German Nazism, then even Austrian Nazis were only really *victims*, as Austrians, of the Germans. Hence the Allies were persecuting upstanding Austrians, who just happened to have been Nazi Party members. And many ex-Nazis, such as the influential Heimito von Doderer, were now falling over themselves to prove their new-found Austrian loyalty. While Jews were resented as being the protégés of the 'liberators', the ex-Nazis were quickly accepted as part of the new Austrian nation: an ex-Nazi was 'one of us' in ways that a Jewish concentration camp survivor was not.

Austrians came to depend on the myth of victimhood to free themselves from their past and their 'liberators'. The Austrian leadership united behind Foreign Minister Karl Gruber's policy of responding to reparation claims from countries such as Yugoslavia, Poland and Greece, where Austrians in the SS and Wehrmacht had indeed participated in horrific military actions, by protesting Austrian innocence and victimhood. Gruber played up Austria's status as the 'first victim of Nazi aggression' and emphasized the heroic resistance of individual Austrians. The small detail that Austrian society generally had been *supportive* of Hitler and his regime was discarded. The victimhood strategy worked: reparation demands were dropped.

It took much longer to persuade the Allies to end the occupation. Negotiations started in early 1947, but eight years passed before the State Treaty was signed. The Soviets had a special incentive for delay in their continuing economic exploitation of eastern Austria, but the main stumbling block was the Cold War stand-off that developed, with neither the Western Allies nor the Soviets prepared to risk strategically placed Austria going over to the other side. Events in Czechoslovakia and Berlin in 1948 only added to Western fears about Austrian susceptibility to a communist coup. Soviet intransigence prevented a deal in 1949, and it was not until the death of Stalin in 1953 that Austria's diplomatic situation began to thaw.

To solve the East–West stand-off, Julius Raab, Austrian chancellor from 1953, began to explore the idea of Austria becoming a non-aligned or neutral country, on the Swiss model. While it still took adroit manoeuvring and luck to extricate Austria from the diplomatic thicket of the Cold War, especially the German problem, this formula eventually broke the logjam. The emergence of Nikita Khrushchev as Soviet leader in 1955, and his initial drive to improve relations with the West, greatly helped Austria. Against Western advice, Raab went to Moscow in April and soon enough emerged with a mutually acceptable agreement, built around Austria's promise to declare itself (separately from the State Treaty) a neutral country. The State Treaty was formally signed on 15 May 1955 at the Upper Belvedere Palace by the foreign ministers of the four powers and Austria.

Three months after the State Treaty was signed, the occupation troops had left. On 26 October 1955, the Austrian parliament, as promised, passed the law of permanent (armed) neutrality. The State Treaty also had a provision to recompense the Soviet Union $150 million for the 'returned' German assets, paid for largely in the form of oil shipments for years after.

Illustration 42. 'Austria is free': State Treaty, 15 May 1955.
Balcony of the Upper Belvedere. The most famous scene in
post-war Austrian history. In this version, Harold Macmillan
(British foreign minister) accepts the applause of the crowd.
To his left, in order: Llewellyn Thompson (US ambassador);
John Foster Dulles (US secretary of state); Antoine Pinay
(French foreign minister); Leopold Figl (Austrian foreign
minister); Adolf Schärf (Austrian vice-chancellor); Vyacheslav
Molotov (Soviet foreign minister); Julius Raab (Austrian
chancellor).

The State Treaty achieved the freeing of Austria from its occupiers, and neutrality, though forced on Austria by circumstance,
also helped free Austria from any remaining wish to rejoin Germany.
Neutrality could have its disadvantages, as Austria was to discover
in the economic sphere, but it provided real independence – for the
first time. The State Treaty also managed, at the last moment, to
free Austria from its more immediate past even under international
law. Almost as an afterthought, in the spirit of letting bygones be
bygones, the Allies agreed to let the clause concerning 'Austrian
responsibility for her participation in World War II', upheld ever
since 1943, be omitted.

Austria ended the occupation on the basis of airbrushing out the horrors of its past, for the sake of its future social harmony, political unity, economic prosperity and new Austrian *national* identity. Even its neutrality was a stepping aside from the Cold War, making Austria a free rider of the West. Both the political amnesia and the international passivity were condoned, even demanded, by the occupiers, but they were also warmly embraced by most Austrians. Individual Austrians might try to counter the consensual repression of the past, but they were far outnumbered by those happy to conform to the new, Allied-sanctioned dispensation, even if, at a deeper level of Austrian collective memory, few really forgot about what had actually happened.

GETTING RICH, 1955–1970

In hindsight we can see that Austria was set fair in 1955 to become by the 1970s a model of prosperity and domestic peace for other countries to emulate. It did not always look that way at the time.

In 1950 there had been a major industrial crisis, instigated by VdU members, and turned by the communists in Vienna into a general strike in October, but the strike had failed. In 1952 the economy had again been in trouble with runaway inflation, but the austere Raab–Kamitz economic reforms and the introduction of the 'social market economy' ushered in a sustained economic boom. In 1956 there was revolution and Soviet suppression in neighbouring Hungary, but there was no invasion of neutral Austria, and 180,000 Hungarian refugees found sanctuary there, many fleeing over the Neusiedler Lake. Austria's image in the West benefited. The East–West summit of Khrushchev and Kennedy in Vienna in 1961 further burnished Austria's image as a bridge between the two ideological camps. (Vienna also served as an important entrepôt in the Cold War's spyworld.)

In 1957 Chancellor Raab suffered a heart attack, but he recovered; in the same year Adolf Schärf was elected president, succeeding Theodor Körner. In trade policy, the creation of the European Economic Community (EEC) in 1957–8 raised concerns that Austria would be excluded from its markets because of its neutrality; but in 1960 Austria joined the European Free Trade Area (EFTA) instead.

In 1962, and again in 1967, recession provoked fears that Austria's economic rise was at an end, but the economy was restructured and growth resumed.

Along the way there were frequent alarums at the corruption of the '*Packelei*' (logrolling) of the '*Proporz* democracy', and ever more frequent spats within the Grand Coalition between the ÖVP as senior partner and the SPÖ as junior. Both parties played with the idea of a 'small coalition' with the only other significant party, the Freedom Party (FPÖ), successor to the VdU and hence largely representing the interests of former Nazis, with some libertarian capitalists thrown in. Yet neither the old guard of the ÖVP nor the socialist leadership ever took the bait. So the politics of compromise went on, and on.

The SPÖ did collaborate with the FPÖ on one issue: the Habsburgs. Otto Habsburg's renunciation of his claims on Austrian sovereignty and his request to visit his historic homeland led to socialist outrage when the Administrative Court adjudicated in 1963 that Otto should be allowed entry. Backed by the FPÖ (anti-Habsburg at this time), they claimed a judicial hijacking of Austrian democracy, while the ÖVP countered that this was the rule of law in action. Eventually Otto was persuaded not to come to Austria.

After 1963 there were major power struggles within both parties, which redounded to the ÖVP's advantage. The victory of Josef Klaus in the 1966 election introduced the innovation of one-party government, but only marginally affected *Proporz* and the social partnership. There were various scandals involving building contractors, some ex-Nazi professors at the university, and an increasingly restive and left-wing student body. That was about as exciting as it got in Austrian politics in this era.

There were just no serious and long-lasting crises that could not be overcome by mutually agreed readjustments. High economic growth and the Grand Coalition's political stability reinforced each other to produce spectacular improvements in Austrian productivity and Austrians' standard of living. In 1955 alone the economy grew by 11.5 per cent, and by 1959 GDP per capita was double that of 1937. The expansion moderated after that, but the average annual growth rate of GDP from 1953 to 1962 was still 6.4 per cent.

Austria undoubtedly piggy-backed on the even greater growth in West Germany, but Austrian prosperity also had many internal causes. A leading factor was technological innovation, especially in industries that had benefited most from development by the Third Reich. The invention in 1949 of the 'Linz–Donawitz Process' for making high-quality steel made the VOEST steelworks in Linz (once the Göring Werke) the top-performing steel producer in the world. It was the basic, nationalized industries that led the economic boom of the 1950s. Part of this was a result of large infrastructure investments encouraged by the Marshall Plan. Yet most investment was internally generated: the investment rate, 17 per cent in the 1950s, 23 per cent in the 1960s, surpassed that of most European states. The nationalized industries themselves, organized on business lines, displayed high levels of enterprise.

The interaction of economics and politics in the nationalized sector, unlike in Britain, was beneficial. The social partnership, though informal and extra-constitutional, became an entrenched part of the polity, in such quasi-official, shadow institutions as the Parity Commission from 1957, and the Board for Economic and Social Questions from 1963. The pact between unions, business and the political parties produced rising living standards and an ever more elaborate welfare state. In 1955 a comprehensive social insurance law was passed; in 1959 the 45-hour work week was introduced; in 1964 the three-week holiday. Austria's neutrality helped here, because the resulting low levels of defence spending allowed more resources for social goods, and reinvestment.

Austria's economic success was primarily down to its industrial sector, but the other major area of spectacular growth had more impact on Austria's image abroad: tourism. Especially in the western Alpine provinces, tourism was a major engine of growth. In 1951 there were 17 million overnight stays in Austria, by 1966 64 million.

Austria's tourism industry benefited immensely from newly prosperous German visitors, but its flourishing was also the result of conscious, politically motivated encouragement of tourism as the engine of growth. Interwar conservatives had been attracted to tourism for its promise of prosperity without social or cultural modernity, and now, in the 1950s, this fitted well with the new, conservative self-image of Austrians as a peace-loving, orderly, church-going, happy-go-lucky people. This made an ironic, but strangely effective complement to the very hard-nosed, class-based, social partnership. The touristic image of Austria was both economically productive, and an important part of the new national identity.

Part of this identity hearkened back to the old image of Austria as a land of culture, especially musical culture, which greatly helped Austrians ingratiate themselves with post-war foreigners. The 1947 tour of Britain by the Vienna Philharmonic and the Vienna Opera was not only an artistic triumph, but also a diplomatic coup, suggesting as it did the rebirth of cultural Austria. The fact that of the fifty members of the Philharmonic who had been Nazi Party members only five were sacked and that the Jewish former members were mostly not invited back escaped notice.

Austrian cultural heritage was dusted off, and a nostalgia for Habsburg Austria was promoted, embodied in figures such as Heimito von Doderer. What was not encouraged was anything too radical. Artists such as Fritz Wotruba, Ingeborg Bachmann and Ilse Aichinger challenged the post-war 'conservative paradigm', but they were largely ignored, as was the more radical side of Vienna 1900's heritage, along with the memory of that culture's wilful destruction. In October 1945 schools in Upper Austria were directed to destroy the school chronicles from the period 1938–45 and rewrite them.

High culture remained important to Austrian identity, but in a conservative, safe version. Even when Friedrich Torberg, a returned Jewish émigré, set up the literary magazine *Forum* in 1954 with CIA money, he ended up playing the Austrian game, emphasizing an anti-avant garde model of 'culture', and exercising severe self-restraint over the Nazi past. The Vienna State Opera reopened on 5 November 1955 with *Fidelio* (conducted by the opera house's director, then and during the Nazi era, Karl Böhm), but the play chosen for the Burgtheater's reopening on 15 October was the more telling choice: Franz Grillparzer's *König Ottokars Glück und Ende*, a product of the Biedermeier time, and most famous for its patriotic hymn to the wonders of the Austrian landscape, Austria as the land of tourism. The figure that was to embody the new Austrian high culture was the maestro of the Salzburg Festival, Herbert von Karajan. Karajan, Böhm's successor as Vienna State Opera director and another former Nazi, survived his Nazi past quite handily, and set about turning himself into a high-cultural, media-savvy superstar and the Salzburg Festival into a forum for the harmless, if technically brilliant rendering of the classical canon: 'motorized Biedermeier'.

Salzburg now outshone Vienna on the stage of international high culture. Eastern Austria had been held back by the Soviet occupation. The Cold War's closing off of Vienna's Central European hinterland also shifted momentum to Austria's western provinces. The context of Austrian high culture changed. Instead of the urban, relatively sophisticated and modern context of Vienna 1900, Austrians now presented themselves to the outside world as a rustic, Alpine people. Austrian high culture was tied to, and largely displaced by, a banal popular culture.

'Austria' became a winter sports wonderland, an image strongly promoted by the Innsbruck Winter Olympics of 1964. The incipient interwar rustication of Austrian identity proceeded apace, with folk costumes, *Trachten*, *Lederhosen* and *Dirndl*, sold proudly as the epitome of Austrian fashion. Tourists were treated to exhibitions of Alpine entertainments such as yodelling and the *Schuhplattler* dance, and came away thinking that this was Austrian culture. It was as if Mozart's hero in *The Magic Flute* was really Papageno.

Austria's touristic image was supported by Broadway and Hollywood. In 1959 Rodgers and Hammerstein's *The Sound of Music* was a smash hit on Broadway. It recounted the highly sentimental story of Maria von Trapp's journey from apprentice nun to political émigré. In 1965 the film version was released and became an even bigger hit. The film was a cinematographic ode to Salzburg and the surrounding Austrian Alpine landscape. It told a personalized version of 'plucky little Austria's' struggle against the German Nazis, and it set in concrete the positive image of Austria in the West.

The one place where the film was not such a great hit was Austria. The story's Catholic and conservative viewpoint would not have appealed in socialist and anti-clerical circles, especially in Vienna, and while foreigners might see the film as praising Austrian resistance to Hitler, Austrians may have noted that the Nazis in the film were Austrians, and that the hero and heroine end up *leaving* Austria in 1938.

The film, for all its sentimentalizing, could be seen as an unwelcome reminder of a past about which the Austrian public remained

Illustration 43. 'Der Herr Karl'. Helmut Qualtinger's most notorious and brilliant performance, an evisceration of the post-war Austrian consensus, was broadcast on Austrian television on 15 November 1961.

extremely touchy. In 1961 the cabaret duo Carl Merz and Helmut Qualtinger wrote a satirical monologue with Qualtinger as *Der Herr Karl*, broadcast on Austrian television. It was a biting satire on the perverse illogic that Austrian Nazi collaborators had employed to rationalize their actions; the outraged viewing public saw it as an attack on themselves, and, as it did skewer the myth of national victimhood, their reaction proved them right.

The filming of *The Sound of Music* itself occasioned a display of the dual consciousness of post-war Austria. Permission was requested to film the entry of German troops in the Residenzplatz, but the authorities refused, arguing that Salzburgers, as staunch anti-Nazis, would be outraged at seeing Nazi paraphernalia displayed. When the film-makers proposed using newsreel from 1938 instead, showing crowds of Salzburgers greeting the German troops with Hitler salutes, the authorities relented, with the proviso that no cheering crowds be shown.

Austrians presented a happy and welcoming face to Western visitors, but they remained wary of the more radical and progressive trends in Western thought and culture. That same thought and culture had meanwhile been shaped to a large degree by Austrian émigrés.

Philosophy had been radically reshaped by Ludwig Wittgenstein and émigré members of the Vienna Circle of Logical Positivism, as well as Karl Popper. Arnold Schoenberg, in Los Angeles, led modern musical theory, while his fellow Austrian Billy Wilder became one of Hollywood's greatest directors. Psychology continued to be heavily influenced by Austrian émigrés, including Anna Freud. Hans Kelsen, at Berkeley, was influential in legal theory; there were many influential economists, including Friedrich Hayek and Joseph Schumpeter. In England especially the Austrian and 'Central European' émigrés, such as Ernst Gombrich and George Weidenfeld, played a key role in the development of modern British culture.

It was not only the stars of the émigré firmament that made such a large impact, but all the lesser known figures, in film, television, theatre, music, business, the various universities and centres of higher education, and also as physicians, research scientists, journalists, German teachers in secondary schools, such as Jan and Herta Palme, who conveyed to their pupils not only the German language but also the great values of the progressive Central European culture in which they had been raised. Hampstead became synonymous with not only intellectual sophistication but also the cosmopolitanism of émigré life, and in this world Austrians played a significant role.

Back in Austria, the Austrians who had stayed in 1938 did very little to embrace this vibrant émigré society and culture. There were attempts to create closer intellectual and cultural ties between the West and the new Austria. The Salzburg Seminar, set up by the émigré Clemens Heller immediately after the war (in the Leopoldskron Palace that had been Max Reinhardt's home and served as the main film set for *The Sound of Music*), became a prestigious forum of international discussion, and did help relations between leading Austrians and their foreign counterparts. Yet most Austrians remained oblivious to its existence. The Alpbach European Forum also facilitated mutual understanding, but it too remained an elite concern. The strands of Austrian culture and thought slashed in the 1930s were inadequately repaired, even as the Salzburg Festival created a conservative cosmopolitanism safe for Austrians.

Some perceptive Austrians decried this neglect of the progressive part of Austria's heritage, in which, as Friedrich Heer insisted, Jews had been so central, and of which the émigrés were now the main representatives. Most Austrians were content at the absence of the troublemakers, and happier to welcome tourists instead.

Leonfelden offers a good example of how tourism could transform the fate of a small Austrian village. Stuck in the remote Mühlviertel, occupied by the Soviets until 1955, cut off from its hinterland to the north, with no spectacular Alpine scenery, Leonfelden appeared unlikely to share in Austria's new-found prosperity. In 1960, however, five of the village's businessmen hit on a remarkably successful solution. In the eighteenth century Leonfelden had been known for the miraculous curative properties of the water at the Bründlkirche, and in the 1880s a nascent spa business had developed. The First World War had brought this to an end, but what if Leonfelden could now rebuild the spa, on modern lines? Linz, the rapidly growing centre of Austrian heavy industry, was fairly close, and there was increasing demand for spa-based water treatments in Austria and also West Germany.

The businessmen formed a company and sought help from the provincial government, which provided subsidies and granted Leonfelden spa status, so that it became Bad Leonfelden in 1962. The new Kurhaus, built on the edge of the forest in the modern Bauhaus style, opened the same year. It followed the balneological practices of the German Sebastian Kneipp, and was an instant success, especially with Germans. By 1990 the Kurhaus's clientele had increased tenfold from 1962.

The Kurhaus's success revived the rest of the village, and made it into a holidaying spot in its own right. Kastner's Café Konditorei gained a regional reputation for its excellent pastries and gingerbread, and became a favourite goal of families from Linz for their Sunday drive. By 1970 the Leonfeldeners were already talking of their ages-old entrepreneurial talent, even if their economic success was based on German and Austrian health tourists using their state-subsidized health benefits, daytrippers from Linz's nationalized industries, and significant economic state aid.

As Bad Leonfelden's success illustrates, Austria's neo-corporatist system could be very enterprising, and nationally there was a continuous, steep rise in the standard of living, and in the quality of life. There was a huge increase in automobile ownership: 6 per thousand in 1949, 151 per thousand in 1969; there was a housing boom: 450,000 units were built in the 1960s, a 25 per cent increase. The car involved might only be a tiny Steyr-Daimler-Puch, but it was a car; the apartment might be in an ugly concrete block, but it was one's own. Soon enough there was a better car, and a refurbished apartment. Life was getting really quite good by the mid-1960s.

By then, however, the system was beginning to flag. Its undemocratic corporatism was increasingly seen as inappropriate for modern Austria. The Grand Coalition could still achieve major compromises, such as the school reform law of 1962, but such successes were becoming frustratingly rare. The motor of Austrian post-war success was now seen as blocking 'healthy' political development.

The passing of the political old guard also loosened the bonds forged after 1945. Raab retired as chancellor in 1961 and in both parties a new generation of more highly educated and technically trained officials began asserting themselves. Modernization, from neo-corporatism to 'techno-corporatism', became the goal of Austrian politics. The question was which party would get there first, and take the leap into the uncharted waters of parliamentary, one-party government.

Franz Olah's unsuccessful play for the SPÖ leadership in 1964 and his subsequent split from the party left it poorly prepared for the national elections of 1966. It was therefore the ÖVP, with its new, modernizing leader, Josef Klaus, chancellor since 1964, that won the 1966 election in a landslide (for Austria's proportional representation system): 48 per cent of the popular vote and a majority of five (ÖVP: 85; SPÖ: 76; FPÖ: 4) in the parliament.

For the first time since the war, the ÖVP chose to govern alone. This was less radical than it appears, for *Proporz* was so woven into the fabric of the Austrian polity that it continued more or less undisturbed outside of the central ministerial positions. Klaus's technocratic approach, putting policy decisions in the hands of experts rather than politicians, also meant that this foray into democratic politics remained a typically Austrian 'enlightenment from above'.

Nevertheless, Klaus's government was serious about modernization. It poured resources into new housing. Austria's university system was greatly expanded, including new universities at Salzburg and Linz. Austria's student numbers, 20,000 in 1955, were to reach 175,000 by 1985. Foundations and institutions for academic research were also created to burnish Austria's profile as a modern, technologically and intellectually advanced nation.

Yet the Klaus government was not a political success. It lost the 1970 elections and a revived SPÖ became the largest party, with 81 seats. Klaus's regime suffered the Heathite fate of just not being modern enough. The recession of 1967 was partly to blame: the austerity package introduced in response by finance minister Stephan Koren limited the modernization programme, and although it proved extremely successful, leading to another extended boom, that helped not Klaus, but his successor. A larger problem was Klaus's image of 'Oberlehrer' to the nation, a sort of moralistic Josephist professor, media-shy to boot, which no longer matched the rapidly changing times. The new generation of university students were no longer the docile ÖVP supporters of the 1950s but shared the left-wing leanings of their Western counterparts.

Even the Catholic Church, in the wake of the Second Vatican Council (1962–5), was in a state of progressive change. An Austrian cleric, Franz König, archbishop of Vienna from 1956 and cardinal from 1958, played a key role in the Council's considerations, and brought an openness to change, and the political Left, that was new to the Austrian Church. The hierarchy's leftward shift reflected Austrian society as a whole. Embracing the West's new consumerism and permissiveness, many Austrians no longer tolerated being lectured at by moralizing modernizers. Klaus, it turned out, was only the harbinger of the new modern Austrian politics; its real master was to be Bruno Kreisky.

ISLAND OF THE BLESSED, 1970–1985

In November 1971, the Austrian president, Franz Jonas, undertook the first state visit of an Austrian head of state to Italy. This marked a major transition in Austria's post-war position, following the resolution of the South Tyrol question. South Tyroleans, and Austrians, had felt 'tricked' by the Italians ever since shortly after the 1946 Gruber–De Gasperi agreement, when Italy had undermined the intended guarantee of (German-speaking) South Tyrolean autonomy by the administrative merger of South Tyrol with Italian-speaking Trentino. Resentment against Italy had even led to terrorist attacks. Under a 1969 agreement, however, the South Tyroleans were finally guaranteed real autonomy, while remaining within Italy. Shortly thereafter Italy lifted its veto on Austria's negotiations with the EEC, and only a few months after the state visit, in July 1972, Austria was to sign a free trade agreement with the EEC that made it an informal economic member.

The state visit to Italy was followed by a state visit to the Vatican. In his audience with Jonas, Pope Paul VI talked of Austria as 'an island of the blessed'.

This papal praise for Austria was understandable. Heavily Catholic Austrian society was still relatively conservative, the Church still a weighty factor in national life. The neo-corporatist social partnership exemplified Catholic teachings on economic organization, and had produced an enviable degree of social peace. Largely unaffected by the turmoil of 1968 in the West, or the Soviet suppression of the Prague Spring in neighbouring Czechoslovakia, Austria had become a haven from the Cold War's storms, literally in the case of 96,000 Czech refugees.

Papal praise for the *status quo* also implied, however, that the SPÖ, which had just a month before gained an absolute parliamentary majority, should not too radically change what was already working so well. The new government, for all its left-wing rhetoric, was happy to oblige. There would be moments of concern for conservatives with the socialists' agenda of social liberalization and democratization, but overall changes were moderate. The SPÖ continued the 'Austrian way' of social partnership and *Proporz*, collaboration and consensus, in more than a decade of prosperity and peace so dominated by its leader, Bruno Kreisky, that it has become known as the Kreisky era.

As the irony of Austrian history would have it, Kreisky came from the Viennese Jewish bourgeoisie destroyed after 1938. Born in

Vienna in 1911, Kreisky had joined the Social Democratic Party in 1926, and was imprisoned by Schuschnigg's regime in 1935–6. From 1938 to 1945 he was a refugee in Sweden. After the war Kreisky became a prominent foreign policy maker in the coalition government, and from 1959 to 1966 foreign minister. Kreisky had played a central role in the eminently successful elaboration of Austrian neutrality. He was also a parliamentary deputy from 1956. Nevertheless, his background as a diplomat and the scion of a Jewish bourgeois family made him an outsider within the socialist ranks. It was the fiasco of the 1966 election campaign that gave Kreisky the opportunity to present himself as the 'modern' candidate to rescue the socialists. The politically savvy Kreisky seized this opening, and, against the odds, he became leader of the SPÖ, and then in 1970 chancellor.

The ÖVP tried to exploit the antisemitic prejudice of many Austrians against Kreisky. In the 1970 election campaign Josef Klaus was presented as 'Ein echter Österreicher', an *authentic* Austrian, a clear, if indirect, play on Kreisky's Jewish origins. Yet Kreisky proved too canny for such attacks: sidelining the Jewish issue, he portrayed himself as the modernizing leader for a New Austria, on the side of youth (despite being almost sixty), and appealing to that youth directly by proposing to cut compulsory military service from nine to six months. The March election left the SPÖ as the largest party for the first time in post-war Austria, but without an absolute majority. Kreisky formed a minority government, in effect relying on FPÖ toleration. When this arrangement broke down over the 1971 budget, Kreisky called another election, and on 10 October the SPÖ gained an absolute majority for the first time in Austria's history. Kreisky went on to lead the SPÖ to absolute majorities in the 1975 and 1979 elections as well. For more than twelve years Austria was under socialist rule. The 'island of the blessed' became shorthand for an eminently successful *socialist*-run mixed economy welfare state.

Economic prosperity was the backbone of SPÖ strength. Hannes Androsch, only thirty-four when he became finance minister, proved one of the era's most adept economic managers. He was able to keep the Koren boom going, despite the 1973 oil crisis and resulting worldwide recession. He pursued an unorthodox economic policy,

combining maintenance of a hard currency (pegging the schilling
to the mark) with large-scale public investment and large budget
deficits. The Austrian economy bucked the trend of the 1970s, continuing to expand at a healthy rate, faster than West Germany. There
were occasional hiccoughs, in 1975 and 1981, but overall Austria
became a textbook economic marvel, attributed by economists to
Androsch's brilliant 'Austro-Keynesianism'.

There were many reasons for Austrian imperviousness to the economic tempests of the 1970s, but chief among them was the absence
of industrial strife. Unlike in three-day week Britain, strikes were virtually unheard of in Austria. This led to high investor confidence,
plentiful foreign investment, and hence easy and cheap financing
of infrastructure investments and the budget deficit. The industrial
placidity was a result of the continuation of the social partnership
and the post-1945 'Austrian way'.

The SPÖ might govern alone, but Kreisky was careful to preserve
the *Proporz* system, and ensure that the ÖVP and business retained
a place at the bargaining table. Kreisky made the ÖVP's Koren the
head of the National Bank. Under Androsch's economic policy businesses actually benefited more from the boom than labour, owing
to the restraint in wage hikes negotiated in the Parity Commission;
but as everyone was doing better, everyone was happy, and Austria
Inc. purred along. By the early 1980s Austria had become one of
the most prosperous countries in the world.

The SPÖ was much more interested in managing a mostly capitalist economy in a socially responsible way than in introducing
socialist reforms. Austria had one of the largest state-owned sectors
among Western nations, at more than one-third of the economy,
but the companies involved, including most banks, were run com-
mercially, rather than as public institutions. The SPÖ expanded the
legal powers of the unions, but it preferred fostering enterprise and
enhancing equality of opportunity to imposing public control. It
gave tax breaks and financial incentives to encourage small business growth in the less prosperous regions of Austria, such as the
Mühlviertel, and businessmen in Bad Leonfelden benefited greatly.
The emphasis on more generous welfare measures, such as expanded
pension and health benefits, and on greater workers' rights, such as
the forty-hour week and four weeks' vacation, were the other side of

Austria Inc., from 1945

a mutually acceptable, graduated restructuring of Austria's economy and society that left all sides better off.

The Kreisky regime's agenda of social reform was similarly marked by a gradualist, consensual approach. The results, while modest, did start to bring Austria up to Western norms. The main figure behind the reforms of the penal code of 1971 and 1975 was Christian Broda, the progressive minister of justice. Broda's radicalism was, however, under the constant restraint of the pragmatic Kreisky, his eyes on electoral politics and intent on preserving good relations with Cardinal König and the Church. Kreisky was especially hesitant about the legalization of abortion, but even this reform gained public acceptance. Cardinal König opposed the law, but did not make too much of an issue of it. The reforms also included many liberalizing measures to match the law to the new social reality. Adultery was decriminalized and the hitherto total prohibition on homosexuality was abolished, although with compromise qualifications which effectively kept Austrian gay men in the closet.

Family law was also overhauled. The hitherto patriarchal definition of marriage became one of equal partnership. The divorce laws were liberalized and a more egalitarian regard of the sexes adopted. The Equal Treatment Law of 1979 provided, in principle, for equal pay for equal work regardless of gender, and this was an era of advances for Austrian women, with female pioneers such as the minister for science and research, Hertha Firnberg.

Firnberg's new ministry was at the centre of the relatively controversial reform of the universities. Education policy was central to SPÖ efforts at creating true equality of opportunity in Austria, and hence a 'classless society'. Schoolchildren were given free books, and guaranteed free travel to school. With ÖVP opposition blocking further reform of primary and secondary education, the SPÖ chose to intervene in higher education. Traditionally the post-war universities had been bastions of conservatism, and many ex-Nazi professors had been able to retain or regain their posts. Despite changes in the late 1960s, the university establishment was still very hierarchical and conservative. The creation of Firnberg's ministry cut the universities off from the Education Ministry's bureaucracy and opened them to serious reform. The University Organization Law (UOG) of 1975 pushed Austrian higher education in the direction of liberalization and democratization, and with the entry of younger, more progressive academics, Austria's academic establishment took on a less hidebound character.

Like the UOG, the 1974 reform of ORF, the state-owned broadcast media establishment, met stiff opposition, but its move towards greater autonomy (and the choice of the ORF board members) set Austrian broadcasting on a more modern (and left-leaning) course.

Kreisky's government was able to establish a more progressive identity for Austria, based largely on gradualist persuasion. Kreisky's support among the roughly 5 per cent of the electorate who were 'bourgeois' but socially liberal allowed the SPÖ to stay in power long enough for the new 'social–liberal consensus' to take root, and it has remained the Austrian consensus to this day.

For all his success at home, Kreisky was best known for his forays into foreign policy. Kreisky had effectively led Austrian foreign policy since the 1950s. Even the foreign minister in the Klaus government after 1966, Kurt Waldheim, had followed Kreisky's general line. Now fully in charge, Kreisky made 'little Austria' a major international player. He was a firm believer in a policy of active neutrality: the best guarantee of Austrian neutrality was actively to foster good relations between the communist East and capitalist West. Kreisky recognized the need for a credible defence force, and the 1975 defence policy advocated a system of national resistance, on Swiss lines. Yet Austria's defence budget was far below the Western European (and Eastern European) norm, and Austria's splendid economic performance was partly reliant on its neutrality never being militarily tested. Good East–West relations were hence a vital Austrian interest.

Sometimes Austria's position as a border neutral had proved tricky, especially when crises occurred in the neighbouring communist countries, as in Hungary in 1956 and Czechoslovakia in 1968. In both cases Austria acted well in giving asylum to thousands of refugees, although there are indications that in 1968 it was only the decision of the Austrian ambassador in Prague, Rudolf Kirchschläger, to ignore an anonymous directive from Vienna (allegedly from Waldheim) to suspend granting visas that saved Austria's reputation as an independent neutral. Kirchschläger became Kreisky's foreign minister, and in 1974 Austrian president, and his probity added to Austria's credibility in the complexities of the Cold War.

Kreisky meanwhile played Austria's neutral status both ways. He used neutrality to foster good relations with Austria's communist neighbours, seeking where possible to open up borders and establish economic links, to mutual benefit. Obversely, he used the evident Soviet displeasure at Austrian attempts to join the EEC to gain a very beneficial free trade agreement in 1972, while retaining Austria's political independence, in effect, allowing Austria to be a free rider on both NATO and the EEC.

Kreisky was an early and strong advocate of staging a Conference for Security and Co-operation in Europe (CSCE) at a time, 1970, when the Western powers were deeply sceptical of this Soviet suggestion. A stable Europe was obviously in Austria's interest, but Kreisky was prescient in seeing how this process, leading to the Helsinki Accords of 1975, would ultimately undermine communist power more than secure it. An element of local patriotism was also involved: subsequent CSCE negotiations took place in Vienna's Hofburg. The OSCE, CSCE's heir, is still headquartered in the Austrian capital.

Kreisky's ambitions for Austrian active neutrality went beyond Central Europe. One of his proudest moments was playing host to the leaders of the two superpowers, Jimmy Carter and Leonid Brezhnev, at the signing of SALT II in June 1979 in Vienna. Yet Kreisky envisioned Vienna not simply as an entrepôt for the two superpowers, but rather as one of the capitals of the international community, and on 23 August 1979 Vienna became the third seat of the United Nations, when the UNO City, a vast complex in Vienna's north-eastern suburbs, was ceremonially handed over to the United Nations' secretary general, Kurt Waldheim.

Building the UNO City was the culmination of Kreisky's goal of putting Vienna (and himself) at the centre of world politics. Vienna had long been notorious as a meeting place for informal actors in international relations: spies. It had also attracted international organizations such as OPEC, which established its headquarters there in 1965. It was, however, playing host to the UN that appealed to Kreisky most.

Austria had long been a diligent member of the UN, and Austrian troops often served as blue-helmeted peacekeepers. Kreisky now used Austria's role in the organization as a platform to connect with the countries of the Third World. His enthusiastic membership of the Socialist International, alongside Olof Palme, Willy Brandt and then Helmut Schmidt, and his support of the movement of non-aligned states promoted Austria as a bridge between North and South as well as East and West. It was in this context that Vienna was granted the status of being the third UN city – and that the Austrian ambassador to the UN, Waldheim, became UN secretary general in 1971. Austria was at the centre of world attention in a way it had not been for a very long time.

While all the above could be seen, broadly, as being part of a policy of active neutrality, Kreisky's deep involvement in the problems of the Middle East went clearly beyond that. OPEC's presence in Vienna and the accruing advantages in the oil crises of the 1970s partly explain Kreisky's interest, as does his involvement in the Socialist International. Yet Kreisky's Jewish background must surely have been a major factor, for the main goal in his Middle Eastern diplomacy was peace between Israel and its Arab neighbours, including the Palestinians. Kreisky maintained that such a peace was only possible on the basis of direct negotiation. Hence he met Yasser Arafat in 1974, and advocated a coupling of Arab recognition of Israel with Western recognition of the PLO. Leading by example, Austria formally recognized that organization in 1980. Such actions endeared Kreisky, and Austria, to the oil-rich Arab states and much of the Third World, but it antagonized Western opinion, and infuriated Israel and many Jews throughout the world.

Kreisky's relations to Jews and the Jewish state were, undoubtedly, highly ambivalent. Israelis saw Kreisky as willing to sacrifice Jewish interests for good relations with the Arabs. The Israeli government was outraged by Kreisky's 'surrender' to Arab terrorists, when he promised in September 1973 to close the Schönau transit camp for Jews leaving the USSR for Israel. Kreisky's handling of an attack on an OPEC meeting in December 1975 was seen in Israel and elsewhere as more craven surrender.

Many Jews also faulted Kreisky for his equivocal attitude to the Austrian past. Simon Wiesenthal, the famed, Vienna-based, Nazi-hunter who had tracked down Adolf Eichmann, gained Kreisky's enmity by intervening in 1970 and 1975 to reveal that members of Kreisky's cabinet (e.g. Hans Öllinger) and prospective coalition partners (e.g. Friedrich Peter) had been members of the SS. Instead of seeing this as an opportunity to open up discussion of Austria's past, Kreisky saw it as an attempt by Wiesenthal, politically affiliated with the ÖVP, to undermine the SPÖ.

Kreisky had from the start accepted the *Lebenslüge* of Austria as the first victim of Nazism, and he had seen himself as a political, not Jewish, refugee. As an agnostic socialist, he saw his Jewishness as insignificant beside the cause of Austrian social democracy and global peace and justice. To realize a better future, he was willing to forget the past, especially as, in his view and by his policies, Austrians really had become more enlightened. In his vendetta with Wiesenthal he saw himself as the progressive vanquisher of a past-obsessed reactionary.

Some of Kreisky's behaviour during the 'Peter Affair' of 1975 was not entirely reasonable, as when he remarked: 'If the Jews are a people, they are a wretched people.'[3] Kreisky defended this statement by arguing that, as a socialist, he had never accepted that there was a Jewish people as such, so its character was merely hypothetical. Yet why see that hypothetical character so negatively? A partial answer comes from his origins in the emancipatory, and assimilatory, Viennese Jewish bourgeoisie. When in 1973 he remarked to Golda Meir, 'You and I belong to different worlds,' he was partly affirming his distance from the kind of Jewish identity that Israel and Meir stood for.

Yet Kreisky also showed great sympathy for Jewish causes and Israeli interests. He was instrumental in Austria becoming a transit country for Soviet Jewish emigrants, despite the threat of Arab terrorism that deterred the Netherlands and Norway from this role. Closing Schönau actually had little or no effect on Austria's role as a transit country. A new camp, under Austrian administration, was

---

[3] Pick, *Guilty Victim*, p. 107.

opened at Wöllersdorf, and more Soviet Jews passed through Austria after the Schönau incident than before. He was also adamant, now that it existed, about the right of Israel to exist and be secure. Austria condemned the UN resolution in 1975 equating Zionism to racism. Kreisky secretly helped secure the release of Israeli soldiers captured during the invasion of Lebanon in 1982, even while Israeli opinion vilified him for his strong criticism of that adventure.

Kreisky also played a major role in persuading Egypt's Anwar Sadat to enter the peace process with Israel, with Klessheim Palace in Salzburg hosting two crucial meetings, in 1975 and early 1978. When the Israel–Egypt peace was signed at Camp David in September 1978, however, Kreisky was one of the few Western leaders not satisfied by it, because it ignored the Palestinians' plight. Dismissed at the time as typical of Kreisky's 'Jewish problem', his criticisms today appear prophetic.

Most Austrians blithely dismissed such foreign policy adventures as 'Emperor Bruno's' peccadillo. Part of being on 'the island of the blessed' meant not being much concerned with politics. The social partnership meant that things went on much as before, regardless, with ever greater prosperity. Many of Austria's burgeoning leisure industries now catered to home-grown consumerism. Bad Leonfelden expanded rapidly, with summer houses of out-of-towners (mainly from Linz) gobbling up what had once been potato fields. A new 'cultural centre' was built, with tennis courts attached. Spurred on by the nearby construction of a natural gas pipeline from Russia to the West, old village pubs turned into fashionable discos; Kreisky's befriending of Austria's communist neighbours resulted in the opening of the border crossing to Czechoslovakia in December 1978. Hotels with indoor swimming pools were built; Kastner's opened up a sizeable factory on the edge of town. By the 1980s Kastner products could be found in stores all over Austria, and abroad, although Leonfeldeners bemoaned the loss of quality.

In Vienna there was a conscious effort to catch up with more prosperous western Austria. A key component of the city's revival was its far-sighted transport policy. Socialist-dominated Vienna bucked the trend towards cars by continuing to emphasize public transport. Having an underground rail system was partly a matter of prestige for a modern capital city, but the U-Bahn (the first section opening

Illustration 44. Leonfelden in a) the 1950s, from the south,
and b) the 1990s, from the south-east.

in 1976) was integrated into a much larger scheme, with pedestrian-
ization in the inner city and the rebirth of Vienna's extensive trolley
system. Unusual at the time, this has since become a model of urban
transportation design.

The relative lateness of Austria's economic development combined felicitously with the 'Austro-Keynesian' strategy of counter-
cyclical public investment to produce an advanced economic infrastructure. Even in 1970, Austria had been economically behind
Britain; by the 1980s Austria had leaped ahead, while preserving its
sense of social homogeneity and political consensus. Its very neutrality was now a prized symbol of its privileged position: prosperously
linked to the West, while acting as a gateway to communist Eastern
Europe.

Tourism continued to expand, in winter and summer. Music and
culture festivals continued to flourish; but the average Austrian
was most excited about the success of skiers such as Annemarie
Moser-Pröll, and the brilliant racing drivers Jochen Rindt and Niki
Lauda. Two sports events became part of the national identity: Franz
Klammer's dramatic winning of the gold medal at the Innsbruck
Olympics of 1976; and the victory of the Austrian football team over
West Germany in the 1978 World Cup Finals in Argentina. *Kaiser
Bruno* ruled over a happy, flourishing and generally contented land.

Cultural and intellectual life also saw interesting developments.
In art, the School of Fantastic Realism made a name for itself,
with painters such as Ernst Fuchs, Arik Brauer and Friedens-
reich Hundertwasser. More avant-garde, and sensational, was the
Actionism of artists such as Hermann Nitsch. Austrian writers, such
as Peter Handke, Thomas Bernhard and Elfriede Jelinek, joined
the avant-garde of German and world literature. There were even
Austrian pop stars who broke through to international fame, such
as Falco with 'Rock me Amadeus' (1985).

It was also in the 1970s that the rediscovery of Vienna 1900
really took hold. The art of the Secession and Austrian Expression-
ism became ever more popular. Interest in the music of Mahler also
boomed, partly as a result of its use in Luchino Visconti's *Death
in Venice* (1971). This renewal of interest in *fin de siècle* Vienna
was greatly helped by its being given a powerful intellectual frame.

An American, Carl Schorske, had started publishing essays in the 1960s delineating *fin de siècle* Vienna as a model for how the political failure of liberalism had given rise to the subjective culture of modernism. By the early 1970s Vienna 1900 was being discussed as perhaps the leading centre of modern culture of the early twentieth century. Not only was this good for tourism, but it also added to contemporary Vienna's prestige, and justified the shift in attention back to Vienna, the SPÖ's bastion.

At first sight it is difficult to see how all this success could go so wrong so quickly in the early 1980s. Yet the election victories on which socialist hegemony rested were won by only a few percentage points. The Kreisky regime needed discipline, skill and considerable luck to stay in power. After the initial, dynamic reform period ended around 1975, the sort of problems that plague all long-lived regimes emerged.

A major difficulty was the falling out between Kreisky and Androsch. This was partly policy-based, with Kreisky emphasizing full employment and Androsch insisting on a hard currency policy, and resisting deficit spending. The main reason was Kreisky's suspicion, from 1974, of Androsch as a usurper. Androsch's growing renown in the financial world only exacerbated Kreisky's mistrust. Eventually, he had Androsch accused of a conflict of interest, and sacked him in 1981. This was a serious political mistake. Without Androsch at the helm, deficit spending rose and international financiers lost confidence in Austria. The economy sputtered: by January 1983 the unemployment rate was approaching 5 per cent, the highest since 1960. In a world increasingly attracted to monetarism and neo-liberalism, Austro-Keynesianism appeared to be failing.

In foreign policy, Reaganite America was not interested in Kreisky's subtleties, and the Socialist International was no longer a major forum. Waldheim was not re-elected as UN secretary general in 1981, and the state visit of Colonel Muammar Gaddafi to Vienna in March 1982 was an embarrassing failure. Meanwhile Kreisky's allegedly pro-Arab policies did not protect Austrians, especially Austrian Jews, from a number of terrorist attacks in 1981 and 1982. Even if Kreisky's policies were prescient, no one was listening.

Illustration 45. Zwentendorf nuclear power station.

The Kreisky regime had achieved so much that the electorate became blasé, and ever harder to please. In early 1983, the Austrian economy was still doing considerably better than most other Western economies, but it was not doing well enough for Austrians. The regime's success in liberalizing Austrian society also worked against it. An Austrian civil society emerged, independent of state or Church, or party authority, and began to talk, or even push, back. One major area of popular initiative was the environment. The Kreisky government, with ÖVP agreement, had built Austria's first nuclear power station at Zwentendorf in 1976. It was never put on line because protests and a popular initiative resulted in a referendum in 1978, with a narrow majority voting against nuclear power. Kreisky abided by the decision, and went on to win the 1979 election. Environmentalists, though, remained dissatisfied with government technocracy. Seeing the onset of ecological crisis all around them, they instituted the Green movement,

eventually the fourth force in Austrian politics, mainly to the socialists' detriment.

Another sign of the perils of success was the series of corruption
scandals that consumed the regime, most prominently concerning
the building of the new general hospital in Vienna, the AKH. The
ambitious goal of returning to the international front rank, as well
as providing first-class socialized medicine, ended up revealing just
how corrupt and self-serving the new elite was; even Androsch was
implicated in the trial of 1981. The socialist leadership was now,
after a decade, viewed as the 'state party'; the Austrian public, richer
and better educated, fed a diet of socialist-related scandals by the
popular press, now saw Kreisky as an intemperate old man, not the
reforming hero. Then in January 1983, in deepest winter, Kreisky
agreed an economic austerity package to respond to the latest financial crisis – while holidaying in his villa in Majorca.

In the national elections of April 1983 the SPÖ lost its absolute
majority in parliament for the first time since 1971. Kreisky resigned,
and was succeeded by Fred Sinowatz. The SPÖ chose to buck precedent and form a coalition with the FPÖ. This had been the party
of the ex-Nazis, but in 1983 the party leader was Norbert Steger,
a moderate, who wanted to turn the FPÖ into a centrist liberal
party. The problem for the coalition was that the FPÖ's nationalist
right wing proved too strong for Steger, and the resulting intra-party
volatility acted like a loose cannon in Austrian politics.

The economy stagnated, and unemployment rose. The budget
deficit grew, exacerbated by ever larger deficits in the 'feather-
bedded' nationalized industries, necessitating more taxation. Environmentalists protested against the construction of a huge hydro-
electric works on the Danube at Hainburg. Corruption scandals
involving the socialist '*Schickeria*' began to mount. The 'Lucona
Affair' around Udo Proksch began in late 1984. Androsch was again
investigated. Austria remained one of the most prosperous, well-run
countries in the world, but to no avail. A dissatisfied Austrian public
deemed Sinowatz a bumbler.

The highpoint of Sinowatz's haplessness came in January 1985.
For the first time since the Second World War, the executive committee of the World Jewish Congress met in Vienna. This should have

been a triumph for Sinowatz, but it proved a public relations disaster, for on 24 January, two days before the WJC meeting, the Austrian defence minister, the FPÖ's Friedhelm Frischenschlager, had personally greeted a war criminal, Walter Reder, on his return from prison in Italy, and had shaken his hand. In the ensuing furore, Frischenschlager apologized, after a fashion, but did not resign, despite the outrage of the WJC and international opinion. It was only the beginning of an upheaval in Austrians' relation to the world, to their past, and to themselves that is still not settled.

BACKING INTO THE FUTURE, 1985 ONWARDS

On 15 May 1985, Austrians looked back with pride at three remarkably successful decades of independence. For the next couple of decades looking back proved much less pleasant. The Austrian past resurfaced in ways that cast a pall on what, otherwise, should have been a period of immense opportunity for a country at the heart of Central Europe. As Austria entered the twenty-first century, it had undergone a rollercoaster of transformative experiences that left it far less 'innocent'. It is still unclear whether this has left Austrians wiser, or better.

The Reder Affair was the first of a string of crises that chipped away at the image of Austria as an island of the blessed. The Burgenland wine scandal started in April, when some wine-makers were discovered to have added diethyleneglycol, potentially lethal anti-freeze, to their best dessert wines, to give them a higher rating and hence higher price. This devastated Austria's burgeoning wine-growing business, and undermined Austria's international trustworthiness.

In Tyrol, in the summer of 1985, the fate of the relics of Anderl of Rinn revealed that problems in the Austrian past, even the far distant past, still festered. Anderl had supposedly been a medieval victim of Jewish ritual murder, and his relics were still on display in Judenstein as an object of pilgrimage, in 1985. The crisis arose when plans to remove the relics were opposed by conservatives apparently unconcerned with perpetuating the blood libel. In a very Austrian compromise, Anderl's remains were removed from the high altar, put in a coffin and then plastered into the wall of the church. Literally plastering over the past did little to counteract Austria's image as an antisemitic nation in denial.

Yet Austrian public life remained largely undisturbed by such reminders of another past. Within the FPÖ, Steger was being attacked by the right-wing, quasi-German nationalist Carinthian party leader, Jörg Haider, but Haider was still only a minor annoyance. The 'Austrian way' still functioned, as did Austria's reliance on neutrality. Austrian foreign policy in 1985 was still dominated by questions of which second-hand fighter planes to buy, relations with the East European neighbours and sanctions against South Africa. There were stirrings over 'Central Europe', but as late as 1985 few took these seriously. There was also a building effort by Austrian and foreign academics to re-examine recent Austrian history more thoroughly. Yet these tremors barely affected post-war Austria's carefully constructed, and apparently rock-solid, image.

The Waldheim Affair changed all that.

When Kurt Waldheim became the ÖVP candidate for Austrian president in November 1985, it was uncontroversial. Waldheim had been Austrian foreign minister and UN secretary general, and had not been party-affiliated. He had worked well with Kreisky, and earlier in 1985 a joint SPÖ/ÖVP Waldheim candidacy had been mooted. Kurt Steyrer became the SPÖ candidate, but Waldheim was the clear favourite. Waldheim was disliked by the American Right and pro-Israel Jewish groups because of his complaisance to the Soviets and Arabs, but this counted for little in Austrian politics. With his record as 'the man the world trusts', and with an unremarkable biography for the period of the 'German occupation', he seemed someone who would make an ideal Austrian president.

Soon after his nomination, this picture changed. In January 1986, at a ceremony commemorating General Alexander Löhr, a convicted and executed war criminal, someone mentioned that Waldheim had been Löhr's aide-de-camp. Socialist strategists had allegedly known about Waldheim's 'brown past' since at least the summer of 1985, but it was only now that journalists, most prominently *profil*'s Hubertus Czernin, began serious investigations. The result was a major exposé, published in March, of Waldheim's actual wartime record, which was in glaring contrast to his official version. Waldheim was shown to have lied about his past, and to have been far more involved in the German war effort than he had ever let on.

This should have forced Waldheim, and Austrians, to come clean about their distortion and denial of the past. Instead, many Western media organizations, and most prominently the World Jewish Congress in late March, after a preliminary viewing of the evidence, over-reached, claiming that Waldheim was a 'war criminal'. This, as it turned out, was not what the documentation proved, strictly and legalistically speaking. Most Austrians responded by largely ignoring Waldheim's obvious mendacity and instead focusing on the 'war criminal' allegations. Even Wiesenthal and Kreisky united in protesting against this 'dastardly' attack. (Kreisky later changed his mind.)

Accusations of deception and forgery flew back and forth, Waldheim did not withdraw, and the president, Kirchschläger, appointed a commission which cleared Waldheim of war crimes. Waldheim defended himself by asserting that he had only done what every Austrian like him at the time had done, which was 'to do my duty'. He thereby implicated the whole wartime generation in his own record, while enabling them to see their own wartime actions forgiven as simply doing their 'duty'. Few asked (but many realized) to what or whom that 'duty' had been done.

The Waldheim camp also played the Austrian demagogue's ace: antisemitism. From among the many opponents, they concentrated on the attacks of the World Jewish Congress. American media criticism was dismissed as from the American 'Ostküste', eastern coast, a phrase which malevolently but brilliantly associated the American media with the formerly despised Ostjuden, East European Jewry. The attacks on poor Waldheim were nothing, in his own words, but 'Jewish lies'. The answer to the 'attack of the Jews' was, as an infamous poster put it: 'We Austrians elect whom we want. Waldheim now more than ever!'[4] In a fit of misguided national self-assertion, Austrians voted Waldheim into office. In the first round on 4 May, Waldheim failed to gain an absolute majority, but on 8 June he was elected president. On 9 June Sinowatz resigned the chancellorship.

[4] Der Spiegel, 14 April 1986, p. 139.

Illustration 46. Manfred Deix, 'Austria on its way to the 1990s'. On the burdened Austrian horse ride President Kurt Waldheim, the conservative Archbishop Hermann Groer, and Jörg Haider, facing backwards, fiddling with his pipe, and giving a Nazi salute.

There was a shift to the right in Austria in the summer of 1986. Waldheim's installation as president in July was followed a week later by the naming of the conservative Hermann Groer to be the successor to Franz König as archbishop of Vienna. Perhaps the most crucial swing was the takeover of the FPÖ on 13 September by Haider's supporters from the moderates around Steger. The Austrian horse seemed headed in a direction not seen for decades.

Yet Austrian politics served up a surprise, in the form of the former finance minister and new chancellor, Franz Vranitzky. Decisive and effective, Vranitzky's first move after Haider's coup in the FPÖ was to end the coalition government and call elections. The result of the November election was a shock. The SPÖ remained the largest party, but suffered big losses; the ÖVP, far from gaining, also lost ground. The biggest gainer was the demagogic, right-wing FPÖ of Haider, with almost 10 per cent of the vote, double its 1983 performance. The shocked leadership of both major parties responded in early 1987 with a circling of the wagons, a return to the Grand Coalition.

This represented a partial success for the ÖVP, yet as junior partner in the coalition they were in the unenviable position of having to accept responsibility for policies in which their socialist partners still had the last say. The SPÖ, while having to stomach their political arch-enemies as governing partners, could now implement economic reforms and blame them on the 'capitalist' ÖVP. This blame game would inevitably erode voter share, but that was initially not a pressing problem, with the two coalition partners having more than 80 per cent of the vote between them. Thus 1987 was a year in which some crucial and much needed decisions were made concerning the economy and Austria's foreign policy. In March talks began on closer relations with the European Community; in April a deal was made on the rationalization and part-privatization of the nationalized industries. In September an austerity budget was agreed for 1988, a year which saw a return to high growth, far exceeding other Western European countries.

The Waldheim Affair refused to go away, however, and Austrians were forced to recognize that domestic decisions did have foreign policy consequences. Western governments imposed an informal ban on meeting with Waldheim, and throughout his six-year term the only countries he visited as head of state were the Vatican,

Cyprus and several Arab countries. On 27 April 1987 Waldheim was put on the US Watch List of suspected war criminals, and hence was banned from entering the United States. Wiesenthal, in an odd if politically explicable reversal of his usually unforgiving approach, decried the Watch List posting of Waldheim, and the leadership of Austria's small, vulnerable Jewish community pleaded in vain with the World Jewish Congress that their attacks were just provoking antisemitism. Combined foreign and domestic pressure eventually led on 19 May to Waldheim's partial admission to mishandling the accusations against him, and the announcement of the convening of an international historians' commission to settle the issue of Wald-heim's war service.

The commission first met in September and by February 1988 was ready with its report, which was damning. It confirmed that Waldheim could not be proved to be a war criminal as such. How-ever, he had been present in the Balkans and in Salonika, as an officer in Wehrmacht units that had perpetrated gross war atrocities. He could not be proved to have taken part in these, but he clearly must have known about them, having initialled various related orders – and he had done nothing to prevent them. As Gerald Fleming, one of the members of the commission wrote, Waldheim had been 'part of the military machine that had brought these events about'. Waldheim did not resign, claiming exoneration from war crimes, but it was nevertheless a crushing blow to him and Austria's image. Waldheim's life history, and post-war Austria's, had been revealed to be based on lies. At the fiftieth anniversary of the *Anschluss* on 11 March, a time was set aside for 'reflection', but the Waldheim Affair had made the events of fifty years ago far too relevant for most Austrians.

Life in Austria went on. The Tauern motorway's opening completed Europe's north–south motorway axis; Austrian skiers notched up many victories. Oscar Bronner's new, progressive daily, *Der Standard*, began publication in October. The economy boomed again, growing at more than 4 per cent per annum. Yet the scan-dal of Austria's past, unleashed by the Waldheim Affair, did not let up. In August, Haider, still a *German* nationalist, called Austria 'an ideological deformation'. Thomas Bernhard's *Heldenplatz* received its premiere at the Burgtheater on 6 November, virtually the anniversary of *Kristallnacht*. The play was an immense *succès de scandale*, with mass booing as Bernhard dissected the hypocrisies of Austrians' view of their past. On Bernhard's death in February 1989, his will banned the performance of his works in Austria. Hrdlicka's *Memorial against War and Fascism* also faced mass protest, but in turn was criticized for only perpetuating the perverse distortions of the received Austrian past. When the former Empress Zita was buried in the Capuchin Crypt on 1 April 1989, there was almost nostalgia for the 'better times' of the Monarchy. The days of the 'island of the blessed' seemed past.

Meanwhile, international developments were radically changing post-war Austria's external situation. With Mikhail Gorbachev's overhauling of the Soviet Union, and his announced policy of non-intervention in the Eastern European states, 'Central Europe' began to take on a previously unknown practicality. In May 1988 plans were announced for a joint Vienna–Budapest World Expo '95, and there was talk of Austria re-establishing its cultural and historic links with the other successor states of the Habsburg Monarchy, a 'project' that was boosted in April 1989 by the appointment of Erhard Busek as science minister. Yet few if any foresaw the dramatic change that came over Eastern, and Central, Europe during 1989.

In April the Polish government's invitation of Solidarity to talks signalled the start of what became capitulation by autumn. In May partially liberalized Hungary began dismantling the 'Iron Curtain' on its Austrian border, but it was not until August that the full consequences of this were seen. At a 'Picnic' of the Paneuropean Union (headed by Otto Habsburg) held on both sides of the Austro-Hungarian border, the barbed wire separating the two countries was ceremoniously cut, and the Hungarian authorities were persuaded to allow 'tourists' from East Germany to cross the frontier without a visa. East Germans raced to Hungary to escape to the West, and communist Eastern Europe imploded: the Berlin Wall came down in November; the Velvet Revolution triumphed in Prague; there was revolution in Romania. By the end of the year Eastern Europe was transformed.

In Austria these were joyous events. The thousands of Czechs who streamed to Vienna in early December to enjoy the pre-Christmas splendours of the former Habsburg capital were welcomed warmly, for this also meant liberation for Austrians. In Vienna, the street signs on the Ring to Prague, Brno, Bratislava and Budapest made sense in a way they had not for many decades. Vienna could regain some of its Central European lustre. The plan for a joint Expo with Budapest was given the go-ahead; a Europa Roundtable was convened to discuss the emerging new Europe. The Czech president, Václav Havel, and the German president, Richard von Weizsäcker, together attended the Salzburg Festival in July 1990 (as Waldheim's guests).

Yet pleasure at the turn of events did not long remain unalloyed. The welcome to the newly freed peoples of the East soon gave way to a fear of the borders being flooded by cheap foreign labour and fake asylum seekers wanting to live off the Austrian state. Austrian xenophobia was stoked by cynical politicians, chief among them Haider. As early as September 1990 the Austrian army was directed to help reinforce the border guard against illegal immigrants.

Austria's role in Central European politics was also completely overshadowed by a soon reunited Germany. Austria was left strategically worse off by 1989, exposed to world events in a way it had not been before. It could no longer rely on neutrality to avoid the currents of world events; nor could it play the West off against the East, as Kreisky had done so well. Instead, it was faced with being left on the sidelines. This year gave Austrians a huge opportunity to rethink themselves, but it also forced them to do so.

Some effort was made by the government to reposition Austria as the friendly, non-threatening collegial mentor of the other Central European states, in a post-Habsburg identification through history and culture. For this the recent revival of interest in turn-of-the-century Vienna and Central Europe was encouraged. Cultural and economic linkages proved mutually reinforcing. Yet the greater hopes of the 'Central European' lobby were thwarted by Austrian diffidence. In May 1991 the Viennese rejected the plan to co-host the 1995 Expo with Budapest, and Austrians proved reluctant to embrace their post-communist neighbours all that closely.

The main thrust of Austrian foreign policy from 1989 was aimed westwards, at the European Community. Since its inception in the 1950s, there had been a strong lobby within Austria to join the

Common Market. The Europa Bridge, built south of Innsbruck in 1963, was testimony to a certain Europhile pathos in Austria. Being part of 'Europe' made increasing economic sense as Austria became ever more tied into the West German economy, and entry into the European Community was seen as further anchoring Austria into the West.

Yet there were also strong forces opposed to Austria joining 'Europe'. Until well into the 1980s there had been an effective Soviet veto, but this obstacle receded with the rise of Gorbachev and Austria had already started negotiations about closer ties with the EC in 1987, without much Soviet resistance. It is hardly coincidental that Austria applied for full membership of the EC on 17 July 1989, as the Soviet East European empire was falling apart, and opportunity was beckoning for Austria to escape *its* East European fate.

There were also domestic considerations against joining the EC. Neutrality had become part of Austrian identity, and EC entry would inevitably mean less independence in policy-making. Some on the Left viewed EC entry as a threat to Austria's now very elaborate welfare state. Austrians' hard-won *national* identity was also seen as threatened by EC entry: Austrians would be swallowed up not only economically but also culturally and linguistically by Germany.

The government was quite cognizant of these issues. One of the more peculiar clauses in the accession treaty of 1995 was to be a list of specific products, such as apricots, which could be sold in Austria only under their Austrian name, *Marillen*, not the German *Aprikosen*. Yet the reverberations of 1989 had persuaded the leadership in both parties that there was no alternative to EC membership, a conclusion only strengthened when the breakup of Yugoslavia resulted in gunshots and bombs landing on Austrian soil in 1991. They also saw that the EC was becoming a more integrated and stronger institution, and, as the protracted dispute over transit rights showed, being outside the EC was a weak bargaining position.

There were also domestic considerations: joining the EC involved accepting the whole *acquis* of EC law, and overhauling Austrian law, often in a modernizing and liberalizing direction. A striking example of the liberalizing effect of the adoption of European norms was the decriminalization of male homosexuality, leading rapidly to a much more accepting attitude of Austrians to their lesbian and gay citizens. The onset of the AIDS crisis made this change in approach particularly appropriate.

The years leading to Austrian accession were also used to 'prepare Austria for Europe', which meant privatizing and rationalizing the nationalized industries, and reform and consolidation of the 'social state', including wide-ranging pensions reform. Reform of the universities and the federal museums, offering increased autonomy for lower direct federal funding, also began. Austria remained among Europe's best performing economies, but the modernization had costs, and there were constant battles between the coalition partners over finances, and much opposition among Austria's various interest groups, especially over the 'savings package' agreed in late 1994. 'Preparing for Europe' was often used as an excuse to enact policies which were necessary anyway, or pursued for ideological reasons. The anti-EC constituency, meanwhile, was now courted by Haider, who almost overnight turned from a quasi-German nationalist into a fervent *Austrian* nationalist against European and German meddling in Austria.

The elections of October 1990 suggested that Haider's tactic had paid off. The SPÖ maintained its voter share at 43 per cent, with the Greens gaining a respectable 5 per cent. Yet the ÖVP had seen a sharp reduction, to a mere 32 per cent. The main beneficiary was Haider's FPÖ with 17 per cent, now the main magnet of the Austrian protest vote. With EC entry on the horizon, the Grand Coalition held, and the government was still intent on pushing through its modernization programme, but the coalition partners, especially a skittish ÖVP, were clearly looking over their shoulders.

Then in June 1991 a series of events gave the coalition unexpected breathing space, and shifted it in a more liberal direction. On 13 June, Haider went too far in his cynical dalliance with the taboos of the Austrian past. In the Carinthian provincial assembly he spoke approvingly of the 'proper employment policy of the Third Reich'. The resulting outrage in Austria's political establishment led to Haider's forced resignation as governor of Carinthia.

The coalition parties took steps at almost the same time to readjust their identity to the new, post-1989 circumstances. The SPÖ's move was purely symbolic, changing the party's name *back* to the Social

Democratic Party of Austria. The ÖVP, on the other hand, made a quite dramatic gesture by electing the liberal Erhard Busek as their leader. With Waldheim in the same month announcing that he would not be running for re-election, the decks could be cleared to make Austria truly ready for EC entry.

Given the Waldheim Affair, a key part of this national overhaul was recognition of what Austrians had perpetrated between 1938 and 1945. During the Waldheim Affair many Austrian intellectuals and academics campaigned for recognizing that Austrians too had been responsible for their part in the Third Reich's crimes. The government had soon made noises in this direction, instructing, for instance, that the events from 1938–45 should be mandatory teaching in Austrian classrooms, and many within the government argued for an admission of Austrian responsibility as a first step to re-establishing Austria's international standing and allowing Austria to get on with its European future. The change in attitude did occur, but slowly.

In 1988 the government had made a paltry gesture to Holocaust survivors of a one-time 'payment of honour' of 2,500–5,000 schillings ($200–400), which hardly remedied the notorious procrastination of Austria's bureaucracy concerning restitution and compensation. Meanwhile, a British historian, Robert Knight, published damning evidence revealing this procrastination to have been *official* Austrian policy since the 1940s. In 1990, the government made more money available to pay survivors' pensions and fund Jewish old people's homes, but it was only on 8 July 1991, five years after Waldheim's election, that Vranitzky, in a speech in parliament, accepted that Austrians shared a collective responsibility for the good and the bad in the past.

For the first time, an Austrian leader acknowledged Austrians' participation in the Holocaust, and the moral consequences for Austria that followed from this. The material consequences, in the form of a new system of compensation, took another four years to be organized, but in 1995 a National Fund for the Victims of the National Socialists was established at $50 million, and each surviving Austrian Jew was given $6,000. This was only the beginning of a transformation of the issue of restitution and compensation.

The change of approach went much further than just money. It involved a recasting of the basis on which the Second Republic understood itself. Where previously there had been considerable resistance to seeing any distinctly Jewish aspect to Austrian history and culture, now, haltingly, there was recognition of the Jewish side to the contribution of the many Jews to Austria's economy, culture and society. A Jewish Museum in Vienna was (re-)established on 18 November 1993, and a greater appreciation fostered for the Jewish side to Austria's cultural heritage.

There was also a concerted effort at reconciliation with Israel. In May 1992, Thomas Klestil replaced Waldheim as president. A couple of months later full diplomatic relations between Austria and Israel were restored. Then in June 1993 Vranitzky made a state visit to Israel, the first Austrian chancellor to do so, and in November 1994 Klestil spoke before the Knesset. A few months before, in February 1994, Erhard Busek had presided at the inauguration of the Cardinal König Chair for Austrian Studies at the Hebrew University, Jerusalem. Austria, officially at least, appeared to have come to terms with the Jewish aspect of its past.

Austrian accession to the European Union (renamed such since 1991) was in the end relatively easy. Austria first agreed to be a member of the European Economic Area in 1992, together with the other EFTA members, but Austria wanted full membership. With the South Tyrol question finally, completely settled in May 1992, and Austria accepting the security and foreign policy clauses in the Maastricht Treaty, negotiations for Austrian EU entry began in 1993. Agriculture and the old transit dispute proved major stumbling blocks, and negotiations dragged on, but in March 1994 agreement was reached, and in the referendum on 12 June 1994 67 per cent voted 'yes' to Europe. On 1 January 1995, Austria became a full member of the European Union. No longer bordering the Iron Curtain, or shunned by the West for its Nazi past, it appeared headed for the sort of easy, unproblematic life of consensus politics and economic prosperity enjoyed by other small country members of the EU, or so many in the Austrian establishment wanted to think. There appeared only one problem with this scenario: Jörg Haider.

No matter how successful the Vranitzky–Busek Grand Coalition government was in navigating the shoals of the post-Waldheim, post-Cold War world, and bringing Austria safely into the European Union, many Austrians, encouraged by opinion-makers such as the right-wing *Kronenzeitung*, were increasingly dissatisfied with it. Rationalization of the nationalized industries and austerity budgets had improved Austria's economy and finances, but were deeply unpopular. The change from an industrial to a service economy created prosperity but left many losers, especially in the blue-collar working class.

The Grand Coalition also neutered any democratic input of the electorate, for however they voted, they got the same government. Both major parties had sworn not to partner with Haider's extremist FPÖ, and so Austrian politics was stuck with no practical alternative to the Grand Coalition. The undemocratic structures of the postwar consensus were reconstituted. The corporatist system of social partnership was now more transparent, with the partners making their agreement public in November 1992, but this still showed up Austria as only a pseudo-democracy.

Meanwhile the transformation of Central Europe and the breakup of Yugoslavia had produced a flood of migrants, mostly refugees and asylum seekers, for many of whom Austria, next door and with relatively liberal immigration and asylum laws, was an obvious destination. In 1991, of Austria's population of 7.8 million, some 518,000, or 6.6 per cent, were foreign, and that was before the large influx of refugees from Yugoslavia. By 1994 some estimates put the proportion of foreigners in Austria at some 10 per cent, which was very high by European standards, and many Austrians saw this as a threat to their Austrian national identity, and their jobs.

Haider, the root cause of the stalemate that had necessitated the Grand Coalition, was ruthlessly brilliant in taking advantage of the rising xenophobia in the electorate. Haider's removal from the scene in the summer of 1991 proved very short-lived. In the autumn his FPÖ achieved staggering advances in the provincial elections in Upper Austria and Vienna, becoming the second largest party in the capital. Then in March 1992 he muscled his way back into parliament and took over the FPÖ's latest venture, its demagogic campaign against what an FPÖ deputy, Andreas Mölzer, had called in February, with language reminiscent of the Nazis, the 'Umvolkung' (national perversion) of the 'German people and cultural community'.

Unfortunately, the government responded to this exploitation of the asylum emergency by trying to compete. The law on Foreigner Right of Residence of June 1992 constituted a sharp turn away from a liberal policy. In July 1993 this law came into effect and another law, further limiting quotas for foreign guest workers, was also passed. While Austria was coming to terms with what xenophobia had done to its past Jewish outsiders, it was succumbing to the sorcerers of a new xenophobia.

The FPÖ, spurred by government imitation, launched a petition drive in November 1992 with the title of 'Austria first', demanding a harsher crackdown on foreigners. As in 1991, FPÖ extremism, redolent with racist assumptions about Austrian identity, proved too much for Austrian public opinion. For once, Haider's demagoguery found an effective response on the Austrian liberal left. In December the group SOS Mitmensch-Anständigkeit zuerst (SOS Fellow Human-Decency First) was formed, and in January it organized a candlelight procession in Vienna's inner city that was attended by upwards of 250,000 people, forming a veritable 'sea of lights'. The campaign against the FPÖ initiative was joined by the major parties, and on 1 February 1993 it failed. The FPÖ's resistible rise seemed even more resistible a few days later when Heide Schmidt, leader of the party's remaining moderates, left to form her own Liberal Forum. This split in the FPÖ helped smooth Austria's path into the new Europe – because the Haider threat had apparently gone away again.

This proved an illusion. Resentment in the electorate continued to grow, and the coalition parties continued to lose votes. In early 1994 the FPÖ made more gains in Carinthia and Salzburg. The referendum on Europe passed by two-thirds in June, but this still left one-third opposed. Haider continued his opportunistic, xenophobic populism. When national elections were held in October 1994 the result was another shock: the SPÖ were at 35 per cent; ÖVP at 28 per cent; the Liberal Forum had done quite well at 6 per cent; also the Greens at 7 per cent; but Haider's FPÖ was at 23 per cent, biting at the heels of the major parties. Even before Austria's entry into the EU, the domestic situation was headed for a crisis.

A crisis within the coalition over the budget led to a new election in December 1995, which left things more or less the same. From then to the next national elections in 1999 little changed in the dynamics of Austrian politics. The personnel changed: Busek had been replaced by Wolfgang Schüssel as ÖVP leader and vice-chancellor in early 1995; Vranitzky eventually retired in 1997 and was succeeded by Viktor Klima; but the political geometry remained the same. The tension between government liberalization and conservative reaction in the electorate worsened. The government, under increasing international pressure, was ever more intent on sorting out the painful legacy of the past. In 1997 a Day of Remembrance for the Victims of National Socialism, 5 May, was proclaimed. The building of a new Holocaust Memorial in the Judenplatz in Vienna's city centre was agreed, and, after complex disagreements, eventually dedicated in 2000. An International Commission of Experts, including eventually Robert Knight, was set up to look into the issue of Jewish expropriation and restitution. A new refugee nationality law made it easier for 'old Austrians' living still in exile to regain their Austrian citizenship. The restitution process was speeded up, and in 1999 Austrian banks set aside $40 million for Holocaust claims. The collection of expropriated art at Mauerbach, kept hidden by the Austrian government until the secret was revealed in 1984, was handed over to Vienna's Jewish Community in 1994, and the proceeds from the auction in 1996 went to Holocaust victims. In 1998 the exhibition on Austrian participation in the German Wehrmacht, including its criminal actions, marked a new stage in public Austria's coming to terms with its past.

Restitution procedures were still painfully, and suspiciously, slow, and some cases still met large resistance. There was a major change in 1998 when two Schiele paintings on loan for exhibition in New York were confiscated by the American authorities as possibly stolen property. This case was pursued by the Austrian government, but it sparked a radical change in policy by the minister for culture, Elisabeth Gehrer, who decided to abandon the bureaucracy's procrastinations and give back to expropriated Jewish owners what was rightfully theirs. The Rothschilds' property was returned in 1999, and many other restitutions followed.

Even here, though, old habits died hard, and in a restitution case concerning several Klimt paintings, including the golden portrait of Adele Bloch-Bauer, by now an icon of Vienna 1900, legal niceties

Illustration 47. Austrian authority past and present: Viktor Klima (centre) and Wolfgang Schüssel (to his right) at the inauguration of the Austrian EU presidency, 1 July 1998, in the Hofburg – under a portrait of the young, neo-absolutist Francis Joseph.

were manipulated to deny the paintings' rightful return to their owner, Maria Altmann, heir to Ferdinand Bloch-Bauer. (That case has recently been arbitrated in Altmann's favour.) Overall, however, with the Austrian Jewish community being given more support and a much more prominent place in Austrian identity, official Austria had, on the face of it, radically changed its approach to its past and Austrian Jewry.

Austria apparently was becoming an ever more internationalized, open country. Austria's EU presidency in 1998 was a pinnacle of prestige for the Second Republic. Austria again had its budget under control and, with good growth, was confident of success under the new European currency, the euro, introduced on 1 January 1999. With Franz Fischler as a well-respected agricultural commissioner, and other Austrians, including Busek, heavily involved in preparing for EU enlargement into East Central Europe as well as with the Balkan crisis, Austria was an active new member of the Union. There was even a cultural reawakening, headlined by the impressive Museum Quarter, which provided lavish exhibition space for Austria's modern art legacy.

None of this affected the domestic political stalemate in Austrian politics. The Grand Coalition became increasingly frayed and unpopular. Neo-liberals objected to the continuing power of the 'out-dated' social partnership, while a reaction built against the very internationalization and increase in diversity which made the new Austria so much more attractive than the inward-looking Austria of before. This all played into the hands of Haider. Schmidt's Liberal Forum was never able to get beyond the liberal intelligentsia, and even then was ineffective. The Greens remained too far to the left to attract the protest vote, which was a version of the politics of economic despair. So disaffected Austrians voted for Haider's FPÖ, and Haider did his part by being a gadfly on the government. He was greatly helped by the *Kronenzeitung* supporting his cause against 'corruption' and too many foreigners. In March 1999, the FPÖ captured 42 per cent of the vote in Carinthia; in September they gained 27.5 per cent in Upper Austria; in the national elections of October 1999 they gained 27.2 per cent. They had succeeded, just barely, in driving the ÖVP into third place.

Since then there has been another radical shift in Austrian politics. The key figure of the last six years has been the ÖVP leader, Wolfgang Schüssel. Instead of renewing the Grand Coalition, in February 2000 Schüssel chose to break the central taboo of Austrian politics and formed a coalition with Haider's FPÖ. There were mass demonstrations in Austria to protest at what was seen as an illegitimate, and cynical, abuse of the political system. The international community was also deeply disturbed by this entry of a purportedly extreme right-wing organization into the democratic government of an EU member state. The other fourteen members of the EU, many themselves facing pressure from quasi-fascist, xenophobic rightist movements and concerned at the example set to the prospective EU members of post-communist East Central Europe, instituted their own diplomatic sanctions against Austria. The American, Israeli and other Western governments also protested against this apparent atavistic relapse. Some spoke of Haider as a new Hitler.

Yet Haider was not Hitler. Schüssel and Haider himself were aware of their operating limits, but President Klestil made sure they were. In a humiliating move, Klestil forced Schüssel and Haider to sign a declaration promising to uphold constitutional and human rights before he approved the new government. Haider never became a member of the government, not even vice-chancellor. He remained governor of Carinthia, and left his deputy, Susanne Riess-Passer, as vice-chancellor. Despite the fact that the FPÖ had won (just) more votes than the ÖVP in the election, the FPÖ was the *de facto* junior partner in the new government.

Although Schüssel and the ÖVP objected to the domestic demonstrations and the foreign sanctions, these protests aided the ÖVP in setting the new framework of Austrian politics in their favour. FPÖ inexperience in government and the party's fractiousness left it at a disadvantage relative to its coalition partner, but the ÖVP could also use the threat of foreign pressure to exert control over it. Obversely, the claim that the EU Fourteen were 'picking on' Austria yet again for exercising its democratic right of self-determination resonated with the public, even though the argument was highly dubious.

Most Austrians probably still think that the sanctions of the Fourteen were EU sanctions, and represented an undemocratic attack on

Austrian sovereignty. In reality the other fourteen member states exercised their own sovereignty in expressing their displeasure at a democratic party ignoring the apparent popular will and letting a party whose democratic *bona fides* were questionable into a government that had a veto over EU policy, and hence over their (the Fourteen's) freedom of action.

No matter: the international protests and sanctions were characterized as interference, and only gained the government popularity. The domestic demonstrations continued for a long time, but the government rode them out, and after six months the EU Fourteen lifted their sanctions. The political revolution in Austria was complete.

The worst fears raised by the FPÖ's entry into power have failed to materialize. Once in power and faced with responsibility, the FPÖ self-destructed. Haider continued to control his party from the sidelines, and continued to provoke. Meanwhile Schüssel went along with the FPÖ in following a more right-wing programme of tax reform, spending cuts, privatization, university reform and more tightening of asylum and immigration laws, but he retained firm control of the government.

Moreover, partly to neutralize international concern, the Schüssel government continued and broadened restitution and compensation policies, regarding not only Jews but also slave labourers. In January 2001 an agreement was reached with Austria's Jewish communities whereby a fund of $360 million was established by the government and Austrian companies to settle expropriation claims. Haider now made much of fostering good relations with Jews.

Endemic squabbling in the FPÖ eventually resulted in the Knittelfeld Putsch in September 2002, when Riess-Passer left the party. Schüssel ended the coalition in response and called elections for November. Schüssel persuaded his 'whiz kid' finance minister, Karl-Heinz Grasser, to leave the FPÖ for the ÖVP, but with the economy limping along under the black–blue coalition, and discontent over radical new policies, Schüssel was vulnerable. Had the SPÖ leader Alfred Gusenbauer's campaign been more effective, the Schüssel government might have fallen, but it did not.

The results of the 24 November election were nevertheless spectacular. Both the SPÖ, at 36.5 per cent, and the Greens, at 9.5 per cent, gained votes, but their combined forces fell short of a majority. On the government side, however, there had been a land-slide, with the ÖVP gaining over 15 per cent, at 42.3 per cent. This was all owing to the collapse of the FPÖ vote, dropping 17 per cent to a measly 10 per cent. The FPÖ and Haider, it appeared, had been tamed at last.

Many hoped that this radical shift would lead the ÖVP to rethink its position, and for an extended period Schüssel contemplated a Grand Coalition, and even a black–green coalition. In the end he went back to the tamed FPÖ. The second black–blue coalition government was initially much more stable, because neither party wanted to risk facing an electorate which at the local and provincial level has voted in ever larger numbers for the SPÖ and Greens. In the elections for the European Union Assembly in June 2004 the FPÖ only won 6.4 per cent of the vote, and the ÖVP was overtaken by the SPÖ. This followed the election of the SPÖ's Heinz Fischer as president in April. The very fragility of the coalition's position meant, ironically, that there was a steady stream of legislation that has brought major changes.

Grasser has used the budget process to try and cut back on Austria's welfare state. Tax reform, delayed in 2002, has now begun, with the aim of reducing the state's share of national income to 40 per cent. This has been paid for with significant cuts in educa-tion expenditures, with the reform of higher education appearing as largely a means to reduce funding. The continued privatization of the nationalized industries has been seen as a Thatcherite ruse to generate one-time revenue while achieving ideological goals. Not coincidentally, cuts have targeted sectors in the Red–Green camp, while other state sectors have seen increased expenditure, such as defence, even though Austria is still neutral and with no obvious enemy on its border.

This neo-liberal, rightward shift has not gone by without protest. The pension reform plans led in 2003 to the first general strike in Austria's post-war history, forcing a compromise in the eventual law. Railway reform, though also vehemently opposed, has gone through, as has reform of the national broadcast media and the police. These reforms were justified on the basis of deregulation and liberalization, but have often served more prosaic political ends. The suspicion of corruption, which once dogged the SPÖ, has now moved on to the current government, most notably Grasser's dealings concerning his own tax payments.

The government also passed, in October 2003, a very restrictive asylum law, earning the public criticism of the UNHCR. This pandering to xenophobia can also be seen in the restrictive policy towards economic migration from the new Central European EU member states. The opposition to Turkish membership of the EU also feeds into this relapse into an introverted, 'among ourselves' Austrian self-understanding. Schüssel at times has disinterred the idea of Austria as a victim of the Nazis, and there has been a resurgence of the sentiment that Austrians should forget the past, and look forward.

There are also many Austrians who want to learn from the past, and work for a more open, inclusive, welcoming Austrian polity. Yet the main opposition group, the SPÖ, has chosen the path of protectionism in the labour market, even at a time when Austria's relatively good economic performance is largely a result of the encouragement afforded by the opportunities and growth in the new EU member states.

The net effect of government policy changes should not be exaggerated. Despite cutbacks, Austria's welfare state remains one of the most comprehensive and generous in the world, based on a widespread social consensus, shared by the government. Schüssel, criticizing Tony Blair's 'Anglo-Saxon' neo-liberalism, recently reaffirmed his belief in the 'European' social model. Anti-European sentiment, despite being high, has also failed to make much of a dent on policy. Austria is a fully integrated member of 'Euroland', with euros being Austria's actual, physical money since 2002. Austria also benefited greatly from the EU enlargement in 2004. The Austrian Benita Ferraro-Waldner is the current EU foreign policy commissioner.

Politics is currently again in turmoil. The government is pushing ahead with its 'right-wing' agenda, but the FPÖ has, again, unravelled. After severe intra-party disputes, Haider and the party's federal leadership left the party to form a new 'Alliance for the Future of Austria' (BZÖ). In provincial elections in autumn 2005 the SPÖ made more gains, and Haider's BZÖ got nowhere, but the FPÖ, led by Heinz-Christian Strache, even more extreme than Haider, did

Illustration 48. Brave new world: Leonfelden 2004

better than expected. With national elections looming in the autumn of 2006, Austrian politics is once again in the balance.

As Robert Menasse predicted, and Anton Pelinka has confirmed, the 'coup' of 2000 has led to an unblocking of the Austrian political system, and a further modernization of Austrian society. Yet there is deep ambivalence in the most recent trends. The re-emergence of xenophobia, now aimed at Muslims and Turks, remains troubling, as does the apparent relapse of many Austrians into a Euro-sceptical, 'little Austrian' identity. Not enough Austrians seem yet to appreciate the European Union, despite its 'democratic deficit', as the resolution of Austria's search for legitimacy and authority. Instead they rely on the chimera of their narrow, exclusory national identity. In this, unfortunately, modern Austrians are much like other Europeans.

Culturally and socially, however, Austria has become a more secularized, modern society. Pope John Paul II's attempt to inject more conservative backbone into the Austrian Catholic hierarchy has backfired, with child pornography scandals claiming leading churchmen and church attendance declining. The Austrian public is mostly concerned with post-modern social problems arising from a

Illustration 49.   Austria's future? Max Zettler and his cousin, Nathaniel Brimmer-Beller, at a wedding in Bad Leonfelden, summer 2004

material success undreamt of in 1945. While political life has seen a surge in xenophobia, the society appears much more cosmopolitan and open to international influences. How these contradictory trends will play out is unpredictable.

In Bad Leonfelden the tourist industry, based on the Kurhaus, still does well. Kastner's still draws crowds and sells gingerbread around the world, although the business is no longer family-owned. Linzers still come to the village to escape their smog-plagued city, although the village's expansion means it takes longer to get into open country. There are now other easily reached distractions. Just over the Czech border lie such attractions as the fairytale town of Krumlov or Rožmberk castle. A traveller from Linz to such destinations does not even have to go through Bad Leonfelden anymore, but can take the bypass. Yet Bad Leonfelden continues to thrive, because now it has been designated as the region's education centre.

It is also a modern, or even post-modern village. At a recent wedding, the guests were asked to wear national costume, if liberally defined. Yet at the Catholic service there was American Gospel music, and at the civil ceremony Van Morrison's 'You Ease my Burden'. At the reception an R&B band played. Two cousins, aged seven and six, of quite different cultural and racial backgrounds, had a splendid time dancing along. Bad Leonfelden, and Austria, do seem to have come a long way in the past half-century.

Map 8.   Austria and Europe, 1955–2004

CONCLUSION

At the end of January 1996 excavation at a hydroelectric power project at Lambach on the Traun unearthed a mass grave. It was immediately suspected that the human remains were from concentration camp inmates, and Simon Wiesenthal was interviewed on the discovery. He commented that, if one searched, one could find such mass graves 'everywhere' in Upper Austria. 'If you dig in Austria, you can find Roman ruins. You can just as easily find people who were shot to death. After all, Mauthausen had over forty subsidiary camps.'[1]

It turned out that the remains were not those of victims of the Nazis, but of watermen from the nineteenth century. Yet Wiesenthal's comment reminds us of how just scratching the Austrian surface can reveal layer upon layer of a past that has often proved difficult for present-day Austrians to come to terms with. This is true anywhere, but it is particularly poignant for Austria, both because its past is so much greater than the current small republic, and also because the more recent past contains a period, from 1938 to 1945, of national disgrace.

History weighs heavily on Austria. Austrian history is the story of the search for authority; in this search the Habsburg dynasty must play a central role. The Habsburgs took a reasonably successful feudal agglomeration and turned it into the base for imperial power and splendour. The brilliant success of imperial Austria was nevertheless

---

[1] Cited in Associated Press Austria report, 31 January 1996.

ephemeral, and made Austria problematic when the imperial model no longer held sway, and was superseded by the modern nation-state. As a supra-national dynastic power, even as a supra-national state, the Habsburg Monarchy became abnormal, on the wrong side of 'Progress', as most Europeans came to understand it.

In the era of the nation-state, with its decisive logic of the excluded middle, that one either belonged to the nation or not and that other identities and loyalties could not controvert this overarching one, Austria, and Austrians, had the further problem that they fell in-between. The indecisiveness of Austria's German identity hobbled the Monarchy in the nineteenth century, but it became a particularly acute problem when the Monarchy collapsed and the Austrian problem was reduced to German Austria, and the Austrian Republic. The solution to this problem was found after 1945 by the construction and adoption of a separate Austrian national identity. While Austria thus became a 'normal' nation-state, the history of post-1945 Europe reversed direction, towards the supra-national entity of today's European Union.

Austrian history has been characterized by complex dialectical developments, whether it be the religious dialectic between Reformation and Counter Reformation of the sixteenth and seventeenth centuries, or the ensuing contest between Reform and Counter Reform in the eighteenth and nineteenth centuries. The relationship between supra-nationality and nationality that has characterized the nineteenth and twentieth centuries seems now to have finally reached some sort of synthesis in Austria's membership, as a nation-state, in the supra-national European Union. Yet there are still obvious tensions in this relationship, as evidenced by Austrians' Euro-scepticism as well as the persistence of a narrow, exclusive, 'among ourselves' Austrian self-understanding, and a very defensive attitude to the surrounding, formerly 'Austrian' lands of Central Europe.

Austrians are still uncomfortable with their heritage, partly because that heritage is so much larger than the small nation-state that is modern-day Austria. The heritage is supra-national, multi-national and multi-ethnic. It is a heritage that extends to almost all parts of the world: what is reputed to be Montezuma's feather-crown sits not in Mexico but in Vienna, a gift of the conquistadors to the (Habsburg) king. Conversely, the brightest parts of Austria's

Illustration 50. Austrian identity 1: Gustav Klimt, 'Adele Bloch-Bauer I', 1907.

cultural heritage were only saved after 1938 by escaping to the rest of the world, and much of Austria's contribution to the modern world took root not in Vienna but in Hampstead, Berkeley or Jerusalem. The emigration has meant to this day that Austria's heritage exists around the world in a way which many modern-day Austrians still only partly grasp. Moreover, when it comes to the very large part of Austria's modern cultural heritage that was produced, encouraged or paid for by Austrian Jewry, it is not even clear, given the heinous mass crime of expropriation, expulsion and elimination of Jews in which the Austrian populace took full part between 1938 and 1945, in what way, or even whether, this part of the Austrian heritage really 'belongs' to the *current* Austrian nation.

The recent controversy over Klimt's golden portrait of Adele Bloch-Bauer, whether it belonged to 'Austria' or to the Jewish family from which it had been stolen in 1938, is exemplary of the problem of 'Austrian' heritage. That problem was on one level a purely legal one, but there was also a moral dimension, for by hiding behind mere legalities the Austrian government, once more, appeared to be trying to deny the obvious wrong which *Austrians* had done to a family of Austrian Jews, and which the *Austrian state* perpetuated *after* 1945, partly by going back to *before* 1938, and pretending that nothing had happened after that to change matters.

That case has, in its latest stage, been resolved in favour of the Jewish owners, but, more generally, it is still unclear whether Austrians are up to their own heritage. It would be churlish to claim that Austrians have made no progress towards resolving their problematic relationship with their own history; the situation now is qualitatively different from that of a mere twenty years ago, for the better. Yet the rather abrupt approach taken to the negotiations over the Klimt pictures suggests that official Austria, at least, is still more intent on getting over its history and moving on rather than fully embracing that heritage and the responsibilities, including expenditures, associated with it.

Current negative attitudes to the rest of the European Union, especially to the new neighbouring Central European member states, also suggest an insularity and a lack of national and cultural self-confidence. It would appear that Austrians are still reliant on a narrow *national* identity because they are still unsure of their own. Instead of the independence and confidence that comes with a proper sense of citizenship, they still at times exhibit the reflexes of dependent subjects, still beholden to a state to which they belong, rather than one that belongs to them.

Were more Austrians to have a greater sense of their self-worth, then it would be much easier for them to embrace what is, despite the notorious horrors marked in this book, a really most attractive heritage in many respects, and one, moreover, most relevant to today's European Union and the international community. Instead of persisting in a cramped, xenophobic defence of Austrian 'national property', Austria and Austrians could adapt the supra-national and multi-national heritage of the Austrian Habsburg Monarchy and the cosmopolitan and inclusive culture of Vienna 1900 to see the contemporary European Union and the enlargement into Central Europe not only as a great opportunity for their material interests, but also as a realization of what is best in the Austrian tradition, broadly defined.

We started with a paradox, and perhaps the largest paradox is that while Austrians are today among the proudest of their national identity, their history and heritage remain most suited to going beyond, above and between the narrow confines of mere nationality. It is the 'problem' that Austrians thought they had solved, of the Monarchy's supra-nationality, and their own ethnic heterogeneity and lack of national coherence after 1918, their 'in-betweenness', that was actually at the heart of the most positive and significant contributions of Austria to the modern world. It is precisely the experience of multi-faceted identity, of connections across categories and differences, of relations across divisions, of the acceptance of diversity within unity, that typifies what, for want of a better term, we call post-modernism's insight, and this is what that history of the other Europe, Austrian history and Austrian heritage is ultimately about. It should be something cherished and embraced, not solved.

Perhaps modern Austrians will realize this larger meaning to Austrian history. The major parties might today all be competing to be as restrictive about foreign (Central European) workers as possible, but Europe's internal labour market is scheduled to be free in 2011; Austrian voters might still respond to Muslim- and minority-bashing, but the extremist parties seem tamed, and Austrian minority policy is still among the more liberal in Europe. Attitudes in the tabloid press might still be defensive and insular concerning the new Central European member states, but Austrian companies are nevertheless investing heavily there. After the relapse of 2000, the facts on the ground might be leading Austria back to the positive, outward-going approach that appeared to have established itself back in 1999. Let us hope so – it would be truer to all those who thought and did their best for the Austrian ideal if it were so, and the alternative is far less attractive.

In January 2006 Austrians celebrated the 250th anniversary of the birth of the greatest Austrian who ever lived, Wolfgang Amadeus Mozart. Except that Mozart was not really an Austrian, strictly

Illustration 51. Austrian identity 2: Auguste Rodin, 'Mozart', 1911.

speaking. Salzburg was not part of Austria at the time, and although Mozart spent most of his mature career in Vienna, he was really a German composer, much as Beethoven, also resident in Vienna, was a German composer. So should the Austrians celebrate Mozart as an Austrian? They certainly should, if they do so in the spirit of the larger, open, inclusive and cosmopolitan Austrian heritage of which Mozart most definitely was a part, indeed a model. As a child prodigy, Mozart was from early on a cosmopolitan; he was a

Freemason, advocate with Emanuel Schikaneder of Enlightenment humanism; his favourite librettist, Lorenzo da Ponte, was a Jewish convert, friend of Casanova and ex-priest who ended up in New York.

There is even a strange connection to the modern culture of Vienna 1900. In 1911, Auguste Rodin, the great French sculptor, created a bust which he came to title 'Mozart'. Rising out of the block of marble, it is an essay in the spirituality of the musical composer, but the figure actually has the features of Gustav Mahler, a bronze bust of whom Rodin had sculpted in 1909. When Austrians can fully celebrate that conflation, in all its richness, irony, diversity and profundity, and when they fully recognize and act on what this means for their approach to those outside Austria's borders, and the outsiders within those borders, then they will truly be fulfilling their duty.

GUIDE TO FURTHER READING

Much of the literature on which this book is based is only available in German. There is, however, also an extensive literature on Austrian history available in English, of which the following is a selection.

JOURNALS

Austrian History Yearbook (New York: Berghahn)
Austrian Studies (Leeds: Maney)
Central Europe (Leeds: Maney)
Central European History (Boston: Brill)
Contemporary Austrian Studies (New Brunswick: Transaction)

GENERAL

Barea, I. *Vienna* (New York: Knopf, 1966)
Brook-Shepherd, G. *The Austrians* (London: HarperCollins, 1996)
James, L. *Xenophobe's Guide to the Austrians* (London: Ravette, 1994)
Jelavich, B. *Modern Austria: Empire and Republic, 1800–1986* (Cambridge: Cambridge University Press, 1987)
Johnson, L. *Central Europe* (Oxford: Oxford University Press, 1996)
    Introducing Austria (Vienna: Bundesverlag, 1987)
Kann, R. A. *A History of the Habsburg Empire, 1526–1918* (Berkeley: University of California Press, 1977)
Pelinka, A. *Austria: Out of the Shadow of the Past* (Boulder: Westview Press, 1998)
Solsten E., and D. E. McClave. *Austria: a Country Study* (Washington, DC: Library of Congress, 1994)

BEFORE 1740

Barker, T. M. *Double Eagle and Crescent* (Albany: SUNY Press, 1967)

Benecke, G. *Maximilian I* (London: Routledge & Kegan Paul, 1982)

Bérenger, J. *A History of the Habsburg Empire, 1273–1700* (Harlow: Longman, 1994)

Blanning, T. C. W. *The Culture of Power and the Power of Culture: Old Regime Europe, 1660–1789* (Oxford: Oxford University Press, 2003)

Evans, R. J. W. *The Making of the Habsburg Monarchy, 1550–1700* (Oxford: Clarendon Press, 1979)

    Rudolf II and his World (Oxford: Clarendon Press, 1973)

Evans, R. J. W., and T. V. Thomas (eds.). *Crown, Church and Estates: Central European Politics in the Sixteenth and Seventeenth Centuries* (New York: St Martin's Press, 1991)

Fichtner, P. S. *Ferdinand I* (Boulder: East European Monographs, 1982)

    Maximilian II (New Haven: Yale University Press, 2001)

Ingrao, C. *The Habsburg Monarchy, 1618–1815* (Cambridge: Cambridge University Press, 1994)

    In Quest and Crisis: Emperor Joseph I and the Habsburg Monarchy (West Lafayette: Purdue University Press, 1979)

    (ed.). *The State and Society in Early Modern Austria* (West Lafayette: Purdue University Press, 1994)

Kann, R. A. *A Study in Austrian Intellectual History* (New York: Praeger, 1960)

Koenigsberger, H. G. *The Habsburgs and Europe, 1516–1660* (Ithaca: Cornell University Press, 1971)

Leeper, A. W. A. *A History of Medieval Austria* (London: Oxford University Press, 1941)

Lockyer, R. *Habsburg and Bourbon Europe, 1470–1720* (London: Longman, 1974)

McKay, D. *Prince Eugene of Savoy* (London: Thames & Hudson, 1977)

Maltby, W. S. *The Reign of Charles V* (Basingstoke: Palgrave, 2002)

Parker, G. *Europe in Crisis, 1598–1650* (Ithaca: Cornell University Press, 1979)

Spielman, J. P. *The City and the Crown: Vienna and the Imperial Court, 1600–1740* (West Lafayette: Purdue University Press, 1993)

    Leopold I of Austria (London: Thames & Hudson, 1977)

Steinberg, S. H. *The 'Thirty Years' War'* (London: Edward Arnold, 1966)

Stoye, J. *The Siege of Vienna* (New York: Holt, 1965)

Tanner, M. *The Last Descendants of Aeneas: the Habsburgs and the Mythic Image of the Emperor* (New Haven: Yale University Press, 1993)

Wheatcroft, A. *The Habsburgs: Embodying Empire* (Harmondsworth: Penguin, 1995)

1740–1918

Beales, D. *Joseph II, 1741–1780* (Cambridge: Cambridge University Press, 1987)

Beller, S. *Francis Joseph* (Harlow: Longman, 1996)

'The Tragic Carnival: Austrian Culture in the First World War', in A. Roshwald and R. Stites (eds.), *European Culture in the Great War* (Cambridge: Cambridge University Press, 1999)

Vienna and the Jews, 1867–1938: a Cultural History (Cambridge: Cambridge University Press, 1989)

(ed.). *Rethinking Vienna 1900* (Oxford: Berghahn, 2001)

Blanning, T. C. W. *Joseph II* (Harlow: Longman, 1994)

Boyer, J. W. *Culture and Political Crisis in Vienna, 1897–1918* (Chicago: University of Chicago Press, 1995)

Political Radicalism in Late Imperial Vienna, 1848–1897 (Chicago: University of Chicago Press, 1981)

Brauer, K., and W. E. Wright (eds.). *Austria in the Age of the French Revolution, 1789–1815* (Minneapolis: Center for Austrian Studies, 1990)

Bridge, F. R. *The Habsburg Monarchy among the Great Powers, 1815–1918* (Oxford: Berg, 1990)

Browning, R. *The War of the Austrian Succession* (New York: St Martin's Press, 1993)

Cohen, G. B. *Education and Middle-Class Society in Imperial Austria, 1848–1918* (West Lafayette: Purdue University Press, 1996)

Cornwall, M. (ed.). *The Last Years of Austria-Hungary* (Exeter: University of Exeter Press, 2002)

Deák, I. *Beyond Nationalism* (Oxford: Oxford University Press, 1990)

Dickson, P. G. M. *Finance and Government under Maria Theresa, 1740–1780*, 2 vols. (Oxford: Clarendon Press, 1987)

Geehr, R. S. *Karl Lueger* (Detroit: Wayne State University Press, 1990)

Good, D. F. *The Economic Rise of the Habsburg Empire, 1750–1914* (Berkeley: University of California Press, 1984)

Hamann, B. *Hitler's Vienna* (Oxford: Oxford University Press, 2000)

Hanson, A. M. *Musical Life in Biedermeier Vienna* (Cambridge, 1985)

Healy, M. *Vienna and the Fall of the Habsburg Empire* (Cambridge: Cambridge University Press, 2004)

Janik, A., and S. Toulmin. *Wittgenstein's Vienna* (New York: Simon & Schuster, 1973)

Jászi, O. *The Dissolution of the Habsburg Monarchy* (Chicago: University of Chicago Press, 1929)

Jenks, W. A. *Austria under the Iron Ring, 1879–1893* (Charlottesville: University of Virginia Press, 1965)

Johnston, W. M. *The Austrian Mind: an Intellectual and Social History, 1848–1938* (Berkeley: University of California Press, 1972)

Judson, P. M. *Exclusive Revolutionaries* (Ann Arbor: University of Michigan Press, 1996)

King, J. *Budweisers into Czechs and Germans* (Princeton: Princeton University Press, 2002)

Macartney, C. A. *The Habsburg Empire, 1790–1918* (London: Macmillan, 1969)

  Maria Theresa and the House of Austria (London: English University Press, 1969)

McCagg, W. O. *A History of Habsburg Jews, 1670–1918* (Bloomington: Indiana University Press, 1989)

McGrath, W. J. *Dionysian Art and Populist Politics in Austria* (New Haven: Yale University Press, 1974)

  Freud's Discovery of Psychoanalysis: the Politics of Hysteria (Ithaca: Cornell University Press, 1986)

Melton, J. V. H. *Absolutism and the Eighteenth Century Origins of Compulsory Schooling in Prussia and Austria* (Cambridge: Cambridge University Press, 1988)

Okey, R. *The Habsburg Monarchy: From Enlightenment to Eclipse* (New York: St Martin's Press, 2001)

Pulzer, P. *The Rise of Political Antisemitism in Germany and Austria*, rev. edn (London: Halban, 1988)

Rath, J. R. *The Viennese Revolution* (New York: Greenwood, 1969)

Redlich, J. *Emperor Francis Joseph of Austria* (New York: Macmillan, 1929)

Reifowitz, I. *Imagining an Austrian Nation* (Boulder: East European Monographs, 2003)

Rothenberg, G. E. *The Army of Francis Joseph* (West Lafayette: Purdue University Press, 1976)

Schnitzler, A. *The Road to the Open* (Evanston: Northwestern University Press, 1991)

Schorske, C. E. *Fin-de-Siècle Vienna: Politics and Culture* (London: Weidenfeld & Nicolson, 1980)

Shedel, J. *Art and Society: the New Art Movement in Vienna, 1897–1914* (Palo Alto: SPOSS, 1981)

Sked, A. *The Decline and Fall of the Habsburg Empire, 1815–1918* (London: Longman, 1989)

Stone, N. *The Eastern Front, 1914–1917* (London: Hodder & Stoughton, 1975)

Taylor, A. J. P. *The Habsburg Monarchy, 1809–1918* (Harmondsworth: Penguin, 1948)

Varnedoe, K. *Vienna 1900: Art, Architecture and Design* (New York: Museum of Modern Art, 1986)

Vergo, P. *Art in Vienna, 1898–1918* (Oxford: Phaidon, 1981)

Wangermann, E. *The Austrian Achievement, 1700–1800* (London: Thames & Hudson, 1973)

Wawro, G. *The Austro-Prussian War* (Cambridge: Cambridge University Press, 1997)

Williamson, S. R., Jr. *Austria-Hungary and the Origins of the First World War* (London: Macmillan, 1991)

Wistrich, R. S. *The Jews of Vienna in the Age of Franz Joseph* (Oxford: Oxford University Press, 1989)

AFTER 1918

Bassett, R. *Waldheim and Austria* (London: Penguin, 1988)

Bottomore, T., and P. Goode (eds.). *Austro-Marxism* (Oxford: Clarendon Press, 1978)

Bukey, E. B. *Hitler's Austria* (Chapel Hill: University of North Carolina Press, 2000)

Hitler's Hometown (Bloomington: Indiana University Press, 1986)

Bunzl, M. *Symptoms of Modernity: Jews and Queers in Late Twentieth-Century Vienna* (Berkeley: University of California Press, 2004)

Carsten, F. L. *Fascist Movements in Austria* (London: Sage, 1977)

Clare, G. *Last Waltz in Vienna* (London: Macmillan, 1981)

Cronin, A. K. *Great Power Politics and the Struggle over Austria, 1945–1955* (Ithaca: Cornell University Press, 1985)

Field, F. *The Last Days of Mankind: Karl Kraus and his Vienna* (London: Macmillan, 1967)

Gehl, J. *Austria, Germany and the Anschluss, 1931–1938* (London: Oxford University Press, 1963)

Gulick, C. A. *Austria: From Habsburg to Hitler*, 2 vols. (Berkeley: University of California Press, 1948)

Höbelt, L. *Defiant Populist: Jörg Haider and the Politics of Austria* (West Lafayette: Purdue University Press, 2003)

Katzenstein, P. J. *Corporatism and Change: Austria, Switzerland and the Politics of Industry* (Ithaca: Cornell University Press, 1984)

Kitchen, M. *The Coming of Austrian Fascism* (London: Croom Helm, 1980)

Klemperer, K. von *Ignaz von Seipel* (Princeton: Princeton University Press, 1972)

Luft, D. S. *Eros and Inwardness in Vienna: Weininger, Musil, Doderer* (Chicago: University of Chicago Press, 2003)

Robert Musil and the Crisis of European Culture, 1880–1942 (Berkeley: University of California Press, 1980)

Mitten, R. *The Politics of Antisemitic Prejudice: the Waldheim Phenomenon in Austria* (Boulder: Westview, 1992)

Oxaal, I., M. Pollak, and G. Botz (eds.). *Jews, Antisemitism and Culture in Vienna* (London: Routledge & Kegan Paul, 1987)

Pauley, B. F. *Hitler and the Forgotten Nazis* (Chapel Hill: University of North Carolina Press, 1981)

From Prejudice to Persecution: a History of Austrian Anti-Semitism (Chapel Hill: University of North Carolina Press, 1992)

Pick, H. *Guilty Victim: Austria from the Holocaust to Haider* (London: I. B. Tauris, 2000)

Rabinbach, A. (ed.). *The Austrian Socialist Experiment* (Boulder: Westview, 1985)

Robertson, R., and E. Timms (eds.). *The Habsburg Legacy* (Edinburgh: Edinburgh University Press, 1994)

Singer, P. *Pushing Time Away* (New York: HarperCollins, 2003)

Snowman, D. *The Hitler Emigrés* (London: Chatto & Windus, 2002)

Spiel, H. *Vienna's Golden Autumn, 1866–1938* (London: Weidenfeld & Nicolson, 1987)

Stadler, F. *The Vienna Circle* (New York: Springer, 2001)

Stadler, K. *Austria* (Praeger: New York, 1971)

Steiner, K., F. Fellner and H. Feichtlbauer (eds.). *Modern Austria* (Palo Alto: SPOSS, 1981)

Steininger, R., G. Bischof and M. Gehler (eds.). *Austria in the Twentieth Century* (New Brunswick: Transaction, 2002)

Sully, M. *A Contemporary History of Austria* (London: Routledge, 1990)

Vansant, J. *Reclaiming Heimat: Trauma and Mourning in Memoirs by Jewish Austrian Reémigrés* (Detroit: Wayne State University Press, 2001)

Waldheim, K. *The Austrian Example* (London: Weidenfeld & Nicolson, 1973)

Wright, W. E. (ed.). *Austria since 1945* (Minneapolis: Center for Austrian Studies, 1982)

INDEX

CAMBRIDGE CONCISE HISTORIES

Titles in the series:

A Concise History of Poland *2nd edition*
JERZY LUKOWSKI AND HUBERT ZAWADZKI

A Concise History of Portugal *2nd edition*
DAVID BIRMINGHAM

A Concise History of South Africa
ROBERT ROSS